INTERNATIONAL CHEMICAL SERIES

JAMES F. NORRIS, Ph.D., Consulting Editor

THE ELEMENTS

OF

FRACTIONAL DISTILLATION

A Selection of Titles from the

INTERNATIONAL CHEMICAL SERIES

James F. Norris, Ph.D., *Consulting Editor*

The Elements

of

Fractional Distillation

BY

CLARK SHOVE ROBINSON

Associate Professor of Chemical Engineering
Massachusetts Institute of Technology

AND

EDWIN RICHARD GILLILAND

Associate Professor of Chemical Engineering
Massachusetts Institute of Technology

THIRD EDITION

McGRAW-HILL BOOK COMPANY, Inc.

NEW YORK AND LONDON

1939

THE MAPLE PRESS COMPANY, YORK, PA.

PREFACE TO THE THIRD EDITION

In presenting the third edition of this book to the public, the authors wish to repeat that it is an introduction to the study of distillation and not a complete treatise on the subject. Recent advances in the design of distilling apparatus have made it advisable to introduce some of these advances into this book, at the same time omitting certain other methods of treatment which are less satisfactory. The present treatment is believed to represent the best general practice in distillation design at present writing. The new material includes the work of many recent workers in this field.

In the treatment of binary mixtures, the methods of Sorel, McCabe and Thiele, Ponchon, Savarit, Lewis, Smoker, and Fenske are considered and illustrated by several numerical examples.

Multicomponent rectification is represented by the work of Lewis and Matheson, Lewis and Cope, Brown and associates, and Underwood. In several cases the methods of the above workers have been simplified in order to make them easier to use. Methods for predicting the minimum reflux ratio and optimum feed-plate location for these mixtures are developed and presented. Several numerical examples are given in detail in order to aid the reader in calculations of this type.

The performance of plate and packed towers has been considered on the basis of plate efficiencies, pressure drop, allowable liquid and vapor rates, and so forth, making use of the data of numerous investigators.

Rather extensive tables of data on various volatile liquids which appeared at the end of the first and second editions have been largely omitted from this edition because it is felt that other and better sources of data are now available, including such books as Perry's "Chemical Engineers' Handbook."

CAMBRIDGE, MASS.,
December, 1938

C. S. ROBINSON,
E. R. GILLILAND.

PREFACE TO THE FIRST EDITION

The subject of fractional distillation has received but scant attention from writers in the English language since Sidney Young published his book "Fractional Distillation" in 1903 (London). French and German authors have, on the other hand, produced a number of books on the subject, among the more important of which are the following:

"La Rectification et les colonnes rectificatrices en distillerie," E. Barbet, Paris, 1890; 2d ed., 1895.

"Der Wirkungsweise der Rectificir—und Destillir—Apparate," E. Hausbrand, Berlin, 1893; 3d ed., 1916.

"Theorie der Verdampfung und Verflüssung von gemischen und der fraktionierten Destillation," J. P. Kuenen, Leipzig, 1906.

"Theorie der Gewinnung und Trennung der ätherischen Öle durch Destillation," C. von Rechenberg, Leipzig, 1910.

"La Distillation fractionée et la rectification," Charles Mariller, Paris, 1917.

Young's "Fractional Distillation," although a model for its kind, has to do almost entirely with the aspects of the subject as viewed from the chemical laboratory, and there has been literally no work in English available for the engineer and plant operator dealing with the applications of the laboratory processes to the plant.

The use of the modern types of distilling equipment is growing at a very rapid rate. Manufacturers of chemicals are learning that they must refine their products in order to market them successfully, and it is often true that fractional distillation offers the most available if not the only way of accomplishing this. There has consequently arisen a wide demand among engineers and operators for a book which will explain the principles involved in such a way that these principles can be applied to the particular problem at hand.

It has therefore been the purpose of the writer of this book to attempt to explain simply yet accurately, according to the best ideas of physical chemistry and chemical engineering, the principles of fractional distillation, illustrating these principles with a few carefully selected illustrations. This book is to be regarded neither as a complete treatise nor as an encyclopedia on the subject but, as the title indicates, as an introduction to its study.

In general, it has been divided into five parts. The first part deals with fractional distillation from the qualitative standpoint of the phase rule. The second part discusses some of the quantitative aspects from the standpoint of the chemical engineer. Part three discusses the factors involved in the design of distilling equipment. Part four gives a few examples of modern apparatus, while the last portion includes a number of useful reference tables which have been compiled from sources mostly out of print and unavailable except in large libraries.

The writer has drawn at will on the several books mentioned above, some of the tables being taken nearly bodily from them, and has also derived much help from Findlay's "Phase Rule" (London, 1920) and from "The General Principles of Chemistry" by Noyes and Sherrill (Boston, 1917). He wishes especially to express his gratitude for the inspiration and helpful suggestions from Dr. W. K. Lewis of the Massachusetts Institute of Technology and from his other friends and associates at the Institute and of the E. B. Badger & Sons Company. Finally, he wishes to express his appreciation of the assistance of Miss Mildred B. McDonald, without which this book would never have been written.

CLARK SHOVE ROBINSON.

CAMBRIDGE,
June 30, 1920.

CONTENTS

THE ELEMENTS
OF
FRACTIONAL DISTILLATION

INTRODUCTION

Definition of Fractional Distillation.—By the expression fractional distillation was originally meant the process of separating so far as it may be feasible a mixture of two or more volatile substances into its components, by causing the mixture to vaporize by suitable application of heat, condensing the vapors in such a way that fractions of varying boiling points are obtained, revaporizing these fractions and separating their vapors into similar fractions, combining fractions of similar boiling points, and repeating until the desired degree of separation is finally obtained.

Purpose of Book.—Such a process is still occasionally met with in the chemical laboratory, but it is a laborious and time-consuming operation which has its chief value as a problem for the student, for the purpose of familiarizing him with some of the characteristic properties of volatile substances. It is possible to carry on a fractional distillation by means of certain mechanical devices which eliminate almost all of this labor and time, and which permit separations not only equal to those obtained by this more tedious process but far surpassing it in quality and purity of product. The purpose of this book is to indicate how such devices may be profitably used in the solution of distillation problems.

Origin of Fractional Distillation.—Like all of the older industries, fractional distillation is an art that originated in past ages and that developed, as did all the arts, by the gradual accumulation of empirical knowledge. It is probable that its growth took place along with that of the distilled alcoholic beverages, and

1

to the average person today the word "still" is synonymous with apparatus for making rum, brandy, and other distilled liquors. To France, which has been the great producer of brandy, belongs the credit for the initial development of the modern fractionating still.

Physical Chemistry and Fractional Distillation.—Fractional distillation has labored under the same sort of burden that the other industrial arts have borne. Empirical knowledge will carry an industry to a certain point, and then further advances are few and far between. It has been the function of the sciences to come to the rescue of the arts at such times and thus permit advancement to greater usefulness. The science that has raised fractional distillation from an empirical to a theoretical basis is physical chemistry. By its aid the study of fractionation problems becomes relatively simple, and it is on this account that the subject matter in this book is based upon physical chemistry as its foundation.

CHAPTER I

THE PHASE RULE

There is a law of physical chemistry, known as the phase rule, by which it is possible to predict exactly the conditions under which all systems of equilibrium can exist. This law was first stated by Gibbs[1] and has since been applied to a very large number of equilibriums. The rule is so simple and its application gives such an insight into the conditions under which a system may be in equilibrium that it will be of the greatest profit to study fractional distillation in its light.

Definition of Phases.—All systems are considered to consist of one or more separate portions, each portion being separated from the other by definite physical boundaries. For instance, in the system consisting of ice, liquid water, and water vapor, there is a sharp physical boundary between the ice and the water, a sharp boundary between the ice and the water vapor, and a boundary between the liquid and the vapor. It is said that such a system is one of three portions, or *phases*. The ice may be divided into a number of small pieces, separated from each other by liquid, but there still remains only one solid phase. Again, if a piece of iron containing 0.85 per cent carbon is allowed to cool very slowly from a high temperature and its surface is polished, etched, and examined under the microscope, the surface of the metal is found to consist of fine dark and light lines parallel to each other. The light lines consist of an iron-carbon compound called cementite, and the dark lines are pure iron. It is said, therefore, that this metal, apparently homogeneous to the eye, consists of two solid phases.

Types of Phases.—A phase, however, while it must be homogeneous physically, may consist of a number of different kinds of substances. A solution of a mixture of salt and sugar in water consists of but one phase, although three separate substances are present. However, if an excess of salt and sugar were added to

[1] *Trans. Conn. Acad.*, 3, pp. 108–248 (1876); pp. 343–524 (1878).

the water, so that it was unable to dissolve all of them, and some of the salt and sugar remained undissolved, the system then would have four phases—solid salt, solid sugar, the solution, and the water vapor above the solution. In the same way, the vapor present in a system is always considered as one phase, since it is impossible to distinguish between the various components by any ordinary physical means.

Phase Rule Qualitative Only.—It is, of course, evident that the number of phases present in a system is independent of the relative quantities of the respective phases; and, therefore, in discussing equilibrium conditions, the phase rule will give no insight into the quantitative relationship between the phases.

Definition of Components.—A system may consist of one or more pure components, and the maximum number of phases which may be present at equilibrium depends upon the number of components. It is, therefore, important to define what a component is. The components of a system are the *smallest number* of pure chemical compounds out of which it is possible to construct the entire system. For instance, the system ice, water, and water vapor consists of one component, the pure compound H_2O. In the same way, the system solid salt, solid sugar, saturated solution, and vapor, consists of three components, salt, sugar, and water.

Definition of Variants.—The conditions under which a system can exist at equilibrium with respect to its various phases are subject to a certain amount of variation. A system can be subjected to different temperatures; the pressure on the system can be varied; the concentrations of the solutions and vapors can be changed; it is possible to vary the specific gravity and the index of refraction of a solution. Not all of these changes can be made independently of each other, however, and it is customary to distinguish between such by referring to independent and dependent variations or variants; the number of independent variations that it is possible for a system to have are termed its degrees of freedom.

By definition the variants of a system are any physical characteristics or conditions of the whole system or of a single phase that are independent of the amounts of the phases, and the degree of freedom is the number of variants that can be modified without necessitating the disappearance of an old phase or the appearance of a new one.

Degree of Freedom.—The variants will, in this book, be confined to the temperature, pressure, and concentration of the components, and the degrees of freedom that a given system can have is that number of variants that must be fixed arbitrarily in order that the system may be perfectly defined.

The phase rule states that if the number of components of a system be called C, the degrees of freedom or variance V, and the number of phases P, the following relation is true:

$$P + V = C + 2$$

System : Water.—In the system ice, liquid water, and water vapor, there are three phases and one component. Therefore, there can be no degrees of freedom. In other words, neither the temperature nor the pressure can be changed so long as all three phases are present. If, however, one phase, such as the ice, is removed, one degree of freedom is permitted, and it is possible to change either the temperature or the pressure, but not both independently. If the temperature of the system is fixed arbitrarily, the pressure is therefore automatically fixed, and it is said that at any given temperature the water has a definite vapor pressure.

System : Water and Salt.—If, however, salt is added to the foregoing system, it becomes one of two components, and the sum of the number of phases and degrees of freedom is four. If the system has the three phases, solid salt, solution, and vapor, there can be one degree of freedom. Let the temperature be arbitrarily fixed, and the system becomes invariant, neither the pressure nor the concentration of the solution being variable. It is then said that at a given temperature, salt has a definite solubility in water and that the vapor pressure of water over such a saturated solution of salt in water has a definite value. If, however, insufficient salt is added to make a saturated solution at that temperature, there would be but two phases, solution and vapor, and therefore it is possible to fix another variant, either the concentration of the solution or its vapor pressure. Thus it is stated that at 100°C., the vapor pressure of a solution of 1 part of glucose in 20 parts of water is 756 mm. of mercury.

CHAPTER II

ONE-COMPONENT SYSTEMS

Vapor-pressure Curves.—The sum of the number of phases and the number of degrees of freedom in a system of one component is three. In the system water and water vapor, it is therefore possible to fix the temperature and obtain a correspond-

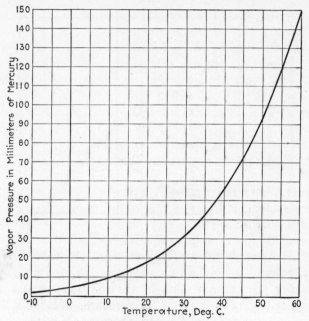

Fig. 1.—Vapor-pressure curve of water.

ing vapor pressure. If this is done over a wide range of temperatures, and the corresponding pressures determined, the results when shown graphically would appear as Fig. 1, which is the well-known vapor-pressure curve for water.

Since in the system ice-water vapor there are two phases as before, it is possible by fixing the temperature to fix the sys-

6

tem, and, therefore, the vapor pressure and the vapor-pressure curve for ice are obtained. These may be plotted as before.

Likewise, the system ice-liquid water is a univariant system, and fixing the pressure, for instance, will determine the temperature at which ice will change into water or the reverse. A plot of such data will give the equilibrium curve between solid and liquid water.

Plot these three curves as on Fig. 2, where the curve ABC is the vapor-pressure curve for liquid water, the curve DB is

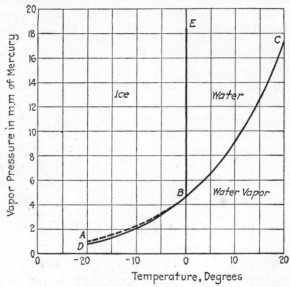

FIG. 2.—Vapor-pressure diagram. System—ice, water, water vapor.

the vapor-pressure curve for ice, and the curve EB is the equilibrium curve for ice and water. At the point B, ice, liquid, and vapor are all in equilibrium, and therefore, both temperature and pressure are fixed, being about 0°C. and 4.60 mm., respectively. The field DBE is the field of stable ice, and within that field both temperature and pressure can be varied provided no liquid or vapor is present. The area EBC is the field where liquid water is stable, and the pressure and temperature can both be varied if neither ice nor vapor is present. The field below the lines DB and BC is the field of superheated water vapor, which behaves like a gas, both temperature and pressure being variable.

The line AB is the line of equilibrium between supercooled water and vapor. The water, however, is not stable at this temperature, and if a crystal of ice is introduced, the water solidifies instantly.

Change of Temperature at Constant Pressure.—If the system water is raised at constant pressure, say 8 mm., from -20 to $+20°$C., the system would first consist wholly of ice. As the temperature was raised, no change of phase would occur until the system reached the temperature corresponding to the intersection of the 8-mm. line and the curve BE, when the ice would start to melt. The temperature would then remain constant until all of the ice was melted, when it would again rise until the line BC was reached. Here the liquid would start to evaporate, and the temperature would remain constant until all was in the form of steam. Further heating would then raise the temperature, and the system would consist of superheated water vapor.

Unstable Conditions.—The line AB—that of supercooled water—lies above the vapor-pressure curve of ice DB; or, the vapor pressure of the unstable liquid below $0°$ is greater than that of ice. It is evident from this that it is not possible for ice, liquid, and vapor to exist together below $0°$C., since the vapor from the water would be supersaturated with respect to the ice and would, therefore, condense upon it, eventually converting all of the liquid to solid through slow evaporation and condensation.

In general, the facts noted with respect to the system water apply to other systems of one component. However, since fractional distillation deals with systems of two or more components, two-component systems will next be considered.

CHAPTER III

TWO-COMPONENT SYSTEMS

Space Model of Two-component Systems.—In systems of two components, the sum of the number of phases and the degrees of freedom is four. Therefore, if but one phase is present, there are three degrees of freedom, and the composition of the phases must be considered in addition to the temperature and pressure of the system. Since any of the variables may be subject to variation, the graphical representation will involve a space model of three coordinates—temperature, pressure, and concentration —as indicated in Fig. 3, where the line OB represents temperature;

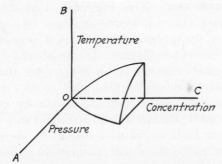

Fig. 3.—Space model—two-component system.

the line OA, pressure; and the line OC, concentration. Any points lying in the plane AOB or any plane parallel to it will have the same composition. Any points in any plane parallel to the plane AOC will have the same temperature, whereas the plane COB and planes parallel to it will be planes of constant pressure. The use, however, of space models is inconvenient, and it is usually customary to fix one condition, such as pressure, and work with a two-dimension diagram, which in this case is usually one of temperature composition.

In the study of fractional distillation, it is usual to deal with liquids and vapors, and it is unusual for solid phases to be of importance. There are two common systems of liquid and vapor where there are two components: first, solution and vapor and, second, two liquids and vapor. In the first case, there are two phases, and the system is bivariant. In the second case, there are three phases, and the system is univariant.

Partially Miscible Liquids.—The univariant system of two liquid phases and the vapor phase is found where two liquids are only partially soluble in each other. The relative solubility of the two components in each other may vary from almost nothing to complete miscibility. Furthermore, the degree to which one component will dissolve in the other changes with the temperature, and univariant systems frequently become bivariant on raising the temperature, owing to the components becoming completely soluble in each other.

Phenol and Water.—The case of phenol and water is a good example of the latter. At 20°C., water will contain 8.40 per cent of phenol. If the temperature be raised to 50°, the solubility will be increased to 12.08 per cent.[1] Similarly, phenol will dissolve water; and at 20°, the amount present amounts to 27.76 per cent, whereas at 50, it has risen to 37.17 per cent. If these solubilities are plotted as on Fig. 4, it will be seen that the respective solubility curves are really one curve which passes through a maximum point at a composition of 35.90 per cent phenol and at a temperature of approximately 68.8°C.

When phenol is added to water, and the temperature kept at 20°, it at first dissolves completely; but when a concentration of 8.40 per cent has been reached, the addition of any more phenol will cause the formation of a second layer, which will have a composition of 72.24 per cent. Further addition of phenol will then have no effect upon the concentration of either liquid phase, the relative amounts of each phase changing to keep the percentages constant, until enough phenol has been added so that the whole system contains phenol and water in the ratio 72.24 to 27.76, when any further addition of phenol will cause the disappearance of the 8.40 per cent phase, and the system will again become a system with one liquid and one vapor phase. Viewed from the standpoint of the phase rule, so long as only one liquid phase is present, it is possible to fix arbitrarily two

[1] ROTHMUND, *Z. Phys. Chem.*, 26, 433.

conditions, such as temperature and composition; but upon the appearance of the second liquid phase, the degrees of freedom are reduced to one; and since the temperature has been fixed in the foregoing example, the compositions of both of the two phases are therefore determined. Above the critical temperature at which both liquid phases have the same composition, the components are miscible in all proportions, and it is possible to vary any two of the temperature, composition, or vapor pressure at will.

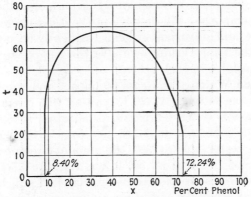

Fɪɢ. 4.—Solubility curve of phenol-water mixtures.

Complete Miscibility.—It is evident that systems of two components which are partly soluble in each other at ordinary temperatures are special cases of the general one of complete miscibility, and within the limits of solubility their behavior is the same as that of the latter.

Liquid Composition.—In the chapter on One-component Systems, it was pointed out that where the system consisted of two phases—liquid and vapor—fixing the temperature gave a definite vapor pressure, the values of which when plotted gave the vapor-pressure curve of the liquid. In the same way, in a system of two components, if the composition of the liquid is fixed, fixing the temperature will determine the vapor pressure, where there is one liquid phase, and the vapor phase. If both components are volatile, fixing the temperature and the composition of the liquid will also determine the composition of the vapor phase.

Temperature-composition Diagram.—By fixing the vapor pressure of a two-component system, a temperature-composition diagram can be made. Figure 5 shows a temperature-composition curve for carbon tetrachloride—carbon bisulphide at a vapor pressure of 760 mm. Any point on the curve ABC gives the composition x, of a mixture of CCl_4 and CS_2 which boils at a pressure of 760 mm. at any given temperature t, where t is in degrees centigrade and x is the mol fraction of CS_2. The use of the "mol fraction" or "molecular fraction" greatly facilitates calculations of vapor-pressure phenomena. By it is meant the

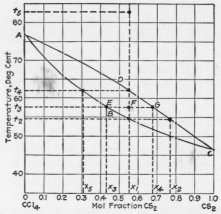

FIG. 5.—Boiling-point curve for CCl_4-CS_2 mixtures.

number of molecular weights of the one component in a mixture in which the sum of the molecular weights of the respective components is 1. Mol per cent is equal to 100 times the mol fraction. The line ADC represents the composition of the vapor that is in equilibrium with the liquid at any given temperature. Thus a liquid with the composition x_1 will have a vapor pressure of 760 mm. at the temperature t_2, and the vapor in equilibrium with it will have the composition x_2.

Starting with a mixture of the composition x_1 and at a temperature below t_2, there can be but one phase present, the liquid mixture of CCl_4 and CS_2. As the temperature is raised, no change but the expansion of the liquid will occur until the vertical line at x_1 hits the curve ABC, when a vapor phase of the composition x_2 will appear. Since there are now two phases and the pressure is fixed, there can be but one variable, temperature, and the composition of the phases will depend upon it. Let the temperature then be raised to some point t_3; and the liquid and vapor compositions, being no longer independent variables must change accordingly, which they do along the curves ABC and ADC, respectively, the liquid now having a composition x_3, and the vapor in equilibrium with it a composition x_4. It should be remembered that the quantity of CCl_4 and CS_2 in the system has not changed during this process, and, therefore, the change in the compositions of the liquid and the vapor includes such a corresponding change in the relative proportions of each phase that the total composition of the system remains the same, x_1. Furthermore, the relative proportions of the liquid phase and vapor phase, at the temperature t_3, are as the distances FG and EF. It will be seen that as the temperature is raised further, the proportion of liquid phase decreases, until when the temperature reaches a point corresponding to the intersection of the vertical line x_1 and the curve ADC, which occurs at a temperature t_4, the vapor has the same composition as the original liquid, and the liquid phase disappears. At higher temperatures, there is but one, the vapor, phase, and the system again becomes trivariant, so that at constant pressure it is possible to vary both the temperature and the composition of the vapor. This is the region of superheated vapor.

If the foregoing process is reversed, the steps can be followed in the same way. Starting with superheated vapor of a composition x_1 and at a temperature t_5, condensation will first occur when the vertical line x_1 cuts the vapor line ADC, when liquid of a composition x_5 will separate out. Further cooling will change both the composition of the liquid and the vapor along the lines ABC and ADC, respectively, until the liquid has reached the composition x_1 when all the vapor will have disappeared.

General Methods of Fractionation.—There are two general methods by which fractionation can be obtained: successive distillation of the condensed distillates, and fractional condensation, both methods depending on the separation of the liquid from the vapor while the phases are in equilibrium.

Successive Distillation.—The first method, successive distillation of the condensed distillates, can be best shown by referring to

Fig. 5.   Starting with a large amount of liquid of the composition x_5 which boils at 760 mm. pressure at a temperature t_4, a small amount of vapor, of the composition x_1, is removed from the apparatus and condensed, giving a liquid of the composition x_1. Let this new liquid again be distilled, and the first portion of the distillate will have the composition x_2. Continuing this process, the successive compositions of the distillate can be estimated by following a series of steps, which eventually approach the point C, pure CS_2, as a limit.

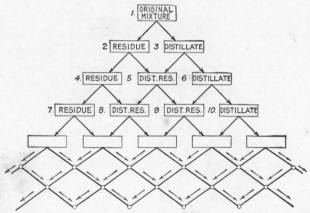

FIG. 6.—Fractionation diagram.

The removal of any vapor of a composition x_1 from the liquid of the composition x_5 will change the composition of the liquid in the direction of pure CCl_4. Therefore, if the distillation of the liquid is continued, the composition will approach pure CCl_4 as a limit, and the last of the liquid to be distilled would have this composition.

It is therefore possible by a systematic series of distillations to separate any mixture of CS_2 and CCl_4 into practically pure CS_2 and pure CCl_4. This systematic fraction may be shown diagrammatically as in Fig. 6, in which the original mixture (1) is divided into a distillate (3) and a residue (2). (3) and (2) are then distilled separately and produce distillates and residues, the distillate from (2) and the residue from (3) being combined into a new liquid (5) which is again distilled with (4) and (6) to continue the separation. This process is continued until practically complete separation is obtained. Such a process is sometimes carried out in the laboratory, but it is extremely tedious, and the same result can be obtained in other, much more convenient ways.

Multiple Distillation.—Suppose an apparatus as in Fig. 7, consisting of a series of distilling kettles A, B, C, etc., each kettle containing a heating coil and necessary connections for vapors and liquids. Suppose that kettle A contains a liquid mixture of CS_2 and CCl_4, of the composition x_5 as in Fig. 5; the kettle B,

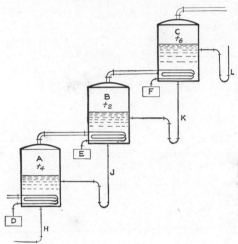

FIG. 7.—Diagram of multiple distillation.

a liquid of the composition x_1; the kettle C, the composition x_2; and so on. The liquid in A boils at t_4, that in B at t_2, and that in C at t_6. Since the vapor leaving A is at a temperature t_4, which is higher than the boiling temperature in B, t_2, then, if the vapor from A is led into the heating coils of B, it will give up its heat to the contents of B, boiling the liquid, and itself being partly condensed. The vapor from B, if led into the heating coils of C, will, in the same way, boil the liquid in C, the vapor being itself condensed as before. The condensed vapors in the coils may be drawn off into receivers D, E, F, etc. However, since the composition of the liquid in B was selected to be the same as that of the vapor coming from the kettle A, from Fig. 5, the condensed vapor in the coils of B can be allowed to mix with the contents of

B instead of being withdrawn into the receiver E. Now, since the vapor from A is being mixed with the liquid in B, and since there is a heat interchange between the two, it is much simpler to blow the vapor directly into the liquid, thus dispensing with the coils.

As the liquid in the kettle B distills, giving off a vapor richer in CS_2 than itself, the concentration of the liquid tends to become poorer in CS_2, in spite of the addition to it of the vapor from A. Therefore, if it is withdrawn continually through the pipe J and run into the kettle A, the tendency for the liquid to become poorer in CS_2 will be reduced, and the contents of the kettle A will, at the same time, be enriched. In the same way, the liquid in C is allowed to flow continuously back into the kettle B.

Continuous Fractional Distillation.—By this process, therefore, if a constant supply of vapor is furnished to the kettle A, a continuous fractional distillation can be obtained. Furthermore, since each kettle represents a change in composition corresponding to one step in the diagram of Fig. 5, if there are as many kettles as there are required steps to pass from practically pure CCl_4 to practically pure CS_2, such an apparatus will separate the mixture into the practically pure components, continuously and with but little labor.

Fractionating Column.—The foregoing device is the basis upon which the fractionating (rectifying or dephlegmating) column of a fractionating still is made. A portion of a simple column is shown in Fig. 8. This column contains perforated plates, dividing it into the sections A, B, C, etc. Each of these sections has the same function as a kettle in the previous apparatus. The vapor from the liquid on the plate A passes through the small holes in the plate B and, coming into contact with the colder liquid on the plate B, is condensed, thereby giving up its heat to the liquid on the plate and causing it to boil. The excess liquid on the plate B overflows on to the plate below through the pipe F.

The analogy between this fractionating column and the series of kettles would be better if the vapor leaving the liquid on the plate had the equilibrium composition as predicted from curves as on Fig. 5. But, unfortunately, no design has been able wholly to prevent some of the vapor from the plate below from passing through the liquid on the plate without coming into equilibrium with it. The vapor above any plate, therefore, is a mixture of the vapor from the liquid on that plate and of the vapor from the plate below, and, therefore, it will contain less of the volatile component than would be the case if complete equilibrium were reached. The ratio of the actual composition of the vapor over the plate, when the *reflux ratio*, which will be explained in Chap. XIII, is infinite, to the equilibrium composition of the vapor is a measure of the efficiency of the plate as a fractionating device.

The numerous modifications of the fractionating column will be discussed in the chapter devoted to that subject.

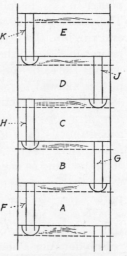

FIG. 8.—Diagram of fractionating column.

Fractional Condensation.—The second general method by which fractionating can be obtained is fractional condensation. Referring again to Fig. 5, suppose a mixture of CS_2 and CCl_4 vapor with the composition x_1 and at the temperature t_5. It was stated that, upon cooling, condensation would begin when the x_1 vertical line reached the vapor line ADC and that the liquid that appeared would have the composition x_5. If, now, the liquid is removed from contact with the vapor as rapidly as it appears, and since the liquid is poorer in the more volatile component CS_2 than the vapor, the vapor will grow progressively richer in CS_2 as the temperature drops until, as the last of the vapor condenses, its composition will have reached that of pure CS_2. It is, therefore, possible to separate the pure more volatile component from a mixture by vaporizing the mixture and then condensing the vapor gradually, withdrawing the condensate as rapidly as it appears. But it is obvious that such a process would be most inefficient, since all of the liquid must be vaporized and condensed in order to obtain the last portion of remaining vapor as practically pure component. Actually, fractional condensation is combined with successive vaporization and with a modification of successive condensation, known as washing or scrubbing which will be discussed below, to produce efficient fractionation.

Classes of Binary Mixtures.—Binary mixtures of volatile liquids, miscible in all proportions, are divided into three main classes. These three classes are illustrated by Fig. 9, where curve I is the liquid-vapor curve for carbon tetrachloride—carbon bisulphide mixtures at 760 mm. which was shown on Fig. 5. This type of mixture can be separated into its components by fractional distillation.

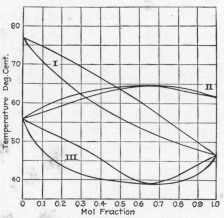

Fig. 9.—Types of binary mixtures.

Maximum Boiling Point.—Curve II is the boiling-point curve for mixtures of acetone and chloroform. This curve passes through a maximum point at approximately a composition of 65 mol per cent chloroform, at a temperature 64.6°C., which is higher than the boiling temperature of either pure component, and the liquid and vapor curves touch each other at this maximum point. Evidently, a liquid of a composition corresponding to this maximum, when raised to its boiling point, would produce a vapor of the same composition as the liquid, and, therefore, the two components cannot be separated by fractional distillation.

If a vertical line is drawn through this maximum boiling point, the diagram will be divided into two parts, and the section of the curve in each part will resemble the simple type of curve I. It can, therefore, be stated that in such a system of two components, where there exists a maximum boiling point, any mixture of these components can be separated by fractional distillation into one pure component and the mixture of constant-boiling point but that it is impossible, by fractional distillation alone, to separate such a mixture into both of its components. Furthermore, in a fractional distillation of such a mixture, the distillate will be richer in the pure component, since it boils at the lower temperature, and the residue will be richer in the constant-boiling mixture (C.B.M.).

Minimum Boiling Point.—Mixtures represented by curve III are the type having minimum boiling points. Such mixtures behave exactly like those of maximum boiling points, except that upon distillation the distillate is richer in the constant-boiling mixture, while the residue is richer in the pure component. The best known case of such a mixture is that of ethyl alcohol and water, which will be discussed later in detail.

Since in such systems there are two phases, liquid and vapor, and if the condition is fixed so that both phases have the same composition, as is the case with the mixtures of constant-boiling point, then there can be but one other degree of freedom; and if the pressure is fixed, then the system is invariant, and it is impossible to change the composition of the constant-boiling-point mixture. But changing the pressure will allow a change in the composition of the mixture. Also, the addition of another component, such as a salt, to the liquid, will allow a change in the composition. This latter method is in common use, industrially, for this purpose and will be discussed later.

CHAPTER IV

MORE COMPLEX SYSTEMS

Two-component systems have thus far been the subject of consideration, but fractional distillation is by no means confined exclusively to such systems, since most industrial mixtures contain greater or lesser amounts of impurities, and fractional distillation is often depended upon to separate the products from them. It is frequently true, however, that the mixtures to be separated consist largely of two components and that the other components are present in relatively small amounts. If this is the case, it is customary to consider the system preliminarily as a two-component system and then modify the design to allow for the other components. In many cases, however, this cannot be done, and the system must be considered from the start as a multicomponent system.

Three-component Systems.—In systems of three components, the sum of the number of phases and the degrees of freedom is five. In order that such a system may be invariant, five phases must be present. In systems consisting of liquids and vapors, however, it is rare that more than two liquid phases and one vapor phase are present, and such a system, therefore, has two degrees of freedom. For instance, ethyl ether and water are partially soluble in each other and when mixed in proportions greater than the limits of solubility form two liquid phases: one a solution of water in ether, and the other a solution of ether in water. Such a system of two components, with two liquid phases and one vapor phase, has one degree of freedom, and, therefore, if the temperature is chosen, the system becomes fixed, and the compositions of the liquids and of the vapor and the vapor pressure of the system are fixed. If, however, some ethyl alcohol is added to the system, it now becomes one of three components, and it is possible to fix some other condition in addition to the temperature, for instance, the vapor pressure.

Or, in other words, the temperature at which such a mixture will boil at atmospheric pressure, *i.e.*, the temperature at which the vapor pressure becomes equal to the barometric pressure, may also be varied. If the temperature and pressure are fixed, the compositions of the liquid and vapor phases become fixed.

System : Ether, Alcohol, Water.—In the system ether, water, alcohol, if alcohol is added to the ether and water, the solubility of ether in the water is increased, and the solubility of the water in the ether is increased. If sufficient alcohol is added, a point is reached when the ether phase and the water phase contain the same amounts of ether, alcohol, and water, and any further increase in the amount of alcohol will produce a system of one liquid phase, where ether, water, and alcohol are completely soluble in each other. Under this condition, there are three degrees of freedom, and the temperature, pressure, and composition of the liquid, for example, can be fixed. This will fix the composition of the vapor phase in equilibrium with the liquid phase. It is difficult to show diagrammatically three-component systems. One method of graphical representation is shown in Fig. 10, which consists of a prism erected on an equilateral triangle *ABC*. The sides of the triangle are divided into 10 or 100 equal divisions, representing mol fractions of the components. Thus the line *CB* represents mixtures of the pure components C and B, and any point on the line indicates their mol fractions. Also, any point on the line *AC* represents mixtures of the components A and C; and any point on the line *AB*, mixtures of the components A and B.

It is a property of such a triangle that if the length of the perpendicular from any apex to the opposite side is unity, the sum of the perpendiculars from any point within the triangle to the three sides will also equal unity. Therefore, since the sides are divided uniformly as mol fractions, the length of the perpendiculars from any point within the triangle to the respective sides will indicate the mol fraction of the component, whose apex lies opposite the side of the triangle to which the perpendicular is drawn. Thus, the point *O* has the perpendicular line *OK* drawn to the line *AC*, having a length equal to 0.2. Therefore, the mol fraction of the component B is 0.2. In the same way, the mol fraction of C is 0.3, and the mol fraction of A is 0.5, totaling 1.0. Any mixture of A, B, and C may, therefore, be indicated by properly locating its composition on this triangle.

If the vertical dimension of the prism represents temperature, on such a space model, it is possible to illustrate changes in temperature and composition but not changes in pressure.

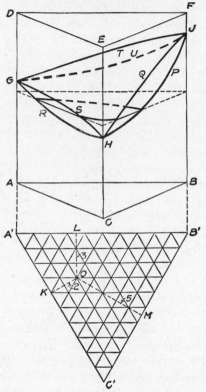

Fig. 10.—Diagram of three-component system.

Just as in a two-component system the temperature-composition diagram was at constant pressure, so in this case the whole space model is at constant pressure. The pure component B boils at atmospheric pressure at a temperature corresponding to the point J. Pure C boils at a temperature corresponding to H, while pure A boils at the temperature G. The plane surface *CEFB* of the prism, then, is exactly the same as the temperature-composition diagram used for two-component systems, and the boiling-point curve for mixtures of C and B can be drawn as before, together with the vapor curve in equilibrium with it, as shown by the curves *HPJ* and *HQJ*, respectively. In the same way, the boiling-point and vapor curves for mixtures of A and C can be drawn in the plane *ADEC*, and the boiling-point and vapor curves of mixtures of A and B can be drawn in the plane *ADFB*. It will be seen that the three boiling-point curves *HPJ*, *GRH*, and *GUJ* form the boundaries of a surface. This surface represents the boiling temperatures of mixtures of A, B, and C, whose compositions are determined as above. In the same way, the vapor lines *HQJ*, *GSH*, and *GTJ* form another surface which represents the vapor in equilibrium with the liquid mixture. A horizontal plane represents a plane of constant temperature, and such a plane, cutting both liquid and vapor surfaces, will form lines that indicate compositions of the vapor phase which are in equilibrium with the liquid mixtures which boil at that temperature. Such an intersection of a constant-temperature plane

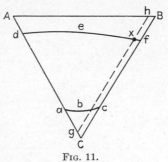

Fig. 11.

with the liquid and vapor surfaces is shown in Fig. 11, where the line *abc* is the intercept with the vapor surface, and the line *def* that with the liquid surface. Since there are two phases, liquid and vapor, and the pressure and temperature have been fixed, there is one degree of freedom. If, now, the composition of the liquid with respect to one component is fixed, say 10 mol per cent of A, the line representing a mol fraction of A of 0.10, *gh*, will cut the liquid line *def* at some point *x*. A liquid of this composition will boil at the fixed temperature and pressure. The vapor in equilibrium with the liquid *x* will have some fixed composition on the line *abc*.

Ternary Constant-boiling Mixtures.—The system illustrated in Fig. 10 is one in which there are no constant-boiling mixtures, and separation by fractional distillation can be complete. Very commonly, however, one pair of the three will have a constant-boiling mixture, and often two pairs of the three will have such mixtures. When this latter occurs, constant-boiling mixtures of the three components will be obtained.   This is very common in cases where one of the components is only partly soluble in the others, *e.g.*, the mixture of benzene, ethyl alcohol, and water. This system has a constant-boiling mixture, boiling at a temperature considerably below any of the pure components and containing more water than the constant-boiling mixture of alcohol and water.   This system may be used in the manufacture of absolute alcohol.

Partially Miscible Components.—Occasionally, the presence of a partly soluble component and a binary constant-boiling mixture fails to produce a ternary C.B.M.   For instance, isoamyl alcohol is only partly soluble in water, and ethyl alcohol forms a C.B.M. with water; but no ternary C.B.M. is formed, since the alcohol-water C.B.M. has a lower boiling temperature than the isoamyl alcohol-water mixture in the presence of alcohol.   This permits the separation of the isoamyl alcohol from the ethyl alcohol and water, as illustrated in the recovery of fusel oil in the rectification of fermentation alcohol.

CHAPTER V

THE GAS LAWS

The principles involved in fractional distillation are fundamentally the elementary laws of physics and thermodynamics. Many of the so-called physical laws are, however, very limited in their applications and do not apply exactly throughout the whole range of conditions included under distillation. Often, the laws hold exactly only for the nonexistent perfect gases and for perfect solutions and hold only approximately for actual gases and solutions which are said to approach perfect gases and solutions to a greater or lesser degree according to their behavior in relation to the perfect-gas and -solution laws. However, in engineering work, the large number of more or less indeterminate factors that come into every problem render exact solutions very difficult, and approximate solutions are usually necessary and satisfactory. Under these circumstances, the perfect-gas and -solution laws often give results that are sufficiently close for engineering purposes.

Boyle's Law.—The first of the theoretical laws of importance in distillation is the law of Boyle, which states that at constant temperature the volume of a given gas is inversely proportionate to its pressure, or

$$PV = \text{constant}$$

Thus, doubling the pressure on a given amount of a gas at constant temperature should halve its volume.

Gay-Lussac's Law.—If, however, the temperature of a given amount of a gas is raised, either the gas will expand or its pressure will increase, and it has been found that at 0°C., raising the temperature 1°C. will cause a gas to increase in volume $\frac{1}{273}$ of its volume, at constant pressure; or inversely, the pressure will be increased $\frac{1}{273}$ of its pressure at 0°C., if heated at constant volume. This temperature effect is known as the law of Gay-Lussac.

25

Absolute Zero.—Since the volume of a gas diminishes $\frac{1}{273}$ of its volume at 0°C. for each degree that it is cooled, when the gas has been cooled to −273°C., or −273.1°C. exactly, its volume should be zero. −273°C. is, therefore, known as the absolute zero. In English units, this corresponds to −459.6°F. This would occur only with a perfect gas, however, and it has been found that actual gases condense to the liquid state before −273°C. is reached.

Perfect-gas Equation.—The laws of Boyle and Gay-Lussac can be combined to give the equation

$$PV = NRT$$

where P is the absolute pressure exerted by the gas, V is its volume, N is the number of molecular weights or mols of the gas present, T is the temperature at which the gas exists, when measured from absolute zero, and R is some constant, known as the gas constant, whose value varies according to the units which are selected for P, V, and T. Thus, when T is in degrees centigrade absolute, P is in atmospheres pressure, and V is in liters, R will have the value of 0.08207 (0.082). $R = 1,543$ when T is in degrees Rankine (degrees Fahrenheit + 459.6), P is in pounds per square foot absolute pressure, N is in pound mols, and V is in cubic feet.

Molal Volume.—The volume that one molecular weight in grams of a gas will occupy at 0°C. and 1 atm. (atmospheric) pressure may be found as follows:

$$1 \times V = 1 \times 0.08207 \times 273.1$$
$$V = 22.41 \text{ l.}$$

The value 22.4 l. of 1 g. mol of a gas at 0°C. and 1 atm. pressure is a very convenient figure to remember, and frequent use will be made of it. In the same way, the value of the mol in English units may be determined and has been found to be 359.0 for 1 lb. mol of a gas at standard conditions (32°F. and 29.92 in. of mercury, normal barometer).

As has been stated above, no gases follow the laws of the $PV = NRT$ equation exactly. The greater the distance of a gas above its saturation temperature, and the lower the pressure, the more nearly will the gas behave like a perfect gas. For the so-called permanent gases such as oxygen, hydrogen, and nitrogen, the $PV = NRT$ equation holds almost exactly for ordinary temperatures and pressures. But even these show marked deviations as the pressures increase and the temperatures approach the liquefying point. Consequently, other equations have been worked out to describe the behavior of these gases more exactly, the most notable being that of Van der Waals

$$\left(P + \frac{a}{V^2}\right)(V - b) = RT$$

which is the $PV = NRT$ equation with $N = 1$, and P and V corrected for the internal-pressure effect of the molecules of a gas and for the actual volumes of the molecules of the gas themselves. This equation holds very well for most gases up to extremely high pressures, and in some cases for the liquefied gases also, but it is a difficult equation to handle and is used very little in engineering work.

In order to show the applicability of the equation $PV = NRT$, the following table has been calculated for 1 lb. of steam. Thus it is evident that for similar saturated vapors, the foregoing

Temperature, degrees Fahrenheit	Pressure, pounds per square inch	Specific volume, cubic feet		Difference	Condition of vapor
		Actual	Calculated		
212	14.70	26.81	27.21	0.40	Saturated
250	15.00	27.84	28.18	0.34	Superheated
400	15.00	33.96	34.13	0.17	Superheated
600	15.00	41.98	42.09	0.11	Superheated

equation is good to about 2 per cent; whereas for superheated vapors, it becomes increasingly more accurate as the degree of superheat increases. Since, in most low-pressure distillation work, errors of 2 per cent in the volume of vapors are not serious, the use of this equation may be permitted.

A method that is useful for approximating the P-V-T relations where the perfect-gas laws are not sufficiently accurate is to use the formula $PV = \mu NRT$ where μ is an empirical correction factor obtained from the reduced temperature (T_R) and the reduced pressure (P_R) of the gas in question. The reduced temperature is obtained by dividing the absolute temperature of the gas by its critical temperature, and the reduced pressure by dividing the absolute pressure of the gas by its critical pressure, in corresponding units. The value of μ is then obtained from the following chart (Fig. 12).

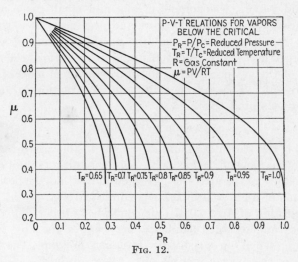

P-V-T RELATIONS FOR VAPORS
BELOW THE CRITICAL
$P_R = P/P_c$ = Reduced Pressure
$T_R = T/T_c$ = Reduced Temperature
R = Gas Constant
$\mu = PV/RT$

T_R=0.65 T_R=0.7 T_R=0.75 T_R=0.8 T_R=0.85 T_R=0.9 T_R=0.95 T_R=1.0

Fig. 12.

As an example, calculate the specific volume in cubic feet per pound for steam at 1,000 lb. per square inch absolute pressure and 600°F. The critical pressure and temperature for steam are 3,200 lb. per square inch and 1165°R. (degrees Fahrenheit absolute), respectively.

$$P_R = \frac{1,000}{3,200} = 0.313 \qquad T_R = \frac{600 + 459.6}{1,165} = 0.919$$

The μ chart, Fig. 12, gives $\mu = 0.815$

$$1,000 \times 144 \times V = 0.815 \times \frac{1}{18} \times 1,543 \times 1,059.6$$
$$V = 0.515 \text{ cu. ft. per pound}$$

The actual value from the steam tables is 0.514.

Dalton's Law.—When ideal gases are mixed together, it has been found that each gas exerts a pressure exactly the same as if that same amount of gas were present in the same space alone and that the total pressure exerted by the mixture of the gases is exactly equal to the sum of the individual pressures of each of the gases if each were present alone in the same space. The pressure of the individual gas is called its partial pressure, and the foregoing law is known as Dalton's law of partial pressures.

Since the equation $PV = NRT$ is substantially correct for all gases and vapors, the volume of one mol of all gases must be the same at the same temperature and pressure. It is therefore evident from Dalton's law that the partial pressure of a gas in a mixture of gases must be proportional to the ratio of the number of mols of the gas present to the total number of mols of all the gases present. This ratio is called the mol fraction (y), and the rule may be stated

$$p = Py$$

where p is the partial pressure of the gas in the mixture of gases containing y mols of the gas per mol of the mixture, and P is the total pressure of the mixture. It also follows that the percentage by volume of a gas in a mixture is equal to $100y$.

Composition of Air.—Thus, air contains 21.0 per cent oxygen, 78.0 per cent nitrogen, and 1.0 per cent argon, by volume. Therefore, when air exists at 760 mm. pressure, the partial pressure of the oxygen will be

$$\frac{21.0}{100} \times 760 = 159.6 \text{ mm.}$$

It is often necessary to convert percentage by volume of a gas to percentage by weight, or the reverse. The method is indicated by the following example.

Calculation of Weight Per Cent.—Calculate the weight composition of the oxygen, nitrogen, and argon in air.

The molecular weight of oxygen is 32.00.
The molecular weight of nitrogen is 28.02.
The molecular weight of argon is 39.88.

If 100 mols of air is used, the weight of the

Oxygen will be $21.0 \times 32.00 = $ 672.0
Nitrogen will be $78.0 \times 28.02 = 2,185.6$
Argon will be $1.0 \times 39.88 = $ 39.88
Sum 2,897.5

The weight per cent of the

$$\text{Oxygen will be } \frac{672.0}{2{,}897.5} \times 100 = 23.2 \text{ per cent}$$

$$\text{Nitrogen will be } \frac{2{,}185.6}{2{,}897.5} \times 100 = 75.5 \text{ per cent}$$

$$\text{Argon will be } \frac{39.88}{2{,}897.5} \times 100 = 1.38 \text{ per cent}$$

Calculation of Mol Per Cent.—The reverse calculation, the conversion of weight per cent to mol or volume per cent is shown as follows:

What is the mol per cent of the acetone and ethyl alcohol in a vapor containing equal parts by weight of each?

$$\text{Molecular weight of alcohol } (C_2H_5OH) = 46.06$$
$$\text{Molecular weight of acetone } ((CH_3)_2CO) = 58.07$$

If 100 parts of the mixture is used, the mols of each vapor will be

$$\frac{50}{46.06} = 1.110 \text{ mols alcohol}$$

$$\frac{50}{58.07} = 0.860 \text{ mol acetone}$$

$$\text{Sum } \overline{1.970}$$

$$\text{Mol per cent alcohol} = \frac{1.110}{1.970} \times 100 = 56.3 \text{ per cent}$$

$$\text{Mol per cent acetone} = \frac{0.860}{1.970} \times 100 = 43.7 \text{ per cent}$$

CHAPTER VI

SOLUTIONS

Clapeyron Equation.—It was shown that where a pure liquid is in contact with its vapor, the vapor pressure of the liquid is fixed at any given temperature. The change of the vapor pressure with the temperature is shown exactly by the Clapeyron equation, which may be developed thermodynamically:

$$\frac{dp}{dT} = \frac{L}{(V - V_0)T}$$

where dp/dT is the change in pressure with the temperature, L is the latent heat of vaporization of 1 mol of the liquid, V is the volume of one mol of the vapor, V_0 the volume of 1 mol of the liquid, and T the absolute temperature at which vaporization takes place.

The heat of vaporization changes with the temperature but not rapidly; and for small temperature ranges, it is possible to consider L a constant. Also, $PV = NRT$ may be considered to hold for moderate pressures, and V_0 is usually very small compared with V, so that $V - V_0$ practically equals V.

Approximate Clapeyron Equation.—Making use of these approximations, the Clapeyron equation may be written

$$\frac{dp}{dt} = \frac{L}{RT^2/p}$$

which when integrated between limits gives

$$\ln \frac{p_2}{p_1} = \frac{L}{R}\left(\frac{1}{T_1} - \frac{1}{T_2}\right)$$

where ln represents Napierian logarithms or $\log_e$ and $\log_e = \log_{10} \times 2.303$.

Benzene.—An example of the use of this equation is given for benzene, C_6H_6, which boils at 80.36°C. under 760 mm. pressure

31

and whose latent heat of vaporization at that temperature is 7,250 cal. per gram mol. When L is measured in calories, R must be used in corresponding units, and it has the value 1.9885 (1.99)

$$\ln \frac{p_2}{760} = \frac{7,250}{1.99}\left(\frac{1}{273.1 + 80.36} - \frac{1}{T_2}\right)$$

Pressure in millimeters	Temperature degrees Centigrade		Difference, degrees
	Observed	Calculated	
181	40.0	37.5	−2.5
389	60.0	59.0	−1.0
760	80.36		
1,748	110.0	111.1	+1.1
3,520	140.0	142.3	+2.3

A table giving values of the latent heat of vaporization of the more common volatile liquids will be found in the Appendix (Table II).

It is possible to obtain a closer approximation of the true vapor-pressure curve of a liquid by expressing L as a function of the temperature:

$$L = a + bT + cT^2 + \text{etc.}$$

The approximate Clapeyron equation then becomes

$$\frac{dp/p}{dt} = \frac{a + bT + cT^2 + \text{etc.}}{RT^2}$$

$$\frac{dp/p}{dt} = \frac{a}{RT^2} + \frac{b}{RT} + \frac{c}{R}$$

which when integrated has the form

$$\ln p = -\frac{a}{RT} + \frac{b}{R} \ln T + \frac{c}{R}T + \text{constant}$$

An example of the use of this type of formula is the Marks equation, for steam:

$$\log_{10} p = 10.515354 - \frac{4,873.71}{T} - 0.00405096T +$$

$$0.0000013929664T^2$$

where p and T are expressed in pounds per square inch and degrees Fahrenheit absolute (degrees Rankine) respectively. It must be realized that this type of equation is wholly an empirical one, since it is based on an empirical relation between L and T.

Raoult's Law.—The introduction of a dissolved substance or solute into a volatile liquid lowers the vapor pressure of the liquid if the solute is nonvolatile or lowers the partial vapor pressure of the solvent if the solute is volatile. It has been found that the vapor-pressure lowering for ideal solutions is proportional to the mol fraction of the dissolved substance, and the relation may be expressed by the equation

$$p = p_0 x_0$$

where p is the partial vapor pressure of the solvent, p_0 is the vapor pressure of the pure solvent, and x_0 is the mol fraction of the solvent in the mixture. This is known as Raoult's law of vapor-pressure lowering. It can be predicted qualitatively from the phase rule, since the addition of another substance to a pure liquid makes a two-component system, and it is, therefore, necessary to fix the composition of the liquid (or the vapor) as well as the temperature, in order to fix the vapor pressure.

Vapor Pressure of Sugar Solution.—For example, the vapor pressure of a 10 per cent cane-sugar solution in water at 100°C. is calculated as follows:

$$\text{Molecular weight of water} = 18$$
$$\text{Molecular weight of sugar} = 342$$
$$\frac{0.10}{342} = 0.000292$$
$$\frac{0.90}{18} = 0.050$$
$$\text{Sum} \quad \overline{0.050292}$$

Mol fraction of the sugar $= \dfrac{0.000292}{0.050292} = 0.00580$

Mol fraction of the water $= 1. - 0.00580 = 0.9942$
The vapor pressure of pure water at 100°C. $= 760$ mm.

Therefore vapor pressure of the 10 per cent sugar solution would be $0.9942 \times 760 = 756$ mm. This example for the case of a nonvolatile material dissolved in a volatile solvent is similar to the case of a volatile material dissolved in a volatile solvent, the only difference being that the partial pressure of the solvent and not the total vapor pressure of the mixture must be taken into consideration. For instance, in order to calculate the partial pressure of benzene over a mixture containing 5 per cent by weight of toluene in the benzene at 80°C., a similar method is used. The molecular weight of benzene is 78.1, and the molecular weight of toluene is 92.1. In 100 parts by weight of the mixture there will be $5/92.1 = 0.0543$ mol of toluene and $95/78.1 = 1.216$ mols of benzene. The total number of mols present in 100 parts of the mixture is 1.270.

The mol fraction of the toluene $= 0.0543/1.270 = 0.0427$
The mol fraction of the benzene $= 1.0 - 0.0427 = 0.9573$

The vapor pressure of pure benzene at 80°C. is 753.6 mm. Therefore, the partial pressure of benzene over this mixture will be $753.6 \times 0.9573 = 721.5$ mm.

Limits of Raoult's Law.—The use of Raoult's law for the purpose of calculating the partial pressure of the solvent in any solution is limited in application to dilute solutions, usually of less than 5 mol per cent dissolved solute. In some cases, however, as for instance the case of mixtures of benzene and toluene, Raoult's law applies to considerably higher concentrations, while in others, such as mixtures of alcohol and water, Raoult's law practically does not hold at all. Furthermore, if the dissolved material is an electrolyte, such as an acid, an alkali, or a salt, which is ionized in solution, the vapor-pressure lowering is increased, depending upon the degree of ionization of the dissolved material. For instance, a solution of acetic acid and water will conduct electricity, indicating that the acetic acid is ionized to a certain extent. Experiments have shown that dilute acetic acid of a strength approximately one-tenth of a molecular weight per 1,000 g. of water, that is, 6 g. of acetic acid in 1,000 g. of water, is ionized approximately 1.34 per cent at 25°C. The vapor-pressure lowering of the water in a solution of this concentration, therefore, will be increased by 1.34 per cent over the lowering which would be calculated from the molal concentration of the acetic acid if it were not ionized. Thus, the equivalent number of mols of acetic acid present in this solution would be 1.0134 × $\frac{1}{10}$ mols in 55.5 mols of water. Since the vapor pressure of pure water at 25°C. is 23.55 mm., the vapor-pressure lowering would be

$$\frac{23.55 \times 0.10134}{55.5 + 0.10134} = 0.429 \text{ mm.}$$

The partial pressure of the water vapor, therefore, over this solution would be 23.55 − 0.429 = 23.12 mm.

Henry's Law.—There is another rule for solutions known as Henry's law which states that the partial pressure over the mixture of a volatile solute dissolved in a solvent is proportional to the mol fraction of the solute in the mixture, or

$$p = ax$$

where p is the partial pressure of the dissolved substance, x is the mol fraction of the dissolved substance in the mixture, and a is a constant. If the constant a has the same value as the vapor pressure of the pure solute at the same temperature, the equation becomes the expression for Raoult's law which is, therefore, a limiting case of Henry's law. It is not common, however, for a mixture of two volatile materials to follow Raoult's law throughout the entire range of compositions. Therefore, the constant a is usually different from p_0, the vapor pressure of the pure material. In the case of benzene and toluene, for instance, a is practically equal to p_0, and the partial pressure of the dissolved substance present in the smaller proportion can be calculated from Raoult's law with considerable precision. Thus, in the case cited above, 5 per cent by weight solution of toluene in benzene, it was noted that the mol fraction of toluene was 0.0427. Therefore, if the vapor pressure of pure toluene at this temperature be multiplied by this figure, the partial pressure of toluene in the vapor above this mixture will be obtained. The vapor pressure of pure toluene at 80° is 291 mm., giving a partial pressure of the toluene of 12.4 mm. The total vapor pressure of the liquid, which is the sum of the partial pressures of the two components, will be the sum of the partial pressures of the benzene and toluene, or 735.9 mm.

Partial Pressure of Ammonia over Water.—In most cases, however, the constant a is not equal to p_0, and it is necessary to determine experimentally the value of a at any given temperature. This has been done for a large number of mixtures. For instance, the partial pressure of ammonia, NH_3, above an aqueous solution of ammonia containing one molecular weight, 17 g., per 1,000 g. of water at 25° is 13.47 mm.

In the expression $p = ax$, $p = 13.47$ mm.

$$x = \frac{1}{1 + \dfrac{1,000}{18}} = 0.018$$

The value of the constant a, therefore, is $13.47/0.018 = 748$.

Using this value of a, it would be possible to calculate by Henry's law the partial pressure of ammonia over a 0.5 M solution at the same temperature.

$$p = 748 \times \frac{0.5}{1,000/18} = 6.74$$

The experimentally determined value for this strength is 6.65. In the same way, the partial pressure of ammonia over a 0.25 M solution would be 3.37 mm., and the experimentally determined figure is 3.32 mm.

Chemical Combinations.—The foregoing figures indicate the reliability of Henry's law and its application to very dilute ammonia solutions. It should be noted, however, that ammonia combines with water to form ammonium hydroxide according to the reaction $NH_3 + H_2O = NH_4OH$. It should be expected from this equation that the more dilute the solution of ammonia the greater the proportion of ammonia in the solution that will be present in the form of NH_4OH rather than NH_3. In other words, where a volatile material combines chemically with the solvent, the vapor pressure of the volatile material will tend to be less than that calculated from Raoult's law, and the divergence will be greater the more dilute the solution. It is, therefore, safe to use Henry's law only for dilute solutions.

Limits of Henry's Law.—Where the volatile materials do not combine chemically, as in the case of mixtures of benzene and toluene, Henry's law will be found to apply nearly exactly over a fairly wide range of concentrations. In general, however, its range of accuracy has an upper limit of somewhere between 5 and 10 mol per cent of the dissolved substance.

It will be seen, therefore, that Raoult's law and Henry's law apply for very great and very small concentrations, respectively. For intermediate concentrations, however, there are no physical laws that are applicable, and recourse must be had to experimentally determined data. It is possible, in some cases, to derive equations that fit the data very closely between the two extremes covered by Raoult's and Henry's laws. These equations are frequently of considerable value in vapor-pressure calculations.

The Duhem equation

$$\frac{d \ln p_1}{d \ln p_2} = -\frac{1-x}{x}$$

is the best known of these equations. In it, p_1 and p_2 are the partial pressures of the more and of the less volatile components, respectively, and x is the mol fraction of the former in the liquid phase.

CHAPTER VII

CONCENTRATED SOLUTIONS

Mixtures of certain liquids, especially mixtures of substances that are closely related chemically, *e.g.*, substances in the same homologous series, as benzene and toluene, follow Raoult's law very closely, so closely, in fact, that it is possible to derive the boiling-point curve of such mixtures from Raoult's and Dalton's laws with a very small percentage of error.

Vapor-pressure Curves for Benzene-toluene.—Figure 13 shows the vapor-pressure curves of benzene and toluene between the temperatures of 60 and 110°C. It is possible to derive empirical equations based on the Clapeyron equation which will represent these vapor-pressure curves very closely.

The diagram in Fig. 14 shows the total pressure and partial pressure of benzene-toluene mixtures at different temperatures. For instance, the vapor pressure of pure benzene at 100°C. is 1,344 mm. The vapor pressure of pure toluene at 100°C. is 560 mm. On the diagram on Fig. 14, the vapor pressures in millimeters are plotted as ordinates, and the mol percentages of benzene are plotted as abscissas. (A mixture containing 30 mol per cent benzene is a mixture of 30 molecular weights of benzene and 70 molecular weights of toluene. Zero mol per cent benzene is equal to 100 mol per cent toluene.) The pressure of pure toluene, therefore, is plotted on the left-hand side of the diagram, and the pressure of pure benzene is plotted on the right-hand side of the diagram, and a straight line AB is drawn connecting these two pressures. A straight line is also drawn connecting the vapor pressure of pure toluene with a point representing 0 mol per cent toluene and 0 mm. pressure, shown by the dotted line AC. In the same way, a line BD is drawn connecting the vapor pressure of pure benzene and the point representing 0 per cent pure benzene and 0 mm. pressure. From Raoult's law, any point on the line AC represents the partial pressure of

38

toluene in a mixture of benzene and toluene for any given composition. Thus, a solution containing 50 mol per cent toluene will have a partial pressure for the toluene of 280 mm. In the same way, *DB* represents the partial pressures of benzene in the same

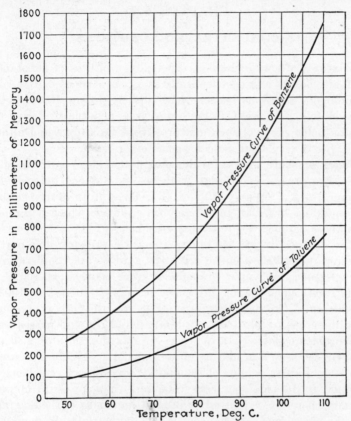

Fig. 13.—Vapor pressure curves of benzene and toluene.

mixture, and a mixture containing 50 mol per cent of benzene will have a partial pressure for the benzene of 673 mm.

Since the total pressure on the system is the sum of the individual partial pressures, the total pressure above such a mixture at 100°C. will be the sum of the two partial pressures, or 953 mm. This total pressure is shown graphically by the straight line *AB*. In the same way, the total pressures and partial pressures of mixtures of benzene and toluene can be drawn for different temperatures, and Fig. 14 indicates such lines for temperatures from 60 to 110.4°C. The partial-pressure lines for the benzene have been omitted from the diagram, since the partial pressure of the

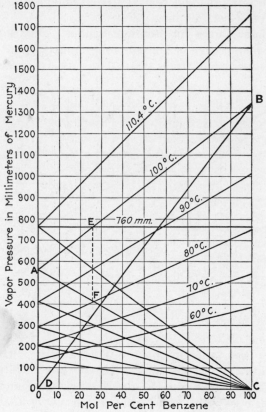

Fig. 14.—Partial-pressure curves of benzene-toluene mixtures.

benzene can be obtained by subtracting from the total pressure the partial pressure of the toluene, lines of which are indicated.

Distillation of Benzene-toluene Mixtures.—Suppose, now, that the distillation of a benzene-toluene mixture is being conducted at a total pressure of 760 mm. The pressure corresponding to 760 mm. is indicated on Fig. 14, and it will be noted that it cuts the total-pressure line at 110.4°C. at 0 mol per cent benzene, at 100°C. at 26 mol per cent benzene, and at 90°C. at 58 mol per cent benzene.

In other words, mixtures of these three compositions will have a total pressure of 760 mm. at the respective temperatures. Thus, these mixtures will boil at these temperatures under an external pressure of 760 mm.

Boiling-point Curve for Benzene-toluene.—Figure 15 shows the boiling-point curve of benzene-toluene mixtures at 760 mm. pressure, constructed from these data. Several intermediate

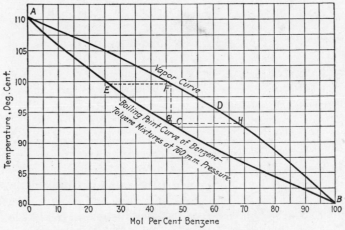

Fig. 15.—Boiling-point curve for benzene-toluene mixtures.

points have been taken in order to determine the curve exactly. This boiling-point curve is indicated by the line ACB, where mol per cents benzene are plotted as abscissas, as before, and temperatures in degrees centigrade are plotted as ordinates. This diagram is one of constant pressure and corresponds exactly to the phase-rule diagram discussed previously. Any point on the line ACB, therefore, indicates the boiling point of that composition at 760 mm. pressure. The partial pressure of toluene at 100° over a liquid boiling at this temperature at 760 mm. is found to be 415 mm., as determined by the intersection of the dotted line EF (Fig. 14) with the partial-pressure line AC, point E being taken where the chosen temperature cuts the total-pressure line, 760 mm. This means that over a solution con-

taining 25.7 mol per cent of benzene, at 100°C., the partial
pressure of toluene is 415 mm.   Therefore, the partial pressure of
the benzene will be the difference of 760 and 415 mm., or 345 mm.
Since the mol fraction of substances in the vapor state is proportional to the partial pressure, the mol fraction of toluene in
the vapor above this solution will be equal to 415/760 = 0.546.
In the same way, the mol fraction of toluene in the vapor above
a number of solutions of these two substances which boil at
760 mm. pressure can be determined, and some are tabulated in
the following table.

Temperature	Composition of the liquid	Partial pressure of toluene	Mol fraction of toluene
105	12.5	567	0.746
100	25.7	415	0.546
95	40.3	285	0.375
90	58.	173	0.228
85	77.	85	0.112

Vapor-composition Curve.—It is now possible to construct
a curve showing the composition of the vapor in equilibrium with
any mixture of benzene and toluene boiling at 760 mm. pressure,
and such a curve will be found to have the form ADB in Fig. 15.
The two curves meet at two points A and B, the boiling points of
toluene and benzene, respectively.   Therefore, the point E on the
liquid line ACB indicates that a mixture containing 26.5 mol per
cent of benzene will boil at 99.7°C. at 760 mm. pressure, and the
vapor in equilibrium with it will have the composition indicated
by the point F at this temperature, or 46.5 mol per cent benzene.
As was pointed out before, if such a vapor were condensed, it
would boil at a temperature corresponding to the point G and
would itself produce a vapor at some temperature corresponding
with the point H.   The relative ease of separating mixtures of
benzene and toluene by fractional distillation, therefore, may be
indicated by the number of steps that would be required to pass
from near the point A, pure toluene, to near the point B, pure
benzene.   It is obvious, of course, that it is impossible to produce
absolutely pure A and B by such a process.

Effect of Pressure.—Mixtures of volatile liquids do not, as a rule, follow Raoult's and Dalton's laws completely, and the variations are very irregular. Even mixtures that do conform satisfactorily at low pressures are found to deviate quite widely at high pressures, largely because of the failure of the vapor to obey the gas laws. This is particularly important in petroleum work where high-pressure operations are used in stabili-

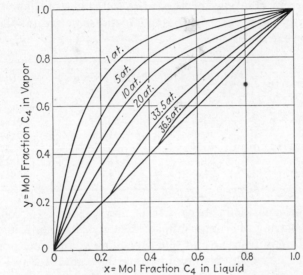

Fig. 16.—Effect of pressure on vapor-liquid equilibriums.

zation, absorption, natural-gasoline manufacture, and similar operations.

In general, as the temperature (or pressure) is increased, the relative volatility decreases. This is most clearly brought out by plotting y-x curves, $i.e.$, the mol fraction of the light component in the vapor vs. the mol fraction of the light component in the liquid. Figure 16 is a y-x plot for n-C_4H_{10} − n-C_6H_{14} based on the data of Cummings.[1] At a given liquid composition, the mol fraction of n-C_4 in the vapor decreases as the pressure increases. This decrease makes it more difficult to separate the components by distillation. Although an increase of pressure makes the separation more difficult, it makes the condensa-

[1] CUMMINGS, Sc. D. thesis in Chemical Engineering, M.I.T., 1933.

tion of the overhead vapor much easier, and for this reason pressure is commonly used in the distillation of low-boiling materials which would be difficult or impossible to condense at low pressure without the use of refrigeration. In Fig. 16, it is noted that the curves for 33.5 and 36.5 atm. do not cover the whole region. This is due to the fact that 33.5 atm. is above the critical pressures of all mixtures containing less than 23 per cent butane, and in this region only one phase is present. Mixtures with more than 23 per cent butane are below their critical pressure at 33.5 atm., and two phases of different composition are possible. Separation by distillation is possible only within the limits of the two-phase region. As the pressure is increased, the two-phase region decreases until at pressures higher than the maximum critical pressure of butane-hexane mixtures only one phase is possible for all compositions, and separation by distillation is no longer possible. It has been found possible largely to correct for these deviations due to pressure by the use of fugacities based on μ charts (see page 28).[1] Such corrections are best expressed as the relation between the mol fraction of a component in the vapor y and the mol fraction in the liquid x.

$$y = Kx$$

where K is the equilibrium constant. The table on pages 45 and 46 contains values of K for the lower hydrocarbons.

It should be emphasized that these K values become unsatisfactory at pressures approaching the critical pressure of the mixture, since in this region the K values for a given component are a function not only of the temperature and pressure but also of the other components present. Experimental data on various mixtures agree satisfactorily with these K values up to about 350 lb. per square inch, but at pressures higher than this the deviations become large.

[1] Lewis and Luke, *Ind. Eng. Chem.*, 25, 725 (1933).

K VALUES

Temperature, degrees Fahrenheit	Absolute pressures, atmospheres				
	1	5	10	20	50
CH₄					
20	114	23.0	11.5	6.00	2.60
200	305	61.0	32.0	15.5	6.30
400	580	116	58.0	29.0	12.0
600	850	170	85.0	43.0	17.5
C₂H₄					
20	24.5	5.10	2.60	1.44	0.840
200	103	20.5	10.4	5.30	2.35
400	265	54.0	27.0	14.0	5.60
600	510	102	51.0	25.5	10.4
C₂H₆					
20	16.0	3.30	1.75	1.00	0.660
200	71.0	14.5	7.40	3.80	1.75
400	195	40.0	20.0	10.0	4.30
600	380	77.0	39.0	19.5	8.00
C₃H₆					
20	4.50	0.950	0.540	0.340	0.260
200	30.0	6.20	3.20	1.76	0.980
400	100	20.0	10.0	5.20	2.30
600	215	43.0	22.0	11.0	4.70
C₃H₈					
20	3.70	0.800	0.450	0.290	0.235
200	25.0	5.20	2.75	1.52	0.850
400	85.0	17.0	8.80	4.50	2.00
600	185	37.0	18.6	9.40	4.10
n-C₄H₁₀					
20	0.810	0.190	0.110	0.074	0.078
200	10.5	2.25	1.25	0.770	0.610
400	43.0	8.80	4.50	2.40	1.25
600	(110)	22.0	11.0	5.60	2.50

K Values.—(*Continued*)

Temperature, degrees Fahrenheit	Absolute pressures, atmospheres				
	1	5	10	20	50
$i\text{-}C_4H_{10}$					
20	1.20	0.280	0.162	0.110	0.110
200	13.0	2.80	1.52	0.910	0.670
400	51.0	10.5	5.30	2.85	1.36
600	125	25.5	13.0	6.60	2.85
$n\text{-}C_5H_{12}$					
20	0.175	0.042	0.026	0.018	0.022
200	4.30	0.960	0.550	0.360	0.345
400	22.5	4.75	2.50	1.42	0.890
600	65.0	13.4	6.90	3.60	1.70
$i\text{-}C_5H_{12}$					
20	0.255	0.061	0.037	0.026	0.032
200	5.20	1.15	0.650	0.425	0.400
400	25.5	5.40	2.75	1.55	0.940
600	69.0	14.0	7.00	3.70	1.72
$n\text{-}C_6H_{14}$					
20	0.040	0.010	0.0064	0.0047	0.008
200	1.85	0.430	0.255	0.180	0.215
400	13.6	2.90	1.60	0.980	0.770
600	42.0	8.60	4.40	2.40	1.30
$n\text{-}C_7H_{16}$					
20	0.010	0.0025	0.0017	0.0013	0.003
200	0.830	0.195	0.120	0.089	0.140
400	8.40	1.80	1.00	0.670	0.670
600	29.0	6.10	3.15	1.75	1.05
$n\text{-}C_8H_{18}$					
20					
200	0.390	0.094	0.060	0.042	0.094
400	5.30	1.15	0.670	0.470	0.570
600	19.5	4.15	2.25	1.30	0.910

CHAPTER VIII

SIMPLE DISTILLATION AND PARTIAL CONDENSATION

If a mixture of two volatile liquids is distilled, the distillate contains a greater proportion of the more volatile material than the residue; and as the distillation proceeds, both distillate and residue become poorer in the more volatile component. This change in composition may be estimated quantitatively if the relation of the composition of the vapor to that of the liquid in equilibrium with it is known. As has been indicated above, the theoretical relations are usually difficult to handle, and empirically determined relations are frequently of value.

The Distillation Equation.—Starting with W parts of a mixture of A and B, containing a parts of A and $W - a$ parts of B, the composition of the liquid x will be a/W with respect to A, and the composition of the vapor will be some function of the composition of the liquid $F(a/W)$, or y. Allow a differential amount dW of the mixture containing a differential amount of A, da to be evaporated; there will remain as a residue $W - dW$ parts of mixture containing $a - da$ parts of A, and the composition of the distillate will be da/dW. Therefore $y = da/dW$, or $y = d(Wx)/dW$. Simplifying this equation as follows:

$$\frac{W dx + x dW}{dW} = y$$

$$\frac{W dx}{dW} = y - x$$

$$\int_{W_0}^{W} \frac{dW}{W} = \int_{X_0}^{X} \frac{dx}{y - x}$$

$$\ln \frac{W}{W_0} = \int_{X_0}^{X} \frac{dx}{y - x}$$

The solution of the problem requiring the value for W when the composition of the liquid has reached the value x can then be found by evaluating this integrated equation. In order to do

47

this there are several methods which may be followed. First, for small temperature and composition ranges the relation between the vapor and liquid may be approximately represented by a straight line, or $y = cx$, where c is some constant.

$$\ln \frac{W}{W_0} = \int_{X_0}^{X} \frac{dx}{cx - x} = \int_{X_0}^{X} \frac{dx}{x(c - 1)} = \frac{1}{c - 1} \ln \frac{x}{x_0}$$

clearing of logarithms

$$\frac{W}{W_0} = \left(\frac{x}{x_0}\right)^{\frac{1}{c-1}} \quad \text{or} \quad \frac{x}{x_0} = \left(\frac{W}{W_0}\right)^{c-1}$$

Acetic Acid–Water.—The following data were taken from Lord Rayleigh,[1] giving the relation between the liquid and the vapor for mixtures of acetic acid and water.

Composition of liquid x	Composition of vapor y	c	α
0.0677	0.0510	0.75	1.35
0.1458	0.1136		
0.2682	0.2035	0.76	1.43
0.3746	0.2810		
0.4998	0.3849	0.77	1.60
0.6156	0.4907		
0.7227	0.6045	0.84	1.70
0.8166	0.7306		
0.9070	0.8622	0.95	1.56

This indicates that for values of x up to 50 per cent for acetic acid, such a procedure is safe. This was shown by an experiment as follows:

$$W_0 = 1{,}010 \text{ g.} \qquad x_0 = 0.0757 \text{ (7.57 per cent)}$$
$$W = 254 \text{ g.} \qquad \text{Assume } c = 0.75$$
$$\left(\frac{254}{1{,}010}\right)^{0.75-1} = \frac{x}{0.0757} \qquad x = 0.107 \text{ (10.7 per cent)}$$

The actual experiment showed $x = 0.110$ (11.0 per cent), which indicates the reliability of this method.

[1] *Phil. Mag.*, p. 534, 1904.

Another method consists in finding an empirical equation
for y. Construct a diagram as in Fig. 17, with composition of
the liquid as abscissas and composition of the vapor as ordinates,
and construct a curve OA from the data as given in the preceding
table. The straight line OB represents the $y = 0.75x$ as used
above. The data are of such nature that it is not possible to fit
one equation to the entire line, as it consists substantially of one
curved and one straight section. In this particular case, the
equation for the straight section will be, as before, $y = 0.75x$,

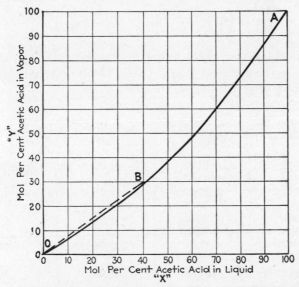

Fig. 17.—Liquid-vapor composition curve for acetic acid-water mixtures.

and the curved section will have the form $y + a = c(x + b)^n$
where a, b, c, and n are constants which can be evaluated from
data. It will be seen, however, that such an equation would be
difficult to handle; and where precise results are required over a
wide range, it is better to use the third, or graphical, method.

Construct a plot of $\dfrac{1}{y - x}$ as ordinates and values of x as
abscissas, as in Fig. 18. The measurement of the area under the
curve between any two limits of x will therefore be the evaluation
of the integral $\displaystyle\int_{X_1}^{X_2} \dfrac{dx}{y - x}$ and will be equal to $\ln\dfrac{W_2}{W_1}$.

A fourth method is by the use of the relative volatility which is defined by the equation

$$\frac{y_A/x_A}{y_B/x_B} = \alpha_{AB}$$

where α_{AB} is the relative volatility of component A to component B. For a large number of mixtures, the variation of α with

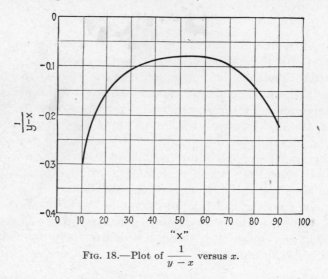

Fig. 18.—Plot of $\dfrac{1}{y - x}$ versus x.

composition is small, and an average value may be employed. For a binary mixture, the expression can be changed to

$$y_A = \frac{\alpha x_A}{1 + (\alpha - 1)x_A}$$

The use of this equation gives

$$\ln \frac{W}{W_0} = \int_{X_0}^{X} \frac{dx}{\dfrac{\alpha x}{1 + (\alpha - 1)x} - x}$$

$$= \frac{1}{\alpha - 1} \ln \frac{x(1 - x_0)}{x_0(1 - x)} + \ln \frac{(1 - x_0)}{(1 - x)}$$

Using $\alpha = 1.35$ in the same example gives $x = 0.115$.

Simple Condensation.—The relation between the weight of a mixture distilled and its composition derived above was based on the assumption that the portion distilled was removed from contact with the liquid immediately, so that equilibrium could not be established afterward. It is possible to condense vapor in the same way, removing the condensate from contact with it as rapidly as it is formed. Analysis of this process leads to similar equation for the relation between the composition of the vapor and the weight condensed:

$$\ln \frac{W}{W_0} = - \int_{y_0}^{y} \frac{dy}{y - x}$$

where W represents the weight of the vapor, and y and x the compositions of the vapor and condensate, respectively.

Partial Condensation.—If a still operates with a partial condenser and a final condenser, so that the vapor condensed in the partial condenser returns to the still as reflux, a certain amount of rectification is obtained without the aid of a rectifying column.

As an example of the application of this method to a specific case, consider an apparatus as indicated diagrammatically in Fig. 84 (page 199), which represents a distilling apparatus for use in the stabilization of absorption naphtha.

In one test, the mol fractions given in the first two columns of the following table were obtained when operating at a pressure of 254 lb. per square inch absolute with a temperature of 117°F. in the reflux drum.

Mol Fraction

Component	Residue gas at $B = y$	Liquid reflux at $A = x$	K^*	$x_{cal.} = y/K$
CH_4	0.053	0.007	12	0.0044
C_2H_4	0.011	0.002	3.6	0.003
C_2H_6	0.146	0.0618	2.55	0.057
C_3H_6	0.140	0.12	1.05	0.133
C_3H_8	0.537	0.580	0.94	0.572
i-C_4	0.081	0.160	0.50	0.162
n-C_4	0.032	0.069	0.40	0.080

* Values of K estimated from page 45 for a pressure of 17.3 atm. and 117°F.

The composition of the liquid in equilibrium with the residue gas can be calculated by the use of the vapor-liquid equilibrium values given on pages 45 and 46. The values of K obtained from this table by interpolation at 17.3 atm. and 117°F. are given in the third column of the preceding table. Since K is equal to y/x, the mol fraction in the liquid is calculated by dividing the mol fraction in the vapor y by the equilibrium constant. Values of the mol fraction in the liquid calculated in this manner are given in the fourth column of this table. These values are seen to be in good agreement with the measured values given in the second column. The close agreement indicates reliability of the experimental data and the applicability of the vapor-liquid equilibrium constants to this system.

The reboiler used in this same test was of the cross-flow type in which the vapor evolved would be swept away and not react to any extent with the remaining liquid. This type of operation should approximate simple distillation instead of partial equilibrium vaporization.

The test data gave the compositions given in the first two columns of the following table.

MOL FRACTION

Component	Liquid from column $= x_0$	Residue from reboiler $= x$	K	$\dfrac{1}{K-1}$	$\left(\dfrac{x}{x_0}\right)^{\frac{1}{K-1}}$
C_3	0.0008	0.0009			
C_4	0.661	0.481	1.34	3.06	0.385
C_5	0.243	0.331	0.66	−3.06	0.387
C_6+	0.0945	0.187	0.314	−1.46	0.368

Since the percentage of the original stock vaporized is fixed, the equation given on page 47 indicates that $(x/x_0)^{\frac{1}{K-1}}$ should be constant and equal to the fraction unvaporized. The C_3 fraction was not considered owing to its being so small in amount that slight errors in analysis would lead to large errors in the calculations. For the C_4 and C_6+ fractions, averaged constants weighted for the portion of the various constituents that they contained were used; thus for the C_6+ fraction, Gunness indicates that it was 72 mol per cent C_6 and 28 per cent higher than C_6; the vapor-liquid equilibrium constant was obtained by taking 72 per cent of the constant for C_6 plus 28 per cent of the constant for C_7 ($0.72 \times 0.35 + 0.28 \times 0.22 = 0.314$).

CHAPTER IX

AMMONIA

The problem of manufacture of pure anhydrous ammonia from crude ammonia liquor obtained from gasworks is one of the most interesting and also complicated problems with which the distillation engineer has to deal.

Sources of Ammonia Impurities.—Crude ammonia obtained from the destructive distillation of coal contains, besides ammonia and water, a large number of other impurities consisting chiefly of compounds of carbon, sulphur, and nitrogen. These impurities are frequently combined together in the form of such compounds as ammonium sulphide, ammonium carbonate, ammonium cyanide, sulphur combinations of the foregoing, and various organic nitrogen compounds such as pyridene bases and other objectionable-smelling substances of this type. There is a certain amount of tarry matter of the general nature of coal tar present in the crude-ammonia liquor. Part of the ammonia in the crude liquor is present as free ammonia, or ammonium hydroxide which can be completely removed from the solution by boiling while the balance of the ammonia may be present as so-called fixed ammonia, *i.e.*, combined with some of the other substances in such a way that some treatment more vigorous than boiling is necessary to drive it out of solution. Most of the organic nitrogen compounds are in this class, it being usually necessary where these are abundant to combine with the boiling the action of a strong base, together with reducing agents of a suitable sort. In general, however, the process of recovering all of the ammonia from the crude liquor consists of boiling the liquor in the presence of milk of lime which decomposes most of the fixed nitrogen compounds in such a way that practically all of the nitrogen available is driven off as ammonia. A part of the impurities present in the solution, however, are volatile and are driven off with the ammonia during this process, and the equipment required to produce pure anhydrous ammonia, therefore, must have provision for the removal of these impurities which may be classed for practical purposes as hydrogen sulphide, carbon dioxide, pyridene, and tar. The hydrogen sulphide and carbon dioxide are usually present in the liquor as ammonium sulphide and ammonium carbonate. Both of these compounds, however, are stable only at low temperatures and decompose at the boiling temperature, giving off, in the vapor, hydrogen sulphide, carbon dioxide, and ammonia. It is also true that the hydrogen sulphide and carbon dioxide are less soluble in water than the ammonia. Therefore, at any given temperature the partial pressure of the hydrogen sulphide and carbon dioxide in the vapor phase in equilibrium with the liquor will be greater than that of the ammonia. By properly arranging a machine, it is possible to get a fairly complete separation of the two volatile gases from the more soluble ammonia by control of temperature and concentration.

The pyridene bases and the tarry oils which are present in small amounts in the ammonia can usually be removed by partial condensation of the vapor, where some of the oils will condense out and can be decanted; and by washing the vapors with some suitable relatively nonvolatile petroleum oil in which the pyridenes are soluble and which will wash them out of the ammonia-water vapor.

The bulk of the impurities having been removed by the foregoing methods, the last traces of the hydrogen sulphide and carbon dioxide can usually be removed by passing the vapor through solutions of caustic soda which will combine with them and render them nonvolatile.

The small amounts of tarry material present are usually removed by absorption on activated charcoal.

Diagram of Continuous Ammonia Still.—A very large number of designs have been utilized for the removal of pure ammonia from crude liquor. In general, it has been found that the continuous system of distillation is the most satisfactory, and the accompanying diagram (Fig. 19) will give an idea of how this system may be utilized for this purpose.

A represents a feed tank for feeding continuously the crude-ammonia liquor to the system. This liquor first is preheated by means of a vapor heater *B*, and then it passes into the central portion of a continuous distilling column *EF*. The columns used in ammonia stills are quite different from those used in the distillation of the finer products such as alcohol, ether, and acetone. In the first place, all apparatus to be used in connection with ammonia must be made of steel or cast iron. It is therefore necessarily of more or less massive nature. Furthermore, owing

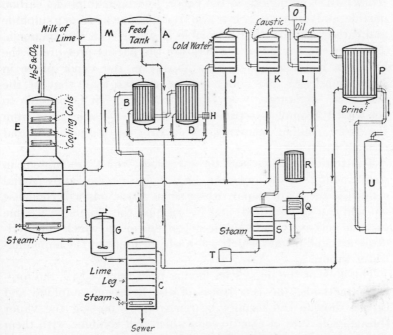

FIG. 19.—Continuous ammonia still.

to the possibility of the formation of solid ammonia compounds with the carbon dioxide and hydrogen sulphide, there is always the possibility of the equipment's clogging. Therefore, if the plate type of fractionating column is to be used, the caps are made large with serrated edges and little attempt is made to obtain the intimacy of contact that is desired in the finer types of distillation equipment.

Removal of Hydrogen Sulphide and Carbon Dioxide.—All parts of the ammonia system are constructed so that they may be opened up for cleaning at any time, and everything is made as accessible as possible. The continuous column *EF* is divided into two parts, the upper part *E* consisting of a number of plates on which there are a number of coils containing cooling water, while the lower part *F* is heated by the introduction of open steam. The crude-ammonia liquor running down over the plates of the column *F* comes into contact with the open steam, and the volatile hydrogen sulphide, carbon dioxide, and ammonia are driven out. Since, however, the hydrogen sulphide and carbon dioxide are less soluble at any given temperature than the ammonia, the two former are driven out more readily, and therefore the vapors passing up through the upper column *E* contain a larger percentage of these gases than is found in the entering feed. The vapors passing up through this column come into contact with the cooling coils whereby they are partially condensed; so that if the temperature at the top of the column *E* is kept sufficiently low, the gases escaping from the top of the column consist almost entirely of carbon dioxide and hydrogen sulphide, and practically none of the ammonia is carried off with them. It is, therefore, usually customary to exhaust these gases directly to the atmosphere, and the loss of ammonia with them is very small indeed. It should be noted, however, in connection with these exhaust gases that both hydrogen sulphide and carbon dioxide are very dangerous gases and should be exhausted outdoors at such a point that they will not be likely to collect and become dangerous.

Treatment with Lime.—The liquor passing down through the column *F* and being diluted by the introduction of steam used for boiling then passes out through the bottom into a mixing tank *G* where it is mixed with a suitable quantity of milk of lime which is supplied from the feed tank *M*. The mixture of ammonia liquor with milk of lime then runs into the exhausting column *C* where it is boiled by the introduction of live steam into the bottom section. This lime leg, as it is called, must be designed so that the solid particles of calcium hydrate will find no opportunity to become lodged on the plates of this column so that it would be clogged up. The column also must be made very accessible for cleaning on account of this danger. The ammoniacal liquor in contact with the lime at the high temperature is freed of all of its ammonia, which escapes from the top of the column through the vapor pipe as indicated, while the excess lime, together with the nonvolatile material, is discharged in the sludge from the bottom of this exhausting column to the sewer.

Removal of Oils.—The vapor from the lime leg passes first to the reflux condenser which is used as the preheater B and then to a second reflux condenser D where it is cooled by cooling water to a fairly low temperature. It has been found that certain oils which are present in the ammonia will condense out at this point in the purification so that the liquor discharged from the condenser D if passed through an oil decanter H will have removed from it a considerable portion of these insoluble compounds. The decanted liquor then runs back into the top of the exhausting column as indicated.

Scrubbers.—The ammoniacal vapor now freed of nearly all of the hydrogen sulphide and carbon dioxide and of a certain amount of oils passes into a compound washing or scrubbing tower indicated by the tower J, K, and L. This column is divided into three sections. In the first section J, the gas is washed by water which removes from it a number of impurities which have escaped previous purifying processes. This water, of course, coming into contact with strong ammonia dissolves a large amount of the gas, and the heat of solution is such that the water would be raised to a higher temperature were it not for the fact that cooling coils are supplied on the plates of the column. The wash water obtained from this column then is allowed to flow back into the central portion of the column F as indicated so that the ammonia thus dissolved of the water is not lost. The gas then passes to the second section where it is washed by a dilute solution of caustic soda which neutralizes all of the remaining hydrogen sulphide and carbon dioxide, forming nonvolatile sodium carbonate and sodium sulphide, the caustic liquor being allowed to return to the column F together with the liquor from the water scrubber J. The vapor now freed from the gases passes into the oil scrubber L where it is washed with a suitable petroleum oil which dissolves out of the gas all of the soluble pyridene bases, thus removing all of these objectionable-smelling pyridenes. The oil from this scrubber, containing but little ammonia, can be used over again, and it is therefore customary to take the oil through a steam-heated oil preheater Q into an oil-exhausting column or oil leg S, as indicated, where it is boiled by the use of open steam, driving off the pyridene which is condensed in the condenser R, while the oil freed from pyridene is discharged from the base of the column into a cooler and oil-supply tank T, from which point the oil-feed tank O shown above is supplied.

Removal of Water.—The vapor from the oil scrubber L now containing only water and a small amount of tarry impurities passes to a condenser P where it is brought into direct contact with brine, the brine condensing out of the ammonia gas nearly all of the water vapor present. The condensed product, ammonia liquor, obtained is allowed to run back through pipe lines indicated into the top of the exhausting column C where the ammonia is handled over again, while the gas, now practically water free, is allowed to pass into an ammonia tower U where it is brought into direct contact with lumps of solid caustic soda which remove from it all of the rest of the water vapor down to the vapor pressure of water which is in equilibrium with solid caustic soda at that low temperature. The ammonia gas is then passed through one or two towers filled with activated charcoal, usually animal charcoal, which has the property of absorbing all of the tarry material present, recovering the gas escaping from these scrubbers, practically pure ammonia. This ammonia is then carried to ammonia compressors where it is compressed, cooled, and liquefied.

CHAPTER X

BENZOLIZED WASH OIL

It is common in the industries to find gaseous mixtures which contain certain condensable vapors which must be separated from the rest of the mixture. Such mixtures as coal gas from the destructive distillation of bituminous coal, and gases from solvent recovery systems, are illustrations of this class of gases. In the former case, there is ammonia, which is removed from the coal gas by washing with water or by passing the gas through sulphuric acid. Coal gas also contains benzene and its homologues, which can be washed out of the gas by the use of any relatively nonvolatile oil in which the benzene is soluble. In the latter case, the gases may contain such vapors as ethyl alcohol which is soluble in water and may be readily washed out by it or such vapors as gasoline or benzol, in which case they can be washed out by some suitable solvent such as oil, as before. It is the case of the vapor that has been dissolved in the relatively nonvolatile oil that will be discussed.

Light-oil Recovery.—Gas plants that recover the "light oil" (benzene and its homologues) usually do so by scrubbing the gas in tall towers down through which the "wash oil" (in this country, wash oil is usually a petroleum oil of high boiling point) is allowed to pass in countercurrent contact with the ascending gas. The wash oil leaving the bottom of the scrubbing tower is, therefore, more or less saturated with the light oil at the partial pressure at which the gas enters the scrubber. This so-called benzolized wash oil must then be subjected to a process of fractional distillation in order to recover the light oil and to render the wash oil fit to be used again in the scrubbing process.

Wash Oil.—The grade of petroleum distillate used for scrubbing may be considered to have a boiling point at atmospheric pressure of about 300°C. In order to study the problem of handling this material, it is advisable to have a boiling point-pressure curve. One method of doing this where the actual vapor-pressure data are not available is to make use of the modified Clapeyron equation noted in a previous chapter:

$$\frac{dp}{dT} = \frac{L}{RT^2}$$

which integrated gives the equation

$$\ln p = -\frac{L}{RT} + \text{constant}$$

For a straw petroleum oil of boiling point 300°C., L may be estimated as 11,750 cal., giving

$$\ln p = -\frac{5,910}{T} + 16.95$$

where p is in millimeters of mercury and T is in degrees centigrade absolute.

The vapor-pressure curve of benzene has been determined, and the relative pressures of benzene and wash oil are given in the following table:

Temperature, degrees Centigrade	Vapor pressure of benzene in millimeters P_s	Vapor pressure of wash oil in millimeters (calculated) P_w
80	760	1.22
100	1,344	3.02
150	4,334	19.7
200	10,663	85.5
250	22,214	282.0
300	40,000	760.0

Boiling-point Curve for Mixture of Benzol and Wash Oil.—
It is possible, by assuming Raoult's law to hold, to get an approximation of the boiling-point curve of mixtures of benzene and wash oil.

Thus on the diagram (Fig. 20), the line AD represents the partial pressure of benzene in the mixture at some given temperature *t*, and *CB* is that for wash oil; the line *CD* is the sum of the two partial pressures, or the total pressure. If *x* represents the mol fraction of the benzene in the mixture, the total pressure will be given by the equation

$$P = P_w + x(P_B - P_w)$$

Thus at different temperatures the mol fraction of benzene in the mixture boiling at a given pressure can be calculated. The following table gives the results of such a calculation for a pressure of 760 mm.:

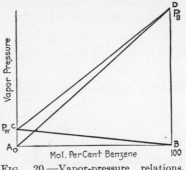

Fig. 20.—Vapor-pressure relations. Benzene-wash oil mixtures.

Temperature, Degrees Centigrade

80	$P = 760 = 1.22 + x(760 - 1.22)$	$x = 1.000$
100	$P = 760 = 3.02 + x(1,344 - 3.02)$	$x = 0.563$
150	$P = 760 = 19.7 + x(4,334 - 19.7)$	$x = 0.172$
200	$P = 760 = 85.5 + x(10,663 - 85.5)$	$x = 0.064$
250	$P = 760 = 282.0 + x(22,214 - 282.0)$	$x = 0.022$
300	$P = 760 = 760.0 + x(40,000 - 760.0)$	$x = 0.000$

The partial pressure of the benzene in the vapor above such mixtures may then be calculated, and the mol fraction in the vapor phase.

$$p_B = xP_B$$

and

$$y_{vapor} = \frac{p_B}{P}$$

For the temperatures selected, the table shown at the top of page 62 can be thus obtained.

Temperature-composition Diagram.—It is now possible to construct a temperature-composition diagram (Fig. 21) for mixtures of benzene and wash oil at 760 mm. pressure.

It is evident from such a diagram that the two components are very readily separated from each other, a dilute solution of 2 mol per cent benzene giving a vapor containing over 60 mol per cent. Such a solution would boil at 250°C. In order to

Temperature, degrees Centigrade	x liquid	pв	y vapor
80	1.000	760	1.000
100	0.563	757	0.997
150	0.172	745	0.981
200	0.064	684	0.899
250	0.022	488	0.642
300	0.000	0	0.000

remove thoroughly all the benzene from the wash oil by boiling at 760 mm., the temperature must be raised to 300°C.

Vacuum Wash-oil Still.—A still to handle wash oil at 300°C. would need a fire-heated kettle; or else hot oil must be used for heating, since saturated steam would require too high a pressure,

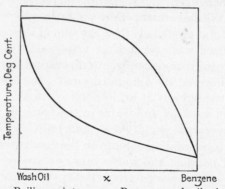

Fig. 21.—Boiling-point curve.   Benzene wash-oil mixtures.

and superheated steam is not a satisfactory agent for heating on account of the high resistance to flow of heat from it to metal. Fire heat is, however, dangerous and is likely to decompose the oil in the kettle, whereas oil heating is often expensive and troublesome. It is therefore advisable to operate this still under as high a vacuum as possible, for instance, 28 in. Hg (50 mm., absolute pressure).

The boiling point of wash oil at 50 mm. may be calculated from the previous equation and will be found to be 180°C.; benzene at the same pressure boils at 12°C. However, 180°C. corresponds to 130 lb. gage steam pressure, which is still high; and, furthermore, in order to condense the benzene vapor, cooling water below 12°C. must be available, and this is not common in warm weather. These difficulties can be avoided, however, by the use of open steam injected into the boiling mixture of benzene and wash oil, thus converting the system from one of two to one of three components. Water is practically insoluble in both benzene and wash oil, and there will, therefore, appear two liquid phases, thus limiting the degrees of freedom of the system to two as before, so that fixing the pressure and the composition of the benzene wash-oil phase will fix the boiling temperature of the mixture.

Since the water is practically insoluble in the other two components, their partial pressures at any temperature will remain practically unchanged, and therefore the presence of the water or water vapor will have little effect upon the problem of fractionation. The total pressure is then the sum of the partial pressures of the benzolized wash oil and the water; and by regulating the amount of steam introduced, the temperature needed for operation may be lowered the amount desired. Such a steam distillation may be carried out at atmospheric pressure. In such case, the mixture of wash oil and water in the kettle of the still would boil at a temperature slightly less than 100°C. The vapor passing from the fractionating column to the condenser would consist essentially of benzene and water vapor at atmospheric pressure, and it would be necessary to cool these vapors down to a temperature somewhat below the boiling point of pure benzene in order to condense them. The weight of steam needed to vaporize a pound of benzene would be the ratio of the vapor pressures at that temperature times the ratio of their molecular weights times the reflux ratio.

Steam Consumption of Vacuum Stills.—The question whether or not the use of a vacuum-steam distillation would affect the ratio of water vapor to benzene vapor in the mixture of vapors passing to the condenser depends upon the relative changes in vapor pressures with the temperature. The following table will indicate how these vapor pressures vary.

Temperature, degrees Centigrade	Water, millimeters	Benzene, millimeters	Ratio B/W neglecting reflux
100	760	1,344	1.77
80	355	754	2.12
60	149	389	2.61
40	55	181	3.29

It is evident from this table that if the total pressure is so regulated that the mixture of water vapor and benzene vapor comes over at 40°C., about one-half as much steam will be needed per pound of benzene as if the steam distillation were carried out at 100°.

There is another economy in the use of steam distillation under a vacuum. It is always necessary to heat the benzolized wash oil up to its boiling point before injecting it into the still. This may be partly accomplished by means of heat interchangers, utilizing the waste heat in the debenzolized oil, but high-pressure steam is always necessary to complete the preheating. It is obvious that the higher the vacuum at which the still operates the lower the temperature to which the oil must be heated, and the less the steam pressure required for such heating. There are other reasons, such as freedom from leaks outward and safety, that make the use of a vacuum in the wash oil still highly desirable.

Diagram of Wash-oil Still.—A diagram of a vacuum wash-oil still operating on this principle is shown in Fig. 22.

Benzolized wash oil is held in a constant-level feed tank A, the tank being under the vacuum of the still proper to insure constant rate of feed. From this tank it flows through the regulating valve B to the heat interchanger C where it is heated countercurrent by the hot debenzolized oil issuing from the still. The partially heated oil then is heated to its boiling temperature in the high-pressure steam preheaters D, two of these being furnished so that one may be cleaned without shutting down the still. The hot oil then flows to the top of the exhausting column E where the benzol is boiled out of the wash oil by means of steam blown into the bottom of the column. The exhausted oil passes from the bottom of the column through the heat interchanger C and then is pumped out against atmospheric pressure by the pump *F*, after which it is cooled, the naphthalene being removed by settling, and is then ready for reuse.

The fractionating column *G* serves to hold back the heavy oil, receiving its reflux from the regulating bottle *M*, which is attached to the continuous decanter *J*. This decanter sepa-

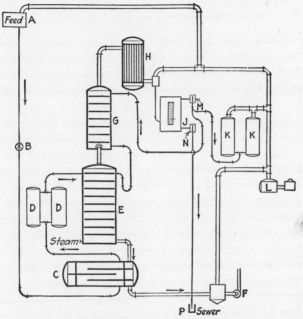

Fig. 22.—Vacuum wash-oil still.

rates the condensed water from the condensed benzol coming from the condenser *H*. The water flows from the decanter through the tester *N* through a barometric seal to the sewer *P*. The benzol is collected in the receiving tanks *K*, from which it is alternately withdrawn by breaking the vacuum on them. The dry-vacuum pump *L* completes the apparatus, except for the usual accessories common to all continuous stills.

CHAPTER XI

METHYL ALCOHOL

Methyl alcohol was formerly made almost exclusively from the destructive distillation of cellulose material, usually hardwoods. Associated with it in the distillate condensed from this process are a large number of other substances, notably water, acetic acid, and acetone, together with smaller amounts of other substances. The problem of the preparation of pure methyl alcohol from this mixture is unquestionably one of the most difficult that the designer of distillation equipment has been called upon to solve, and the solution was not satisfactorily completed until the introduction of the modern continuous still.

Impurities in Wood Alcohol.—Acetic acid and the other organic acids present are, in general, neutralized with lime or some other suitable alkali, thus rendering them nonvolatile. The alcohol, acetone, and the balance of the volatile material are then separated from the salts by a simple distillation. The distillate thus obtained is known as crude wood spirit and has a composition of which the following is an example.

	Per Cent
Methyl alcohol	55 to 50
Acetone	12 to 14
Other impurities	5 to 10
Water	28 to 26

The other impurities consist principally of the following substances:

Aldehydes
Methyl acetate
Ammonia
Amines
Higher ketones (methyl ethyl ketone, etc.)
Allyl alcohol
Wood oils (high-boiling, insoluble, complex substances)

Constant-boiling Mixture or Methyl Alcohol and Acetone.— Methyl alcohol can be separated from water by fractional distillation. This is also true of acetone, but methyl alcohol and acetone together form a binary mixture of minimum boiling point which contains approximately 15 per cent alcohol and 85 per cent acetone. The respective boiling points at 760 mm. pressure are

	Degrees Centigrade
Methyl alcohol	66.5
Acetone	56.5
Constant-boiling mixture	55.93
Allyl alcohol	97

It is therefore impossible to produce a pure acetone from the crude wood spirit by fractional distillation without the addition of some new substances which will modify the respective vapor pressures of the alcohol and acetone in such a way that the constant-boiling mixture is destroyed. This may be done by introducing into the mixture some material like calcium chloride, which combines chemically with the methyl alcohol, thus lowering its vapor pressure, or by some material like sodium hydrogen sulphite, which combines chemically with the acetone, which can then be removed from the solution as a crystalline addition compound, and the alcohol fractionated afterward.

"Methyl Acetone."—The demand for acetone in the past has been largely for its use as a solvent, excepting, of course, the great demand for pure acetone as one of the solvents of cordite smokeless powder; and since the constant-boiling mixture, consisting of 85 per cent acetone, is also an excellent solvent and behaves physically like a pure compound, the latter has satisfied the demands of the trade, and it has therefore been marketed under the name of methyl acetone. The problem to be solved, therefore, consists in the separation of pure methyl alcohol and pure "methyl acetone" from water and from the other impurities. This is essentially a three-component system; and as described under that subject, it is necessary to remove one component first and separate the other two afterward. The method adopted here is to separate the methyl acetone (together with the volatile head products) from the alcohol and water, separate the alcohol from the water, and then finally separate the volatile heads from the methyl acetone.

Diagram of Still.—This method is utilized in the apparatus shown diagrammatically in Fig. 23, with the omission of a number of necessary accessories in order to simplify the drawing.

The function of the double column E_1E_2 is to separate the feed into two portions, one containing the volatile heads and the methyl acetone, and the other the alcohol and water. The

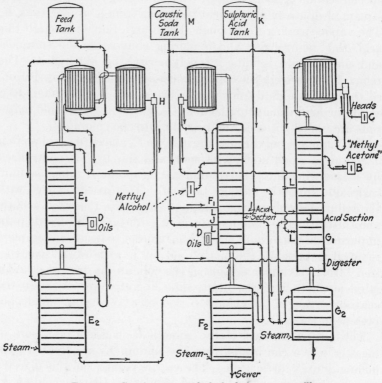

Fig. 23.—Continuous methyl alcohol–acetone still.

heads are delivered from the tester H to the bottom of the column G_1, and the alcohol and water are delivered from the bottom of the column E_2 to the top of the exhausting column F_2. There is an accumulation of insoluble oils in the column E_1, and they are removed by means of a continuous decanter at D, just as fusel oil is removed in the rectification of ethyl alcohol as described under that heading.

The function of the column F_1F_2 is to produce pure methyl alcohol and discharge to waste the water and any nonvolatile substances that may be present. The liquor entering the top of F_2 contains a small amount of heads not removed by the column E_1E_2. These heads consist of ammonia, amines, aldehydes, nitrites, and ethyl acetate. In order to handle them, there is a special section J inserted in the column through which a constant stream of dilute sulphuric acid is flowing from a storage tank K. The vapors passing up through the column bubble through this acid, thus neutralizing and rendering nonvolatile the ammonia and amines and tending to polymerize the aldehydes. The reflux down through the column is by-passed around this section, so the two liquids do not mix. The spent acid is taken to a sulphuric acid exhausting column G_2, where any valuable materials are boiled out of it and pass up into the column G_1.

The vapors rising through the column F_1 above the acid section J contain a small amount of acid, and this is then neutralized by introducing into the column at the point L dilute sodium hydroxide from the storage tank M. This caustic mixes with the reflux, neutralizes the acid, and saponifies the ethyl acetate and nitrite. The vapors are now substantially freed from impurities in the form of heads; but in order to insure as complete removal as possible, the methyl alcohol is withdrawn "pasteurized" from the upper portion of the column (as described under ethyl alcohol), and the heads thus liberated are taken to the central portion of the column G_1 in order to recover the alcohol present in them.

The bottom section of the column G_1 consists of a sort of digester where the heads from the column E_1 are treated with boiling dilute caustic soda. The vapors rising from this digester pass up through an acid section similar to that in column F_1 and are then treated with caustic at a higher point. The purified methyl acetone is then withdrawn pasteurized through the cooler and tester B, any remaining heads accumulating in the upper portion of the column being distilled off and collected at C. The waste sulphuric acid from the column G_1 is withdrawn to the sulphuric acid exhausting column G_2, as before.

Wood oils collect in the column F_1 and are withdrawn through a suitable oil decanter at D, as in the case of the column E_1.

The feed material is therefore separated by this apparatus into pure methyl alcohol, pure constant-boiling mixture (methyl acetone), concentrated head products, wood oils, and waste. This is completed in one operation, with a minimum of labor and heat, and the products are of a degree of purity unobtainable by any intermittent process of fractional distillation.

CHAPTER XII

ETHYL ALCOHOL

The fractional distillation of ethyl alcohol is the classical example in the art of distillation. Nearly all of the earlier technical books on the subject of distillation deal practically exclusively with the problem of producing ethyl alcohol from its various sources, and the problem has unquestionably received more thought than any other phase of the subject.

Sources of Ethyl Alcohol.—Ethyl alcohol is obtained almost wholly from the fermentation of various sugars, as are found in such materials as molasses, hydrolyzed starch, and waste liquor from sulphite-pulp digesters. The conditions under which fermentation of these sugars must be carried out are such that the alcoholic product usually contains from 5 to 10 per cent of alcohol. This mash, as it is usually called, contains in addition to the alcohol and water considerable solid material in suspension, dissolved salts of various kinds, and a number of more or less volatile substances which are by-products of the fermentation. The solid materials and the nonvolatile salts can be readily removed by a simple distillation. The volatile impurities are, however, much more difficult to care for.

It has been the object of manufacturers of stills to produce a commercial alcohol of as high a degree of purity as possible. Only recently, however, has the introduction of the continuous still permitted the production of a really high-grade material. Continuous alcohol stills of the type perfected by Barbet and others are capable of producing continuously and economically alcohol of a high and uniform degree of purity. These stills will be modified in the future as the action of the component parts is studied. The art of still building has suffered in the past from the fact that the problems involved have been studied empirically. The applications of physical chemistry in the future will be sure to be of great assistance in the solution of these problems.

71

Beer Still.—The first process in the production of alcohol from the mash is the removal of all of the nonvolatile material and a good portion of the water. This is usually carried out in what is known as a beer still, which is a simple continuous still of the type indicated in Fig. 24.

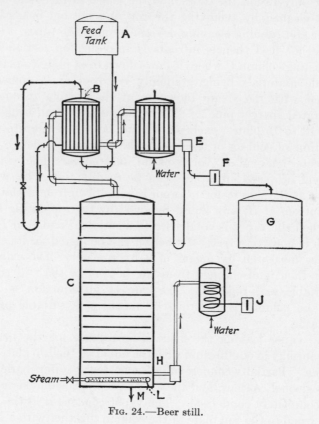

Fig. 24.—Beer still.

The alcoholic feed is supplied by a constant-level feed tank *A*. This tank contains a ball float which operates a steam pump which pumps the feed from the storage tank to *A* as rapidly as it is used. The feed then flows by gravity through the feed heater *B* where it is raised nearly to its boiling point. Continuous stills are often fitted with recuperators where the incoming feed is heated by the outgoing hot waste from the bottom of the exhausting column. Where the liquor contains solid materials which are likely to form deposits on the heating surfaces, recuperators are not always used, on account of the difficulty of cleaning the outside of the tubes. The vapor heater shown at *B* has the liquor only inside the tubes, and the fouled surfaces can be very easily cleaned by removing the top and bottom heads of the heater and running cleaning devices through the tubes.

The hot feed then is introduced into the top section of the exhausting column *C* where it flows down from plate to plate, the volatile materials being gradually removed as it comes into contact with the steam blown in at the bottom through the perforated sparger pipe *L*. The exhausting column usually has from 12 to 15 plates, each plate being large and deep to give a long time of contact of the feed in the column in order to insure complete removal of the volatile substances. The complete removal of these substances can be readily tested by what is known as the slop tester. Vapor is withdrawn from a plate near the bottom at *H*, any liquid removed by the separating bottle, and then the vapor is condensed in a suitable condenser *I*, from which it flows to a tester *J* where it can be tasted, or its specific gravity measured by means of a hydrometer. The exhausted liquor then is discharged from the bottom of the still through a suitable seal pipe *M*. The rate of introduction of steam into the column is governed by means of a suitable pressure regulator.

The vapor leaving the exhausting column for the heater is substantially in equilibrium with the liquid on the top plate of the column. Partially condensed in the heater, it suffers enrichment in its alcohol content, and then it passes to the condenser where it is completely condensed. The vapor condensed in the heater is returned to the top plate of the column together with a greater or lesser portion of the vapor condensed in the condenser, from the regulating bottle *E*. The distillate flows through the tester

	Per Cent
Organic acid measured as acetic acid	0.152
Esters measured as ethyl acetate	0.071
Aldehydes measured as acetaldehyde	0.015
Furfurol	0.00019
Higher alcohols measured as isoamyl alcohol	0.412
Nitrogenous substances measured as ammonia	0.0006

	Original liquor	Heads No. 1	Heads No. 2	Last of heads	High-grade alcohol	Trace of tails	Tails No. 2	Tails No. 3	Tails No. 4
Weight { Per cent of original alcohol in each fraction	100.0	1.58	7.53	21.87	26.43	24.90	10.25	4.20	1.20
Per cent alcohol in fraction	.....	92.0	96.1	96.5	96.5	96.4	96.4	93.6	74.0
Per cent acids (as H Ac)	0.155	0.009	0.0038	0.0038	0.0022	0.0022	0.003	0.007	
Esters	0.074	0.333	0.099	0.017	0.0065	0.011	0.017	0.090	
Aldehydes	0.027	0.58	0.175	0.003	traces	traces	traces	0.010	
Furfurol	0.0002	trace	trace	trace	......	trace	0.0001	0.003	
Higher alcohols	0.42	trace	trace	trace	trace	0.0032	3.13	11.2	
Nitrogen compounds	0.0007	0.0006	0.0003	0.0001	0.00001	0.0001	0.0002	0.002	

F, where its volume and specific gravity may be measured, to the storage tank G. On account of the partial condensation in the heater, the distillate from the 5 to 10 per cent mash will frequently run as high as 30 to 40 per cent alcohol.

The water supply for the condenser is obtained from a constant-level feed tank.

Crude Alcohol.—A sample analysis of such a distillate obtained from a molasses mash showed, in addition to the alcohol and water, the impurities indicated in the table at the bottom of page 73.

Neutralization.—Before this impure alcohol can be refined it must be neutralized with some suitable alkali such as soda ash. The neutralization must be done very carefully, since if the solution is boiled when alkaline the nitrogenous bodies set free amines whose disagreeable odor is hard to remove in the finished alcohol, and which also form blue compounds with copper and color the alcohol. They also tend to combine with the aldehydes forming resins which are likely to gum up the column or color yellow the alcohol withdrawn from the column. On the other hand, if the solution is acid, esters will form, and any undecomposed ammonium acetate will react with strong alcohol forming ethyl acetate and setting free ammonia.

Intermittent Stills.—Formerly, most alcohol was rectified in intermittent stills. The accompanying table gives the results of a rectification in a modern intermittent still (see Fig. 25). The distillate was divided into the fractions indicated.

It will be noted that the fraction entitled "High-grade alcohol" comes rather far from being a pure alcohol and, furthermore, that this fraction contains but 26 per cent of the alcohol in the original liquor. In other words, 74 per cent of the alcohol must be rehandled in order to convert it into high-grade product.

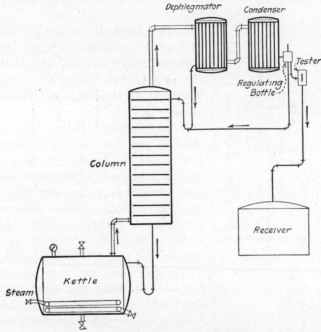

FIG. 25.—Modern intermittent still.

Continuous Stills.—The use of the continuous rectifying still, as developed by Barbet, has enabled alcohol producers to put on the market an alcohol of higher grade than the best produced by the intermittent still without subsequent chemical treatment with charcoal, etc., and to avoid the rehandling of intermediate fraction, at a considerable saving in time, labor, and expense. A simple type of such a still is shown in Fig. 26.

This still consists essentially of a purifying column C and a concentrating and exhausting column D. The function of the purifying column is to remove the volatile head products, which can be separated from alcohol by fractionation. The function of the concentrating column is to separate the alcohol and water, as well as the impurities which are not removed in the heads.

The purifying column is fitted with a reflux condenser G and condenser H and is independent of the rest of the apparatus except that it receives the hot feed continuously from the recupe-

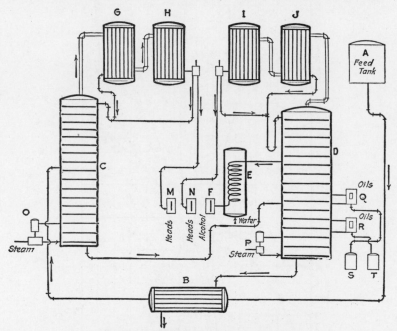

Fig. 26.—Continuous ethyl alcohol still.

rator B and the feed-supply tank A and delivers the purified dilute alcohol continuously from its base to the other column D. It has its own steam regulator O and cooling-water supply, and its rate of operation can be controlled according to the amount of impurities to be removed.

The operation of the purifying column can be readily understood from the following diagram (Fig. 27) which is credited to Barbet. Ordinates represent the plates in the column, there being 13 plates above the plate on which the feed enters and 10 plates below that point, 24 plates in all. Abscissas below represent percentage of alcohol and, above, grams of impurities per hectoliter. The left-hand side of the upper scale is made logarithmic to exaggerate the very low readings, and the right-hand side

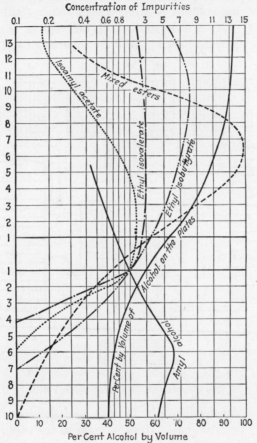

FIG. 27.—Diagram illustrating action of purifying column.

(from 1 to 15) is a normal scale. The lower scale is normal throughout.

The feed consists of a 50 per cent alcohol solution containing heads amounting to 0.5 gram per hectoliter, and higher alcohols (fusel oil) to 2 grams per hectoliter. The mixture distilled from the top of the column is about 95 per cent alcohol, containing

12 grams of head products per hectoliter, and the solution discharged from the bottom contains about 40 per cent alcohol, no head products, and 3 grams of oil per hectoliter. The 40 per cent solution then enters the central portion of the column *D*. This column has the reflux condenser *J* and the condenser *I* and is fitted with a perforated steam pipe and steam regulator *P*, as in the case of the column *C*. This column must remove, as far as possible, the water from the alcohol and remove the impurities left by the purifying column.

Alcohol and water form a binary mixture of constant-boiling point, at a composition of about 96.5 per cent alcohol by weight. This mixture boils about 0.2° below that of pure alcohol, and therefore alcohol can be freed from water only up to that concentration by means of fractional distillation processes.

The impurities left in the alcohol at the entrance to the column *D* consist principally of the higher alcohols propyl, isobutyl, and isoamyl. These alcohols are completely soluble in ethyl alcohol and can be separated from it by fractional distillation. They are, however, only partly soluble in water and are therefore volatile with steam when present in excess of their solubility limit. It should be remembered that in the column *D*, the liquid on the top plates is practically pure alcohol in which these oils are soluble and that the liquid in the bottom of the column is practically all water, in which the oils are practically insoluble. The concentration of alcohol on the intermediate plates varies between these two limits. When the oils are introduced into the column with the dilute alcohol and run down over the plates of the exhausting section of the column, they reach a concentration of alcohol so dilute that they become insoluble and separate out as an oily layer on the plates. The oils are now volatile with steam, and their vapors ascend into the upper portion of the column. Here, however, they are soluble in the higher concentration alcohol and dissolve. But, having a higher boiling point than ethyl alcohol, they are forced back down the column. Since they cannot escape from either the bottom or the top of the column, they therefore collect and accumulate in the central portion of it. It is therefore possible by withdrawing the liquid from these plates, where the oils have accumulated, to separate them from the aqueous layers by decantation and return the

Concentration of Impurities

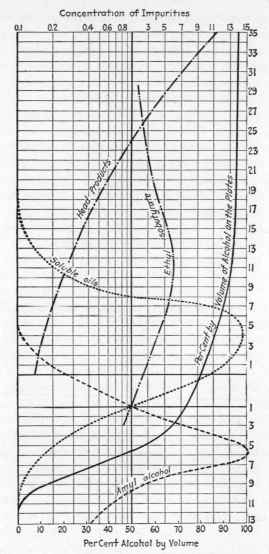

FIG. 28.—Diagram illustrating action of rectifying column.

aqueous alcohol layer to the still.   This is the function of the
continuous oil decanters Q and R, which deliver the decanted
oil to the tanks S and T, respectively.   Since these oils are less
soluble the lower the temperature, the liquid withdrawn from
the column is sometimes cooled on its way to the decanters by
suitable coolers.   There are usually two groups of these oils which
are of quite different solubility.   These collect in two separate
portions of the column and must be withdrawn at these separate
points, as shown, the oils less soluble in water collecting higher
up in the column than those more soluble.

The ethyl alcohol delivered from the top of the column D
would be freed by the removal of the oils from all of its impurities
other than water, were it not for the fact that during the boiling
in the passage through the column more of the volatile esters are
formed than were removed in the purifying column.   These,
therefore, tend to accumulate in the top of the column, being
more volatile than the alcohol itself.   This condition may be
shown by another Barbet diagram similar to the one for the
purifying column (Fig. 28).

It will be seen from this diagram that the alcohol has reached
its maximum strength shortly above the twentieth plate above
feed inlet but that the concentration of heads at that point is
only about one-fifteenth that at the top of the column.   It is
advisable to withdraw the alcohol from the column at this point
rather than from the top, and this act is known as "pasteuri-
zation."   The heads are distilled out of the column and condensed and delivered to a tester N in the same way as the heads
from column C are delivered to the tester M.   The hot liquid
alcohol withdrawn pasteurized from the column is then cooled in
a cooler E and delivered to the tester F.

The waste liquor from the bottom of the column D flows
through the recuperator B and then to the sewer.

CHAPTER XIII

RECTIFICATION OF BINARY MIXTURES

The separation of two liquids from each other by fractional distillation may be accomplished in two general ways: (1) the batch, or intermittent, method; and (2) the continuous method. In the former, the composition and temperature at any point in the system are changing continually; in the latter, conditions at any point are constant.

It will be recalled that a fractionating column consists of a system up through which vapors are passing and down through which a liquid is running, countercurrent to the vapor, the liquid and vapor being in more or less intimate contact with each other. Furthermore, the vapor and liquid tend to be in equilibrium with each other at any point in the column, the liquid and vapor at the bottom of the column being richer in the less volatile component than at the top. It is evident, therefore, that the action of such a column is similar to that of a scrubbing or washing column, where a vapor is removed from a gas that is passing up through the column, by bringing into contact with it, countercurrent, a liquid in which the vapor is soluble, and that will remove it from the gas.

Sorel's Method.—Sorel (15) developed and applied the mathematical theory of the rectifying column for binary mixtures. He calculated the enrichment, the change in composition from plate to plate, by making energy and material balances around each plate and assumed that equilibrium was attained between the vapor and liquid leaving the plate. He proceeded stepwise through the column by applying this method successively from one plate to the next.

Sorel's method will be derived for the case illustrated in Fig. 29. The column is assumed to be operating continuously on a binary mixture with the feed entering on a plate between the top and bottom. The column is provided with heat for reboiling by conduction such as steam coils in the kettle; the case of the use of live or open steam will be considered later. A simple total condenser is assumed where all of the overhead vapor is liquefied, this condensate being divided into two portions, one of which is returned to the column for reflux and the other withdrawn as overhead product. The bottoms are continuously withdrawn from the still or reboiler. The following nomenclature will be used in the derivations:

x = mol fraction of more volatile component in liquid.

y = mol fraction of more volatile component in vapors.

D = mols of distillate withdrawn as overhead products per unit of time.

x_D = mol fraction of more volatile component in distillate.

O = total mols of overflow from one plate to next, per unit of time.

z = mol fraction in feed mixture.

V = total mols of vapor passing from one plate to next, per unit of time.

F = mols of mixture fed to column per unit of time.

W = mols of residue per unit of time.

n = number of plate under consideration, counting up from feed plate.

m = number of plate under consideration, counting up from still.

H = enthalpy, or heat content of vapor.

h = enthalpy, or heat content of liquid.

$p = (O_{f+1} - O_f)/F$.

Subscripts:

n refers to nth plate; *i.e.*, O_n and V_n refer to mols of liquid and vapor leaving nth plate, respectively.

m refers to mth plate.

f refers to feed plate; *i.e.*, x_f is mol fraction of more volatile component in overflow from feed plate.

F refers to feed; *i.e.*, x_F is mol fraction of more volatile component in feed mixture.

D refers to distillate.

R refers to reflux.

W refers to bottoms.

L refers to liquid.

V refers to vapor.

t refers to top plate.

Consider the region bounded by the dotted line in Fig. 29. The only material entering this section is the vapor from the nth plate V_n, while leaving the section is the distillate D and the overflow from the $(n + 1)$th plate O_{n+1}. By material balance,

$$V_n = O_{n+1} + D \tag{1}$$

Considering only the more volatile component, the mols entering this section are the total mols of vapor from the nth plate multi-

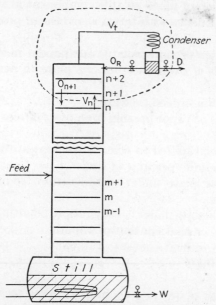

Fig. 29.—Diagram of continuous distillation column.

plied by the mol fraction of the more volatile component in this vapor $V_n y_n$. Likewise, the mols of the more volatile component in the distillate are $D x_D$; and in the overflow from the $(n + 1)$th plate are $O_{n+1} x_{n+1}$. A material balance on the more volatile component for this section therefore gives

$$V_n y_n = O_{n+1} x_{n+1} + D x_D \tag{2}$$

or

$$y_n = \frac{O_{n+1}}{V_n} x_{n+1} + \frac{D}{V_n} x_D \tag{2a}$$

$$y_n = \frac{O_{n+1}}{O_{n+1} + D} x_{n+1} + \frac{D}{O_{n+1} + D} x_D \qquad (2b)$$

Thus, starting at the condenser, the composition of the reflux to the tower, with the type of condenser employed, is the same as the composition of the distillate, which makes the composition of the vapor to the condenser the same as that of the distillate. The mols of vapor from the top plate are equal to $O_R + D$, and the reflux to this plate is O_R. Sorel's assumption of the vapor and liquid leaving the plate being in equilibrium makes it possible to calculate the composition of the liquid leaving the top plate of the tower from the composition of the overhead vapor and vapor-liquid equilibrium data.

In the design of such a tower, it is generally customary to set or fix certain operating variables such as the composition of the distillate and of the bottoms, the reflux ratio O_R/D, and the composition and thermal condition of the feed. With these values and a known quantity of feed per unit time, by over-all material balances it is possible to calculate D, O_R, and W. To calculate the composition of the vapor from the plate below the top plate by Eq. $(2a)$, it is necessary to know the mols of overflow from the top plate and the mols of vapor from the plate below as well as the known quantities D, x_D, and the mol fraction of the more volatile component in the liquid overflow from the top plate. Sorel obtained the mols of overflow from, and the mols of vapor to, the plate by heat (enthalpy) balances. Thus the heat brought into the plate must equal that leaving.

$$O_R h_R + V_{t-1} H_{t-1} = V_t H_t + O_t h_t + \text{losses} \qquad (3)$$

Equation (3) gives a relation between V_{t-1} and O_t; and if the enthalpies are known, this equation can be solved simultaneously with Eq. (1) to give V_{t-1} and O_t. This, in general, involves trial-and-error solutions, since H_{t-1} is not known and must be assumed until the conditions of the next plate are known. The values of V_{t-1} and O_t obtained in this manner are used in Eq. $(2a)$ to give y_{t-1}. From this composition the value of x_{t-1} is obtained from vapor-liquid equilibrium data as well as the temperature on this plate. The value of H_{t-1} can then be accurately checked, and the calculations corrected if necessary. This operation is continued plate by plate down the tower to the feed plate.

A similar derivation for the plates below the feed gives

$$y_m = \frac{O_{m+1}x_{m+1}}{V_m} - \frac{Wx_w}{V_m} \tag{4}$$

$$= \frac{O_{m+1}x_{m+1}}{O_{m+1} - W} - \frac{Wx_w}{O_{m+1} - W} \tag{4a}$$

These equations are used in the same way as Eq. (2).

Because of the complexity of Sorel's method, it is usually modified by certain simplifying assumptions. The heat supply to any section of the column above the feed is solely that of the vapor entering that section. This supply of heat to the next plate goes to supply vapor from this plate, to heat loss from the section of the tower that corresponds to this plate, and to heating up the liquid overflow across this plate. In a properly designed column, the heat loss from the column should be reduced as far as is practicable and is generally small enough to be a negligible quantity relative to the total quantity of heat flowing up the column. It is also assumed that the heats of mixing of the two components both in the liquid and in the vapor are negligible relative to the latent heats of vaporization involved. The sensible heat taken up by the increase in temperature of the overflow as it passes down the column is partly offset by the decrease in sensible heat of the vapor as it flows up the column. The change in the sensible heat of the vapor is usually less than that of the liquid, and the enthalpy of the vapor must decrease sufficiently as it passes up the column to supply the difference of the sensible heats. For binary mixtures of similar properties, *i.e.*, both associating as alcohol or nonassociating as benzene, the molal heat of vaporization at constant pressure decreases with decreasing temperature. Depending on the relative decrease of the molal heat of vaporization and of the enthalpy of the vapor, it is possible for the total mols of vapor to remain substantially constant in passing from plate to plate throughout the column or to increase or decrease.

The available experimental data indicate that if both components are of the same type, up to moderately high pressures, the total mols of vapor (and liquid) are substantially constant except as affected by the introduction of the feed or by the return of cold reflux to the column. Thus in the section above the feed, the mols of vapor and of overflow from plate to plate are substantially constant, and the same applies to the section below the feed, but the mols of both vapor and overflow will not be the same in both sections.

The assumptions leading to this condition, called the usual simplifying assumptions (USA), may be summarized: (1) Heat losses from the column are negligible; (2) the heat of mixing in the vapor and that in the liquid are negligible; and (3) the components are all of the same class, *i.e.*, associating or non-associating, such that their thermal properties are similar.

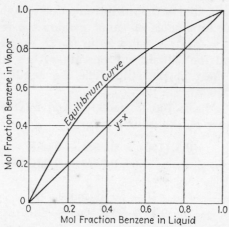

Fig. 30.—Equilibrium curve for benzene-toluene mixture.

Thus, in Eq. (2a), since O_{n+1} and V_n are constant in the section above the feed plate, the relation between y_n and x_{n+1} becomes a straight line with the slope equal to O/V. Similarly, below the feed, y_m is linear in x_{m+1}. On the basis of the operating variables previously fixed, O_{n+1}, V_n, D, and x_D are known, and the equation between y_n and x_{n+1} is completely defined; and likewise for y_m and x_{m+1}.

A plate on which Sorel's conditions of equilibrium are retained is defined as a "theoretical plate," *i.e.*, a plate on which the contact between vapor and liquid is sufficiently good so that the vapor leaving the plate has the same composition as the vapor in equilibrium with the overflow from the plate. For such a plate the vapor and liquid leaving are related by the equilibrium *x-y* curve (see page 43). Rectifying columns designed on this basis serve as a standard for comparing actual columns. By such comparisons it is possible to determine the number of actual plates equivalent to a theoretical plate and then to reapply this factor when designing other columns for similar service.

As an illustration of Sorel's method together with the usual simplifying assumptions, consider the rectification of a 50 mol per cent benzene and 50 mol per cent toluene mixture into a product containing 5 mol per cent toluene and a bottoms containing 5 mol per cent benzene. The feed will enter as a liquid sufficiently preheated so that its introduction into the column does not affect the total mols of vapor passing the feed plate; *i.e.*, such that $V_n = V_m$. A reflux ratio O_n/D, equal to 3, will be employed, and the column will operate with a total condenser and indirect heat in the still. The x-y equilibrium curve is given in Fig. 30.

Taking as a basis 100 lb. mols of feed mixture, an over-all material balance on the column gives

$$(0.5)(100) = 0.95D + 0.05W$$
$$= 0.95D + 0.05(100 - D)$$

gives

$$D = 50 \text{ lb. mols}$$
$$W = 50 \text{ lb. mols}$$

Since

$$\frac{O_n}{D} = 3$$

$$O_n = 150$$
$$V_n = O_n + D = 200$$

by Eq. (2a),

$$y_n = (150/200)x_{n+1} + (50/200)(0.95) = 0.75x_{n+1} + 0.2375 \quad (5)$$

Since a total condenser is used,

$$y_t = x_D = x_R = 0.95$$

from the equilibrium curve at $y = 0.95$, $x = 0.88$, *i.e.*, x_t in equilibrium with y_t is 0.88.

Equation (5) then gives

$$y_{t-1} = 0.75x_t + 0.2375 = 0.75(0.88) + 0.2375 = 0.8975$$

by equilibrium curve, x_{t-1} at $y_{t-1} = 0.8975$ is 0.77 and

$y_{t-2} = 0.75(0.77) + 0.2375 = 0.8145$
$x_{t-2} = 0.64$
$y_{t-3} = 0.75x_{t-2} + 0.2375 = 0.75(0.64) + 0.2375 = 0.7165$
$x_{t-3} = 0.505$

Since the value of x_{t-3} is close to the composition of the feed, this plate will be taken as the feed plate. Below this plate, the equation for the lower portion of the tower must be used. Since the feed was preheated such that

$$V_n = V_m$$
$$V_m = 200$$
$$W = 50$$
$$O_m = 250$$

and

$$y_m = (250/200)x_{m+1} - (50/200)(0.05) = 1.25x_{n+1} - 0.0125$$

since $x_{t-3} = x_f = 0.505$

$y_{f-1} = 1.25(0.505) - 0.0125 = 0.615$
$x_{f-1} = 0.392$ from equilibrium curve
$y_{f-2} = 1.25(0.392) - 0.0125 = 0.478$
$x_{f-2} = 0.275$
$y_{f-3} = 1.25(0.275) - 0.0125 = 0.323$
$x_{f-3} = 0.172$
$y_{f-4} = 1.25(0.172) - 0.0125 = 0.21$
$x_{f-4} = 0.100$
$y_{f-5} = 1.25(0.100) - 0.0125 = 0.122$
$x_{f-5} = 0.058$
$y_{f-6} = 1.25(0.058) - 0.0125 = 0.06$
$x_{f-6} = 0.03$

The desired strength of the bottoms was $x_w = 0.05$; x_{f-5} is too high, and x_{f-6} is too low. Thus it is impossible to satisfy the conditions chosen and introduce the feed on the fourth plate from the top with an even number of theoretical plates. However, by slightly reducing the reflux ratio it would be possible to make x_{f-6} equal to x_w, or by increasing the reflux ratio to make x_{f-5} equal to x_w. In general, such refinements are not necessary, and it is sufficient to say that between eight and nine theoretical plates are required in addition to the still, three plates above feed plates, the feed plate, and four or five plates below the feed, and the still, approximately $8\frac{1}{3}$. The percentage difference between eight and nine is much less than the accuracy with which the ratio of actual to theoretical plates is known; and whichever is used, a sufficient factor of safety must be utilized to cover the variation of this latter factor.

McCabe and Thiele Method (10).—When the usual simplifying assumptions are used with Sorel's method, the relation between y_n and x_{n+1} is a straight line, and the equation of this line may be plotted on the y-x diagram. Thus, for the example worked by Sorel's method in the preceding chapter,

$$y_n = 0.75x_{n+1} + 0.2375$$

This is a straight line of slope $0.75 = O_n/V_n$ which crosses the $y = x$ diagonal at $y_n = x_{n+1} = 0.95 = x_D$. Thus, on the x-y diagram for benzene-toluene, a line of slope 0.75 is drawn through $y = x = x_D$ (see line AB, Fig. 31). Likewise, below the feed,

$$y_m = \frac{O_m}{V_m}x_{m+1} - \frac{W}{V_m}x_w = 1.25x_{m+1} - 0.0125$$

This represents a straight line of slope $O_m/V_m = 1.25$ and passes through the $y = x$ diagonal at $x = x_w = 0.05$ (see line CD, Fig. 31). These two lines are termed the operating lines, since they are determined by the tower operating conditions, AB being the operating line for the enriching section and CD the operating line for the stripping, or exhausting, section. To determine the number of theoretical plates by Fig. 31, start at x_D; as before, $y_t = x_D = 0.95$, and the value of x_t is determined by the intersection of a horizontal line through $y_t = 0.95$ with the equilibrium curve at 1, giving $x_t = 0.88$. Now, instead of using Eq. (2a) algebraically as in the Sorel method, it is used graphically as the line AB. A vertical line at $x_t = 0.88$ intersects this operating line at 2, giving $y_{t-1} = 0.89$. By proceeding horizontally from intersection (2), an intersection is obtained with the equilibrium curve at (3). Since the ordinate of intersection (3) is y_{t-1}, the abscissa must be the composition of the liquid in equilibrium with this vapor, i.e., $x_{t-1} = 0.77$. As before, the intersection of the vertical line through the point (3) with the operating line at (4) gives the y on the plate below, or $y_{t-2} = 0.815$. This stepwise procedure is carried down the tower. At intersection 8, x_{t-3} is approximately equal to x_F; and at this plate, the feed will be introduced. The stepwise method is now continued, using the equilibrium curve and the operating line CD.

Such a stepwise procedure must yield the same answer as the previous calculations, since it is the exact graphical solution of

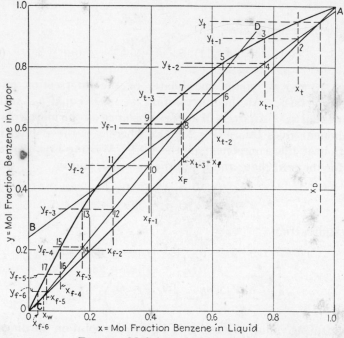

Fig. 31.—McCabe and Thiele diagram.

the algebraic equation previously used. It has a number of advantages over the latter method. First, it allows the effect of changes in equilibrium and operating conditions to be visualized. Second, limiting operating conditions are easily determined; and if a column contains more than two or three plates, it is generally more rapid than the corresponding algebraic procedure. Because of the importance of this diagram it will now be considered in further detail.

Intersection of Operating Lines.—In Fig. 31, the operating lines intersected at $x = x_F$. This intersection is not fortuitous, since the shapes of the two operating lines are not independent but are related to each other by the composition and thermal condition of the feed.   This relation is most easily shown by writing a heat balance around the feed plate.   Let p be the difference between the mols of overflow to and from the feed plate divided by the mols of feed.

$$p = \frac{O_{f+1} - O_f}{F} \tag{6}$$

A material balance gives

$$(p + 1) = \frac{V_f - V_{f-1}}{F} \tag{6a}$$

Let x_i and y_i be the coordinates of the intersection of the operating lines.   At this intersection, y_n must equal y_m, and x_n must equal x_m.   An over-all material balance on the more volatile component gives $Dx_D + Wx_w = Fz_F$, where z_F is the average mol fraction of this component in the feed.   Writing Eqs. (2a) and (4) for the feed plate and using the values y_i and x_i,

$$V_f y_i = O_{f+1}x_i + Dx_D \tag{2a'}$$
$$V_{f-1} y_i = O_f x_i - Wx_w \tag{4'}$$

and subtracting,

$$(V_f - V_{f+1})y_i = (O_{f+1} - O_f)x_i + Dx_D + Wx_w$$
$$= (O_{f+1} - O_f)x_i + Fz_F$$
$$\frac{(V_f - V_{f+1})y_i}{F} = \left(\frac{O_{f+1} - O_f}{F}\right)x_i + z_F$$

Substituting values of p and $p + 1$ gives the point on the diagram at which the intersection must occur.

$$(p + 1)y_i = px_i + z_F$$
$$y_i = \frac{p}{p + 1}x_i + \frac{z_F}{p + 1} \tag{7}$$

Equation (7) together with Eq. (2b) gives

$$x_i = \frac{\left(\frac{O}{D} + 1\right)z_F - (p + 1)x_D}{\left(\frac{O}{D} - p\right)} \tag{8}$$

and

$$y_i = \frac{(O/D)z_F - px_D}{\left(\dfrac{O}{D} - p\right)} \tag{9}$$

This line of intersections crosses the $y = x$ diagonal at

$$y_i = x_i = z_F$$

and has a slope of $\dfrac{p}{p+1}$. The effects of various values of p are

shown in Fig. 32 for a given slope of the operating line above the

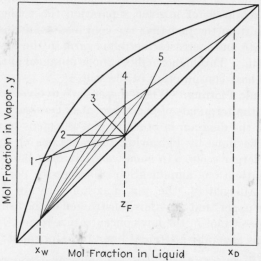

Fig. 32.—The effect of the thermal condition of the feed on the intersection of the operating lines.

1, p is greater than O (superheated vapor feed)
2, $p = O$ $(O_{f+1} = O_f)$
3, $O > p > -1$ (partly vapor feed)
4, $p = -1$ $(V_{f-1} = V_f)$
5, $p < -1$ (cold feed)

feed. Thus, if $p = O$, the mols of overflow above and below the feed are equal, and the operating lines must intersect in a horizontal line through the diagonal at z_F. A value of $p = -1$, i.e., $V_f = V_{f-1}$, would put the intersection on a vertical line at z_F.

The value of p is best obtained by an enthalpy balance around the feed plate. However, when the molal enthalpy of the overflow from the feed plate and the plate above is essentially the same and the enthalpy of the vapor from the feed plate and the plate below is also the same, then, by Eqs. (6) and (6a), $-p$ becomes approximately the heat necessary to vaporize 1 lb. mol of the feed divided by the latent heat of vaporization of the feed. Thus, an all-vapor feed at its boiling point would have a value of $p = O$; for an all-liquid feed at its boiling point, p would equal -1; p would be less than -1 for a cold feed, between -1 and zero for a partially vaporized feed, and greater than zero for a superheated vapor feed.

A little study of Fig. 32 indicates that for a given O/D fewer plates are required for a given separation the colder the feed. This results from the fact that the cold feed condenses vapor at the feed plate and increases the reflux ratio in the lower portion of the column. This higher reflux ratio is obtained at the expense of a higher heat consumption in the still.

Logarithmic Plotting. When the design involves low concentrations at the terminals of the tower, it is necessary to amplify this part of the diagram in order to plot the steps satisfactorily. This may be done by redrawing these regions of the y-x diagram to a larger scale. In some cases, it may be necessary to make more than one amplification of successive portions of the diagram. Alternately, the y-x diagram may be plotted on logarithmic paper, and the steps constructed in the usual manner. On this type of plot in the low-concentration region, the equilibrium curve is generally a straight line, since, for small values of x,

$$y = \frac{\alpha x}{1 + (\alpha - 1)x}$$ becomes $y = \alpha x$; however, the operating line

which is of the form $y_m = ax_{m+1} + b$ is a curved line unless $b = 0$. The operating line is constructed from points calculated from the operating-line equation.

Minimum Number of Plates.—The slope of the operating line above the feed is O_n/V_n, and as this slope approaches unity the number of theoretical plates becomes smaller. When O_n/V_n is equal to 1, O_R/D is equal to infinity, and only an infinitesimal amount of product can be withdrawn from a finite column. Under such conditions the column is said to operate at total reflux or with an infinite reflux ratio, and both operating lines have a slope of unity causing them to coincide with the y-x diagonal.

Since a higher reflux ratio than this is not possible, the size of the steps on the x-y diagram is a maximum, and a minimum number of theoretical plates is determined to give a given separation. This number is determined by simply using the y-x diagonal as the operating line and constructing the steps from x_D to x_w. A column with the minimum number of plates serves as a reference below which no column can give the desired separation, but such a column would have a zero capacity and would require infinite heat consumption per unit of product.

Fenske's Equation for Total Reflux.—Fenske (5) developed an algebraic method of calculating the minimum number of theoretical plates by utilizing the relative volatility together with the fact that at total reflux the operating line becomes the y-x diagonal. Thus, considering the two components x' and x'', and starting with the still,

$$\left(\frac{y'}{y''}\right)_s = \alpha_s \left(\frac{x'}{x''}\right)_s$$

and at total reflux the operating-line equation gives $y_s = x_1$, giving

$$\left(\frac{x'}{x''}\right)_1 = \alpha_s \left(\frac{x'}{x''}\right)_s$$

and

$$\left(\frac{y'}{y''}\right)_1 = \alpha_1 \alpha_s \left(\frac{x'}{x''}\right)_s$$

containing, in the same manner,

$$\left(\frac{x'}{x''}\right)_n = (\alpha_{n-1})(\alpha_{n-2})(\quad)(\quad) \cdots \alpha_1 \alpha_s \left(\frac{x'}{x''}\right)_s$$

Since in most cases the relative volatility does not vary widely, an average value for the entire column is used, giving

$$\left(\frac{x'}{x''}\right)_t = (\alpha_{\text{av.}})^t \left(\frac{x'}{x''}\right)_s$$

where t is the number of plates in the column. This equation can be changed to

$$t = \frac{\log (x'/x'')_t (x''/x')_s}{\log \alpha_{\text{av.}}} \qquad (10)$$

If a total condenser is employed, this becomes

$$t + 1 = \frac{\log (x'/x'')_D (x''/x')_s}{\log \alpha_{av.}} \tag{11}$$

or if a partial condenser equivalent to one theoretical plate is employed,

$$t + 2 = \frac{\log (y'/y'')_D (x''/x')_s}{\log \alpha_{av.}} \tag{12}$$

These equations offer a simple and rapid means of determining the number of theoretical plates at total reflux and avoid the necessity of constructing the y-x diagram. In general, an arithmetic average of the relative volatility at the temperature of the still and the temperature of the top of the tower is satisfactory. For appreciable variations in the relative volatility, the geometric average should be more satisfactory, i.e., $\alpha_{av.} = \sqrt{\alpha_t \alpha_s}$. In the cases of abnormal volatility such as are exhibited by ethyl alcohol and water, the use of an average relative volatility is not satisfactory over an appreciable concentration range; however, the equation may be applied successively to small concentration ranges, but the operation becomes practically as time consuming as constructing the y-x diagram. The use of the y-x diagram has the advantage that it gives a picture of the concentration gradient, and, in addition, after the diagram has been constructed, the number of theoretical plates for other reflux ratios can be easily determined. Fenske's relative-volatility method is not applicable to conditions other than total reflux.

Minimum Reflux Ratio.—In general, it is desired to keep the reflux ratio small in order to conserve heat and cooling requirements. As the reflux ratio O_R/D is reduced from infinity, the slope of the operating line $\dfrac{O_n}{V_n} = \dfrac{O/D}{\left(\dfrac{O}{D} + 1\right)}$ decreases from unity.

Thus, in Fig. 33 a reflux ratio of infinity would correspond to operating lines coinciding with the diagonal as acb, and a lower reflux ratio would correspond to adb. It is obvious that the average size of the steps between the equilibrium curve and the line adb will be much smaller than the size of the steps between the equilibrium curve and the line acb. Thus, a reduction of the reflux ratio requires an increase in the number of theoretical plates to effect a given separation. As the reflux ratio is further decreased, the size of the steps between the operating lines and the equilibrium curve becomes still smaller, and still more theoretical plates are required, until the conditions represented by *aeb* are encountered, when the operating line just touches the equilibrium curve. In this final case, the size of the step at the point of contact would be zero, and an infinite number of plates would be required to travel a finite distance down the operating line.

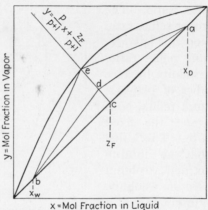

Fig. 33.—Plot for minimum reflux ratio.

The reflux ratio corresponding to this case is called the minimum reflux ratio and represents the theoretical limit below which this ratio cannot be reduced and produce the desired separation even if an infinite column is employed. This reflux ratio is easily determined by laying out the operating line of the flattest slope through x_D that just touches but does not cut the equilibrium curve at any point; the slope of this line $\dfrac{O}{V} = \dfrac{O/D}{\left(\dfrac{O}{D} + 1\right)}$ gives the value of O/D. Alternately, it may be calculated from the equation

$$\frac{O_R}{D} = \frac{x_D - y_c}{y_c - x_c} \tag{13}$$

where x_c and y_c are the coordinates of the point of contact. For mixtures having normal-shaped equilibrium curves, such as benzene-toluene, the point of contact of the operating line with the equilibrium curve will occur at the intersection of the operating lines, and x_c and y_c become x_f and y_f. For cases that deviate widely from Raoult's law, the operating line may become tangent to the equilibrium curve before the intersection of the operating lines touches the equilibrium curve, and in such cases it is usually best to plot the diagram and determine the slope O_n/V_n.

Optimum Reflux Ratio.—The choice of the proper reflux ratio is a matter of economic balance. At the minimum reflux ratio, fixed charges are infinite, because an infinite number of plates is required. At total reflux, both the operating and the fixed charges are infinite. This is due to the fact that an infinite amount of reflux and a column of infinite cross section would be required for the production of a finite amount of product. The

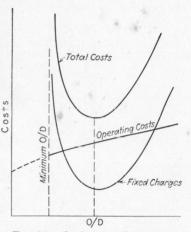

FIG. 34.—Optimum reflux ratio.

tower cost therefore passes through a minimum as the reflux ratio is decreased above the minimum. The costs of the still and condenser both increase as the reflux ratio is increased. The heat and cooling requirements constitute the main operating costs, and the sum of these increases almost proportionally as the reflux ratio is increased. The total cost, the sum of operating and fixed costs, therefore passes through a minimum. These conditions are shown in Fig. 34. Often the operating costs are high relative to the fixed charges, and this causes the minimum in the total cost curve to move toward the minimum O/D.

One of the most important pieces of data needed for such an economic study is the number of theoretical plates as a function of the reflux ratio. When the number of theoretical plates is plotted against the reflux ratio, a hyperbola type of curve is obtained with asymptotes corresponding to the minimum reflux ratio and minimum number of plates. These two asymptotes with a few stepwise calculations allow the entire curve to be sketched with sufficient accuracy for design purposes.

Thus, in the benzene-toluene problem previously solved, the minimum reflux ratio is

$$\left(\frac{O}{D}\right) \text{min.} = \frac{x_D - y_c}{y_c - x_c} = \frac{0.95 - 0.713}{0.713 - 0.5}$$
$$= 1.11$$

and the minimum number of plates can be calculated by Fenske's method. Using a relative volatility of 2.5,

$$t + 1 = \frac{\log (0.95/0.05)(0.95/0.05)}{\log 2.5} = 6.4$$
$$t = 5.4 \text{ plates}$$

The results of stepwise calculations are given in the following table and are plotted in Fig. 35.

O/D	Theoretical Plates
1.11	∞
1.5	13
2.5	9.2
3.0	8.3
5.0	7.0
9.0	6.5
∞	5.4

Feed-plate Location.—One step between the equilibrium curve and the operating line for the enriching section corresponds to one theoretical plate in the enriching section above the feed, and one step between the equilibrium curve and the other operating line corresponds to one theoretical plate below the feed. Therefore the step that passes from one operating line to the other corresponds to the feed plate. Thus, in Fig. 36, when plates are stepped off down the operating line *abc*, it is not possible to step on the operating line *dbe* until the value of x is less than the value corresponding to point *e*. However, as soon as the value of x is less than *e*, it is possible to shift to the other operating line, but it is not necessary to do so at this value, since steps can be continued down *abc* until they are pinched in at *c*, but a value less than *c* cannot be obtained unless the shift is made. The step from one operating line to the other must therefore occur at some value of x between the values corresponding to c and e, and a change at any value within this range will give an operable design. In general, for a given reflux ratio, it is desired to carry out the rectification with as few plates as possible in order to reduce the plant costs; *i.e.*, the minimum number of steps from a to d between the equilibrium curve and the operating line is desired. This minimum number of steps is obtained by taking the largest possible steps at all points between a and d. It is obvious that for values between e and b larger steps will be obtained between the equilibrium curve and operating line abc than would be obtained with operating line dbe.

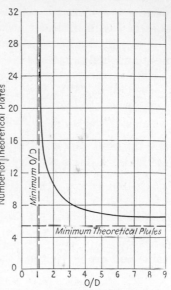

Fig. 35.—Effect of reflux ratio on number of theoretical plates.

Likewise, for values between c and b larger steps will be obtained

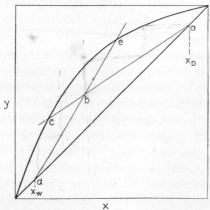

Fig. 36.—Diagram for limits of feed-plate composition.

by using line dbe than by using abc. Therefore it is desirable to use operating line abc for values from a to b, and line dbe for values between d and b; and by making the feed plate, *i.e.*, the shift from one line to the other, straddle the value b, the minimum number of theoretical plates will be obtained for the operating conditions chosen. If a step happens to fall directly on b, then the feed may be introduced either at b or on the plate below without changing conditions.

Partial vs. Total Condenser.—In the foregoing discussion the column was assumed to be operating with a total condenser, *i.e.*, a condenser that completely liquefies the overhead vapor and returns a portion of the condensate as reflux, removing the remainder as product. However, partial condensers are quite frequently used in commercial operations, especially where complete liquefaction of the overhead would be difficult. In this case, only enough condensate for the reflux to the column may be produced, and the product is withdrawn as a vapor. In other cases, mixtures of vapor and liquid are withdrawn. For example, in gasoline stabilizers employed by the petroleum industry, where the overhead contains appreciable percentages of methane, ethane, and ethylene, together with C_3 and C_4 hydrocarbons, in order to condense the methane and C_2 hydrocarbons, very low temperatures would be required with resulting high refrigeration costs. However, sufficient of the C_3 and C_4 hydrocarbons can be liquefied at moderate temperatures and pressures to serve as reflux, and the remainder of the overhead containing a large portion of the C_1 and C_2 hydrocarbons can be removed as vapor and sent to the gas lines.

A partial condenser may operate in any of several ways.

1. The cooling may be so rapid and the contact between condensate and uncondensed vapor so poor that essentially no transfer of components back and forth is obtained, with the result that the condensate and uncondensed vapor are of the same composition. (This is possible if part of the vapor condenses completely and the balance does not condense at all.) In this case, the partial condenser is equivalent to the total condenser with the exception that the product is removed as vapor instead of as liquid.

2. The vapor product may be in sufficiently good contact with the returning reflux for the two to be in equilibrium with each other, in which case the partial condenser acts as a theoretical

plate, and one less theoretical plate may be used above the feed plate in the column when this condition exists than when a total condenser is employed. Such a condition can be approximated by requiring the overhead vapor to bubble through a pool of reflux to the column.

3. The vapor is differentially condensed, and the equilibrium condensate continually removed, giving a differential partial condensation. Alternately, the vapor may be condensed on vertical tubes such that the condensate flows countercurrent to the rising vapor, and fractionation occurs between the vapor and condensate. Theoretically such condenser can be made equal to a number of theoretical plates; however, actually such conditions are seldom employed, since to obtain efficient transfer of components from vapor to liquid, low rates of condensation per unit area are required, thus necessitating large and costly condensers, and, in general, it is found more satisfactory and cheaper to obtain additional rectification by adding more plates to the column and using a condenser to produce condensate rather than make it perform composite duties.

Actual partial condensers usually operate somewhere between cases 1 and 2. For an absorption naphtha stabilizer, Gunness (6) (see page 199) found good agreement with case 2. In actual design calculation, the conservative assumption is to assume operation as in case 1, and any fractionation that does occur will act as a factor of safety; with ordinary condenser design, with the most optimistic assumption, not more than one theoretical plate should be taken for the partial condenser.

Open vs. Closed Steam.—When rectifying mixtures in which the residue is water and in some cases where the mixture undergoing fractionation is immiscible with water, the steam for heating may be introduced directly into the still. Such a procedure may materially reduce the temperature and pressure of the steam necessary for the distillation by giving in effect a steam distillation.

Considering the distillation of an ethyl alcohol water mixture, the operating line when a closed steam heating is used was shown to have a slope of $(O/V)_m$ and to pass through the $y = x$ line at $x = x_w$. In Fig. 37, a column operating with S mols of live steam is shown. A material balance between the m and $m + 1$ plate gives

$$O_{m+1} + S = V_m + W \qquad (14)$$

and with the usual simplifying assumptions, S would equal V_m, making $O = W$. An alcohol balance gives

$$O_{m+1}x_{m+1} = V_m y_m + W x_w$$
$$y_m = \frac{O_{m+1}x_{m+1}}{V_m} - \frac{W}{V_m}x_w$$

This is an operating line of slope O_m/V_m; but at $x = y$, x is equal to $\left(\dfrac{W}{W - S}\right)x_w$ instead of x_w; and at x equal to x_w, y becomes zero corresponding to the composition of the vapor (steam) to the

FIG. 37.—Diagram of column using live steam.

bottom plate. For a given O/D and feed condition, O_m/V_m must be the same whether closed or open steam is used, so that the lower operating line must cross the $y = x$ diagonal at the same x value in both cases, x_w for the live steam being lower than x_w for closed steam because of the dilution effect of the steam. In stepping off theoretical plates, the step must start at $y = 0$ and x_w; i.e., in Fig. 38, the bottom plate corresponds to the step abc. In such a case, the introduction of live steam can eliminate the still, but it dilutes the bottoms and requires more plates in the lower section of the column. Since the steps in the case of live steam start lower, it always requires at least a portion of a step to come up to the intersection of the operating line and the $y = x$ diagonal, and more plates are required with live steam than with closed steam. In Fig. 38, about $1\frac{1}{3}$ more plates would be necessary.

As an example of using open steam to obtain a steam distillation, consider the steam stripping of an oil containing 2.54 mol per cent propane at 20 lb. per square inch. The temperature will be maintained constant at 280°F. by internal heating. The molecular weight of oil may be taken as 300, and 4 mols of steam will be used per 100 mols of oil stripped. It is desired to estimate the number of theoretical plates necessary to reduce the propane content of the oil to 0.05 mol per cent. The oil may be assumed nonvolatile, and the vapor-liquid relation of the propane in the oil may be expressed as $y = 33.4x$.

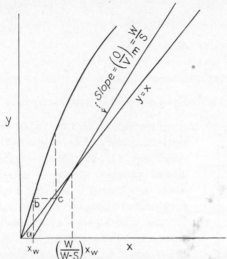

FIG. 38.—McCabe and Thiele diagram for case of live steam.

It is obvious that the mols of vapor will increase up the tower, since the steam does not condense under the conditions given, and the propane vaporizes into it as it passes up the tower. This will cause O/V to vary through the tower, and points on the operating line must be calculated, since it will not be a straight line. This is easily done by taking a basis of 100 mols of entering oil, for which the terminal conditions are given in Fig. 39. Now, assume that the liquid flowing down the tower at some position contains 1.3 mols of C_3H_8. The vapor at this point must then

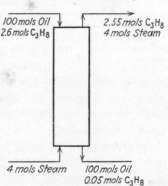

FIG. 39.—Figure for illustration.

contain 1.25 mols of C_3H_8, giving $x_{n+1} = 1.3/101.3 = 0.0128$ and $y_n = 1.25/5.25 = 0.238$. In a similar manner, other values on the operating line are calculated and plotted in Fig. 40

together with the equilibrium curve, and a little more than six steps are required to give the desired stripping.

Side Streams.—Side streams are removed from a column most often in multicomponent mixtures; however, they are occasionally

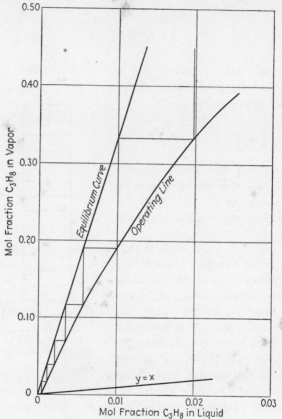

Fig. 40.—Steam stripping diagram.

used in the distillation of binary mixtures. Thus, a plant separating alcohol and water might have uses for both 80 and 95 per cent alcohol mixtures, which of course could be produced by making only 95 per cent alcohol and diluting with water to produce the required 80 per cent; or alternately liquid could be tapped off of a plate in the column on which the concentration was approximately 80 per cent. The proper plate in the tower can be determined by constructing the usual operating lines. Figure 41 illustrates the removal of a liquid side stream L. Considering this figure and making the usual simplifying assumptions, the operating line above the side stream is, as before,

$$y_n = \left(\frac{O}{V}\right)_n x_{n+1} + \frac{Dx_D}{V_n}$$

A material balance around the top of the column and some plate between the feed plate and the side-stream plate gives

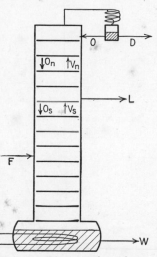

$$y_s = \left(\frac{O}{V}\right)_s x_{s+1} + \frac{Lx_L + Dx_D}{V_s} \quad (15)$$

The operating line above the side stream passes through $y = x = x_D$ and has a slope of $(O/V)_n$, while the operating line below the side stream passes through $y = x = \dfrac{Lx_L + Dx_D}{L + D}$ (*i.e.*, the molal average composition of the product and side stream) and has a slope $(O/V)_s$. Since x_L is less than x_D and O_s is less than O_n, ($O_s = O_n - L$); this latter operating line will cross the $y = x$ diagonal at a lower value than the upper operating line and will have a flatter slope.

Fig. 41.—Diagram of continuous column with side stream.

The two operating lines will intersect at $x = x_L$. Figure 42 illustrates these lines.

Theoretical plates are stepped off in the usual manner, using the operating line between ac from a to c, the operating line bcf from c to some value between e and f, and then the line edg from there to g. Although the feed plate may have any composition between e and f and the feed-plate step may be made at any value between these two, the side-stream step must fall exactly on c. This is because the feed can be actually introduced into plates of different composition, but a side stream has to be of the same composition as the plate from which it was withdrawn unless a partial separation of the side stream is made and a portion returned to the column. By altering the reflux ratio slightly, the step can be made to fall very close to c.

Unequal Molal Overflow.—The usual simplifying assumptions are applicable in most cases, but occasionally a mixture is encountered in which such assumptions are not justified. Sorel treated the problem by making a heat balance on each plate, but such calculations are time consuming. In those cases in which the

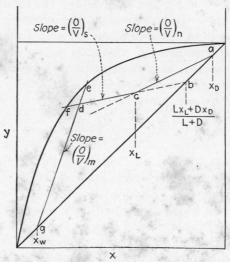

Fig. 42.—y-x diagram for column with side stream.

sensible heat differences and the heats of mixing are negligible, but for which the heats of vaporization of the two components are different, the approximate solution can be obtained by using

$$Q_n = V_n[y_n i_1 + (1 - y_n)i_2]$$

where Q_n is the latent heat of the vapor rising from the nth plate; i.e., i_1 and i_2 are the latent heats of the more and less volatile components, respectively. Neglecting heat losses and changes in sensible heat, Q_n is the same at every section above the feed plate. By rearrangement,

$$V_n = \frac{Q_n}{y_n i_1 + (1 - y_n)i_2} \tag{16}$$

where V_n is a constant only if $i_1 = i_2$; if these two values are not equal, then V_n is a function of y_n. By starting at the condenser for a given O/D, the vapor from the top plate is known. Using the values of V and y for the top plate, Q_n is calculated. This value of Q_n is then used with an assumed value of y_n to calculate V_n. The overflow corresponding to this vapor is calculated by $O_{n+1} = V_n - D$; the assumed value of y_n with the calculated values of V_n and O_{n+1} allows the determination of x_{n+1} by Eq. (2a). By performing this calculation at several assumed values of y_n, a curve of the calculated x_{n+1} values may be plotted vs. the assumed y_n values on the y-x diagram to give an operating line that may be used in the same manner as the operating line based on constant O/V.

In the same manner, below the feed

$$V_m = \frac{Q_m}{y_m i_1 + (1 - y_m) i_2} \tag{17}$$

The operating line for the lower portion of the column is plotted by assuming values of y_m and calculating values of x_{m+1}. The assumed values of y_m and y_n do not have to correspond to the concentration above any actual plate, since they are simply used to construct the operating line.

Method of Ponchon and Savarit.—Ponchon (12) and Savarit (13) developed a graphical method to correct for the variations of the molal overflow.

Equations (1) and (2) are combined with the following heat balance:

$$V_n H_n = V_T H_T + O_{n+1} h_{n+1} - O_R h_R$$

to give

$$\frac{x_D - x_{n+1}}{M - h_{n+1}} = \frac{x_D - y_n}{M - H_n} \tag{18}$$

where M equals $\left(\dfrac{O_R}{D} + 1\right)H_T - \left(\dfrac{O_R}{D}\right)h_R$, which gives the operating equation

$$y_n = \frac{M - H_n}{M - h_{n+1}} x_{n+1} - \frac{H_n - h_{n+1}}{M - h_{n+1}} x_D \tag{19}$$

Equation 18 can be represented graphically on a heat-composition diagram; *e.g.*, in Fig. 43, the molal enthalpy of the vapor and liquid are plotted vs. the vapor and liquid composition, respectively. Now, if a point with ordinate M and abscissa x_D is plotted, and a straight line cutting the curve at a corresponding to x_{n+1}, then $b - a$ is $x_D - x_{n+1}$ and $e - a$ is $M - h_{n+1}$; and by similar triangles $e - c$ must be $M - H_n$ and $d - c$ must be $x_D - y_n$. Thus, a straight line drawn through M to the liquid enthalpy curve at any value of x_{n+1} will cut the vapor curve at a mol fraction y_n corresponding to the vapor rising from the plate below. From this vapor composition and equilibrium, data

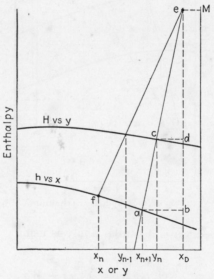

Fig. 43.—Heat-balance diagram.

x_n are determined and plotted on Fig. 43 and the line ef then gives y_{n-1}; such a procedure may be continued down the column.

Such a diagram can be used to construct operating lines for the usual y-x diagram. Thus, by drawing several straight lines through e, the abscissas at which this line cuts the vapor-enthalpy and liquid-enthalpy curves are the ordinate and abscissa of a point on the operating line. Actually, the heat diagram and the y-x diagram can be combined, but it is generally more convenient to use the diagrams separately to avoid confusion.

This method of calculation has the advantage that the H and h curves can be constructed to take account of heat of mixing, sensible heats, and variation of latent heats.

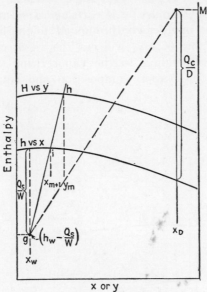

Fig. 44.—Heat-balance diagram.

Below the feed plate, a similar analysis using

$$O_{m+1} = V_m + W$$
$$O_{m+1}x_{m+1} = V_m y_m + W x_w$$
$$O_{m+1}h_{m+1} + Q_s = V_m H_m + W h_w$$

gives

$$\frac{y_m - x_m}{H_m - \left(h_w - \dfrac{Q_s}{W}\right)} = \frac{x_{m+1} - x_w}{h_{m+1} - \left(h_w - \dfrac{Q_s}{W}\right)} \qquad (20)$$

where Q_s is the heat added in the still. This equation may be plotted in the same way as Eq. (18).

Thus, in Fig. 44, where the point x_w, $\left(h_w - \dfrac{Q_s}{W}\right)$ is plotted on the enthalpy diagram, Eq. (20) gives the relation that a straight line through this point will cut the vapor and liquid enthalpy at abscissa values corresponding to y_m and x_{m+1}, respectively; and by drawing several such lines, sufficient coordinates can be obtained to construct the operating line for the lower part of the column.

On Fig. 44, the point M, x_D is also shown, and it can be shown that the enthalpy of the feed and the feed composition must give

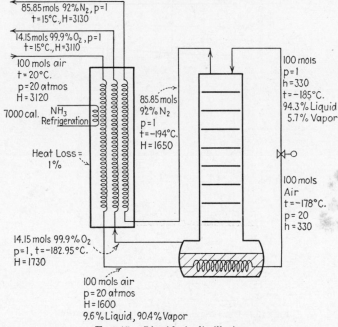

FIG. 45.—Liquid-air distillation.

a point that falls on the straight line connecting x_D, M, and x_w, $\left(h_w - \dfrac{Q_s}{W}\right)$. Thus, fixing the reflux ratio fixes M and the line through the point M, x_D, and the feed intersects the vertical line through x_w at $\left(h_w - \dfrac{Q_s}{W}\right)$, determining the heat load on the still.

Although these heat diagrams can be used to determine the number of plots for a given separation, minimum reflux ratio, minimum number of plates, and other problems, it is generally simpler to use such a diagram to construct the operating lines on an ordinary y-x diagram and then to proceed in stepwise manner.

The heat-balance method is applied to the example given in Fig. 45. Since the liquid-air fractionation involves only the stripping tower, the enthalpy diagram is for the lower portion

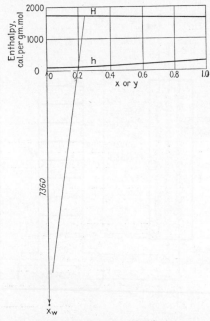

FIG. 46.—Heat diagram for liquid-air separation.

and is given in Fig. 46. The table at the top of page 112 gives values of y_n calculated at assumed values of x_{n+1}, for constant O/V and by heat balance using the data of Keesom (7).

The values of y_n calculated by the two methods agree within the accuracy of the data and the calculations. The operating line is plotted in Fig. 47. Logarithmic plotting is used so that the steps can be satisfactorily made in the low-concentration region. Nine theoretical plates in addition to the still give the desired separation. The y-x data are those of Dodge and Dunbar (4).

x_{n+1}	Calculated y_n	
	Constant O/V	Heat balance
0.001	0.001	
0.002	0.00218	
0.004	0.0045	
0.01	0.0116	
0.02	0.0233	0.024
0.04	0.0468	0.048
0.1	0.1175	0.12
0.2	0.235	0.24
0.4	0.470	0.475
0.6	0.705	0.71
0.8	0.94	0.94

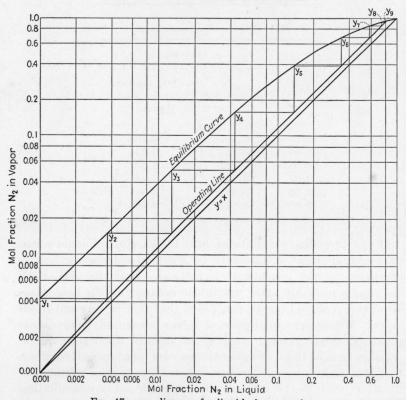

FIG. 47.—x-y diagram for liquid-air separation.

The following table also gives calculated y_n values for other systems.

O_2-N_2 AT 10 ATMOSPHERES

x_{n+1}	y_n calculated	
	Constant O/V	Heat balance, data of Bosnjak-ovic (2)
1.0	1.0	1.0
0.9	0.955	0.953
0.8	0.91	0.91
0.7	0.865	0.867
0.6	0.82	0.823

NH_3-H_2O AT 10 ATMOSPHERES

x_{n+1}	y_n calculated	
	Constant O/V	Heat balance, data of Bosn-jakovic (2)
0.1	0.701	0.705
0.09	0.624	0.625
0.08	0.547	0.547
0.07	0.47	0.46
0.06	0.393	0.385
0.05	0.316	0.305

Of the preceding calculations, only the case of ammonia water gave any appreciable difference by the heat-balance method as compared to the constant-O/V method. Even for NH_3-H_2O, the results probably agree within the accuracy of the heat data. However, it should not be concluded that O/V is constant in all cases. When large quantities of heavy, essentially nonvolatile constituents are present, such as in gasoline debutanizers, the sensible heat of these components may be large enough to affect O/V materially; also in operations where large heats of mixings are involved, such as the concentration of nitric acid by distillation in the presence of sulphuric acid, a variation of O/V would be expected.

Analytical Equation for Finite Reflux Ratio.—Fenske's method for total reflux is rapid and convenient for mixtures in which α does not vary too widely, and it is desirable to have a comparable method that is applicable at other reflux ratios. Two basic equations were used in the total reflux derivation, *viz.*,

$$\left(\frac{y_A}{y_B}\right)_n = \alpha_n\left(\frac{x_A}{x_B}\right)_n$$

and

$$\left(\frac{y_A}{y_B}\right)_n = \left(\frac{x_A}{x_B}\right)_{n+1}$$

The first of these two equations is true at any reflux ratio, but the latter is true only at total reflux. However, new variables may be defined such that

$$\left(\frac{y'_A}{y'_B}\right)_n = A_n\left(\frac{x'_A}{x'_B}\right)_n$$

and

$$\left(\frac{y'_A}{y'_B}\right)_n = \left(\frac{x'_A}{x'_B}\right)_{n+1}$$

and it is obvious that the equation developed from these will be identical in form with the Fenske equation. Thus, above the feed

$$n = \frac{\log\ (x'_A/x'_B)_D(x'_B/x'_A)_F}{\log A_{av.}} \tag{21}$$

It remains to relate the new variables to the usual variables, and this is done by the use of the following relations:

$$\left(\frac{y_A}{y_B}\right)_n = \alpha\left(\frac{x_A}{x_B}\right)_n$$

$$(y_A)_n = \frac{O}{V}(x_A)_{n+1} + \frac{D}{V}x_{AD}$$

$$(y_B)_n = \frac{O}{V}(x_B)_{n+1} + \frac{D}{V}x_{BD}$$

$$y_A + y_B = 1$$
$$x_A + x_B = 1$$

Smoker (14) has obtained a set of solutions to these equations, and the ones tabulated below are equivalent to his published values.

$$A_n = \left(\frac{O}{V}\right)\left(\frac{S^2}{\alpha}\right)$$

$$x'_{An} = x_{An} - \frac{Dx_D}{O(S-1)}; \qquad y'_{An} = \left(\frac{O}{V}\right)x'_{A(n+1)}$$

$$x'_{Bn} = \frac{V}{O} - \frac{[(\alpha-1)/\alpha]S}{[(S^2 O/\alpha V)-1]}x'_{An}; \qquad y'_{Bn} = \left(\frac{O}{V}\right)x'_{Bn+1}$$

where

$$S = \frac{2(D/O)x_D(\alpha-1)}{\left[\alpha\left(\dfrac{V}{O}\right) - 1 - \left(\dfrac{D}{O}\right)x_D(\alpha-1)\right]\left\{1 - \sqrt{1 - \dfrac{4(D/O)x_D(\alpha-1)}{[\alpha(V/O)-1-(D/O)x_D(\alpha-1)]^2}}\right\}} + 1.$$

Similarly, below the feed, O_m and V_m are used instead of O and V, and $-Wx_w/O_m$ instead of Dx_D/O.

Thus, for the benzene-toluene rectification problems of page 87, in which an equimolal mixture was fractionated into a product containing 95 mol per cent benzene and a residue containing 5 mol per cent benzene with $O/D = 3$, and the feed heated such that the mols of vapor above and below the feed were equal, above the feed these conditions give $S = 2.552$, $A_n = 1.95$, $x'_{AD} = 0.746$, $x'_{AF} = 0.296$, $x'_{BD} = 0.132$, $x'_{BF} = 0.856$, giving

$$n = \frac{\log(0.746/0.296)(0.856/0.132)}{\log 1.95} = 4.18$$

Below the feed, $W/O = \frac{1}{5}$, $V/O = \frac{4}{5}$; making the appropriate changes in the equation gives $S = 2.03$, $A_n = 2.06$, $x'_{AF} = 0.510$, $x'_{AW} = 0.0597$, $x'_{BF} = 0.214$, and $x'_{BW} = 0.731$, giving

$$m + 1 = \frac{\log(0.510/0.0597)(0.731/0.214)}{\log 2.03} = 4.93$$

The 1 is added to the left-hand side of the equation to compensate for the enrichment in the still. The total theoretical plates required equals $n + m = 8.1$. This compares with $8\frac{1}{3}$ estimated by the stepwise method (page 89).

These equations are exact solutions for the case of constant relative volatility and constant molal reflux ratio. In general, it is more accurate than the graphical method unless the logarithmic plot is used; however, it is equally time consuming for designs involving a moderate number of theoretical plates; and for cases for which several reflux ratios are to be studied for the same design conditions, the graphical method is usually the simplest to carry out. For designs involving a large number of theoretical plates, the analytical method is much simpler, but even here the calculations must be of high precision, since for this case the difference of two large numbers of approximately equal magnitude is involved. If the components are chosen such that the relative volatility is less than 1, the S equation must be modified by changing the minus sign before the square root to positive.

Lewis's Method.—Lewis (8) expresses the rate of increase of concentration of the liquid in the column from one plate to the next by the differential dx/dn; therefore,

$$x_{n+1} = x_n + \frac{dx}{dn} \tag{22}$$

The material-balance equation

$$V_n y_n = O_{n+1} x_{n+1} + D x_D$$

can be written, using $V = O + D$,

$$y_n = x_{n+1} + \frac{D}{O}(x_D - y_n)$$

From Eq. (22),

$$\frac{dn}{dx} = \frac{1}{x_{n+1} - x_n} = \frac{1}{y_n - x_n - \frac{D}{O}(x_D - y_n)} \tag{23}$$

The integration of this equation gives the number of theoretical plates between the x limits chosen; thus, the number of theoretical plates above the feed n is

$$n = \int_{x_f}^{x_D} \frac{dx}{y_n - x_n - \frac{D}{O}(x_D - y_n)} \tag{24}$$

Similarly, below the feed the theoretical plates m becomes

$$m = \int_{x_w}^{x_f} \frac{dx}{y_m - x_m - \left(\dfrac{F - D}{O - pF}\right)(y_m - x_w)} \qquad (25)$$

The equilibrium y-x curve gives the relation between y_n and x_n and y_m and x_m; thus by assuming values for x_n, values of y_n can be obtained from the equilibrium data, and

$$\frac{1}{\left[y_n - x_n - \dfrac{D}{O}(x_D - y_n)\right]}$$

can be calculated and plotted vs. the assumed values of x. The area under such a curve from x_f to x_D is the number of theoretical plates by the Lewis method.

Although this method is based on a continuous rate of concentration instead of the actual stepwise concentration increase, the error involved is not serious when the change in concentration per plate is small. This latter condition is generally true when the number of plates involved is large.

When the relative volatility is reasonably constant over the range of concentrations involved, the equilibrium curve may be approximated by the relative-volatility relation (see page 50)

$$y = \frac{\alpha_{\text{av.}} x}{1 + x(\alpha_{\text{av.}} - 1)}$$

and the foregoing equation may be integrated directly, avoiding the necessity for the graphical integration. Thus, for total reflux at which $D/O = 0$ and $(F - D)/(O - pF) = 0$, the foregoing equations give

$$n + m = \left(\frac{1}{\alpha - 1}\right) \ln \left(\frac{x_D}{x_w}\right)\left(\frac{1 - x_w}{1 - x_D}\right)^{\alpha} \qquad (26)$$

where $n + m$ is the total number of steps including the still step and any condenser enrichment. Noting that $\ln \alpha$ for values of α near to 1 is approximately equal to $(\alpha - 1)$ makes the foregoing equation approach Fenske's equation for total reflux; but for values of α widely different from 1, Fenske's equation is the more satisfactory. For example, with $\alpha = 1.07$ and $x_D = 0.96$ and $x_w = 0.033$, the true value of the number of theoretical plates as given by Fenske's equation is 93.5 and by Eq. (26), 97. However, Fenske's equation is applicable for total reflux only while the Lewis equation can be integrated for finite reflux ratios. Thus Eq. (24) can be integrated to give

$$n = \frac{\left(1 + \dfrac{b}{2}\right)}{\sqrt{b^2 - 4ac}} \ln \left[\left(\frac{x_D + A}{x_f + A}\right)\left(\frac{x_f + B}{x_D + B}\right) \right] - \tfrac{1}{2} \ln$$
$$\left(\frac{ax_D^2 + bx_D + c}{ax_f^2 + bx_f + c}\right) \quad (27)$$

where $\quad a = (1 - \alpha); \quad b = \{(\alpha - 1)[1 - (D/O)x_D] + \alpha D/O\};$ $c = -(D/O)x_D$

$$A = \frac{b - \sqrt{b^2 - 4ac}}{2a} \quad \text{and} \quad B = \frac{b + \sqrt{b^2 - 4ac}}{2a}$$

A similar equation is obtained below the feed with $-W/O_m$ replacing D/O, $-(W/O_m)x_w$ replacing $(D/O)x_D$, and using x_f instead of x_D and x_w instead of x_f.

The integrated equations are most useful in cases where the number of plates is large and the graphical method would be long and tedious.

The use of these methods will be considered in the following example:

Consider the rectification at atmospheric pressure of an aqueous solution containing 20 mol per cent ethanol into a product containing 75 mol per cent ethanol and a residue containing 2 mol per cent ethanol. For this separation, consider the following calculations, making the usual simplifying assumptions:

1. Minimum reflux ratio for liquid feed at 80°F.
2. Minimum number of plates.
3. Comparison of all vapor feed ($p = 0$) with liquid feed at 80°F. for a reflux ratio of $O/D = 5$.
4. Effect of feed-plate location.
5. Comparison of closed vs. open steam.
6. Comparison of partial vs. total condenser.
7. The withdrawal of 20 per cent of the entering ethanol as a side stream containing 50 mol per cent ethanol.

In addition, a calculation by the heat-balance method will be made for a liquid feed at 80°F. for a reflux ratio of 2. In all of the calculations, O/D has been chosen such that the number of plates will be few and the graphical design of satisfactory accuracy.

Basis: 100 lb. mols of feed:

By over-all material balances:

$$20 = 0.75D + 0.02W$$
$$= 0.75(100 - W) + 0.02W$$
$$= 0.75 - 0.73W$$
$$W = \frac{55}{0.73} = 75.4$$
$$D = 24.6$$

1. Minimum reflux ratio with liquid feed at 80°F.

Using the enthalpy data of Bosnjakovic (2) for the 20 per cent solution,

$$h_{80} = 15\text{kg cal. per kilogram}$$
$$H_{\text{sat. vapor}} = 490\text{kg cal. per kilogram}$$
$$\text{Latent heat} = 418\text{kg cal. per kilogram}$$

This gives a value of $p = -\left(\dfrac{490 - 15}{418}\right) = -1.137$

Thus, for the intersection of the operating lines by Eq. (7),

$$y_i = \frac{-1.137}{-0.137}x_i + \frac{0.2}{-0.137}$$
$$= 8.28x_i - 1.46$$

The y-x diagram for ethanol water of Lewis and Carey (9) is given in Fig. 48. The upper operating line becomes tangent at a before the intersection meets the equilibrium curve, and the minimum reflux ratio is dictated by this tangency. The slope of this line gives

$$\frac{O}{V} = \frac{0.75 - 0.542}{0.75 - 0.24} = 0.408$$

or

$$\frac{O}{D} = \frac{0.408}{0.592} = 0.690$$

2. Minimum number of plates at total reflux.

a. By stepping down the $y = x$ diagonal in Fig. 48; about $4\frac{2}{3}$ steps are required. If a still and total condenser are used, this would correspond to $3\frac{2}{3}$ theoretical plates.

b. Fenske's equation:

$$\alpha_{\text{top}} = \left(\frac{0.783}{0.217}\right)\left(\frac{0.25}{0.75}\right) = 1.203$$
$$\alpha_{\text{still}} = \left(\frac{0.16}{0.84}\right)\left(\frac{0.98}{0.02}\right) = 9.3$$

since the variation is so large because of the abnormal mixture in question. The geometric mean will be used:

$$\alpha_{av.} = \sqrt{(1.203)(9.3)} = 3.08$$

$$t + 1 = \frac{\log (0.75/0.25)(0.98/0.02)}{\log 3.08} = 4.45$$

$$t = 3.45 \text{ theoretical plates}$$

which is in very good agreement with the stepwise calculation, especially when the wide variation of relative volatility is considered. An arithmetic average for α would have given a result somewhat too low.

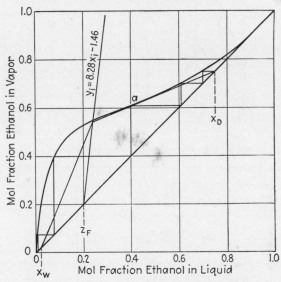

Fig. 48.—Figure for minimum reflux ratio.

3. Comparison of all vapor feed ($p = 0$) with a liquid feed at 80°F. for a reflux ratio of $O/D = 5$.

The operating lines for these two conditions are given in Fig. 49. The lines *abc* are for the cold feed, and *adc* are for the vapor feed. For the cold feed, $5\frac{1}{3}$ steps are required, while for the vapor feed, about six steps are required. The fewer steps are obtained for the cold feed because of the higher heat consumption in the still.

4. *Feed-plate Location.* Considering Fig. 49 and the operating lines for the cold feed, it is obvious that the change from one operating line to the other can be made at liquid compositions between $x = 0.02$ and $x = 0.42$. However, the steps will be large if the change is made near to the intersection *b*.

5. *Closed Steam vs. Open Steam.* Consider the cold-feed conditions of part 3. Figure 50 is an enlarged section of the lower portion of the y-x

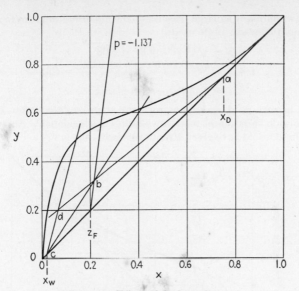

Fig. 49.—Effect of feed condition.

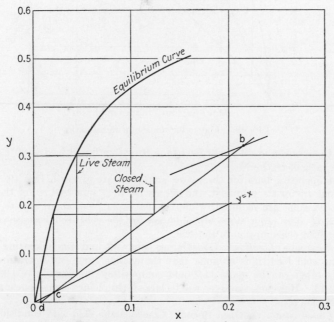

Fig. 50.—Live steam vs. closed steam.

diagram.   Since live steam is added, the concentration of the bottom will be diluted.   Extending the operating line to $y = 0$ gives $x_w' = 0.006$ at point d.   In the case of the closed steam, steps are started at c, and the step corresponding to the still is shown in Fig. 50.   With open steam, the steps are started at d, and the first step is shown.   More steps are required for live steam because of its diluting effect in the still.

6. *Partial Condenser vs. Total Condenser.*   If no enrichment takes place in the partial condenser, the results are the same except that the partial condenser gives a vapor product instead of a liquid product.   If the partial

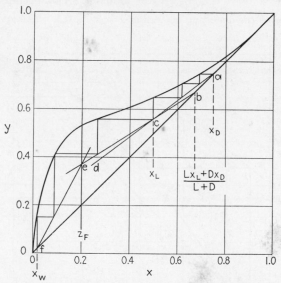

Fig. 51.—Diagram for column with side stream.

condenser gives enrichment equal to one theoretical plate, then the first step down from x_D in Figs. 48 and 49 corresponds to the partial condenser, and one less theoretical plate is needed for the column.

7. A side stream of 20 per cent of the entering ethanol is withdrawn as a liquid containing 50 mol per cent ethanol.   Consider the case of a liquid feed ($p = -1$) and $O/D = 3$.

Since 4 mols of ethanol is in the side stream, the side stream will total 8 mols.

$$16 = 0.75D + 0.02W$$
$$= 0.75(92 - W) + 0.02W$$
$$= 69 - 0.73W$$
$$W = 53/0.73 = 72.6$$
$$D = 19.4$$

giving $O_n = 58.2$ and $V_n = 77.6$.

After the withdrawal of the side stream,

$$Q_s = 50.2, \qquad \text{and} \qquad V_s = 77.6$$

The diagram for these conditions is given in Fig. 51. Starting at $x_D = 0.75$, the operating line acd for the upper section of the tower is drawn with a slope equal to $O/V = 58.2/77.6 = 0.75$. The operating line between the side-stream drawoff and the feed plate will have a slope equal to $50.2/77.6 = 0.648$ and will pass through the $y = x$ diagonal at $\dfrac{Lx_L + Dx_D}{L + D} = \dfrac{8(0.5) + 19.4(0.75)}{8 + 19.4}$, or at 0.677. This operating line bce will also cross the operating line acd at $x = x_L = 0.5$. The operating line

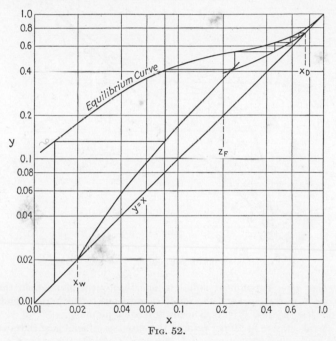

Fig. 52.

bce and the operating line below the feed fe will intersect on the vertical line through z_F. The three operating lines are drawn in this manner on Fig. 51. Plates are stepped off starting at x_D, using the operating line acd down to c, after which the operating line bce is used from c down to below e, and then the operating line fe is used to x_w. Starting at x_w, the first step corresponds to the still; and since the next step straddles z_F, this step is the feed plate, the concentration on the feed plate being 0.09 mol per cent ethanol. The second theoretical plate above the feed plate is the plate from which the side stream is removed, and then two theoretical plates above the side-stream plate together with the total condenser complete the column. Thus, five theoretical plates, a still, and total condenser are required for the separation.

A comparison of the heat-balance method will be made with the constant O/V method at a reflux ratio of 2, using a still and total condenser. The feed will enter at 80°F. The results will be used on a logarithmic plot to amplify the lower portion of the curve. Since the operating lines are not straight, coordinates will be calculated and plotted on Fig. 52.

a. Constant molal overflow for the enriching section:

$$y_n = 0.667x_{n+1} + 0.333(0.75) = 0.667x_{n+1} + 0.25$$

for the exhausting section:

$$y_m = 1.853x_{m+1} - 0.853(0.02) = 1.853x_{m+1} = 0.0171$$

x_{n+1}	y_n	x_{m+1}	y_m
0.75	0.75	0.02	0.02
0.7	0.716	0.04	0.057
0.6	0.65	0.06	0.094
0.5	0.584	0.10	0.168
0.4	0.517	0.15	0.261
0.3	0.45	0.2	0.354
0.2	0.385	0.25	0.446

b. Heat balance.—The enthalpy data for the saturated vapor and liquid given by Bosnjakovic are plotted in Fig. 53. The point A corresponds to x_D and M, where $x_D = 0.75$ and

$$M = \left(\frac{O}{D} + 1\right)H_T - \left(\frac{O}{D}\right)h_R = (2 + 1)11{,}550 - (2)(2{,}000)$$
$$= 34{,}650 - 4{,}000 = 30{,}650 \text{ cal. per gram mol.}$$

Point B corresponds to the feed condition, and point C is determined by drawing a line through A and B, the intersection of which with the vertical line through x_W is C.

x_{n+1}	y_n	x_{m+1}	y_m
0.75	0.75	0.02	0.02
0.7	0.716	0.04	0.056
0.6	0.65	0.06	0.095
0.5	0.582	0.10	0.170
0.4	0.52	0.15	0.262
0.3	0.452	0.20	0.358
0.2	0.385	0.25	0.453

The values of y_n and x_{n+1} in the table at the bottom of page 124 are determined by drawing lines through A, the intersection with the vapor line being y_n and the intersection with the liquid line being x_{n+1}. *EF* is one such line, giving $y_n = 0.65$ at $x_{n+1} = 0.6$. Other values are obtained in the same manner. Below, the feed values of y_m and y_{m+1} are obtained in the same manner, using the point C.

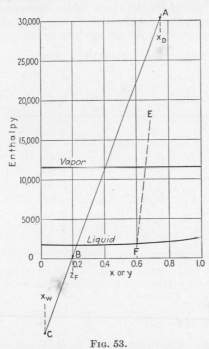

Fig. 53.

A comparison of the values in this table with those obtained for constant molal overflow in part a shows that the values are almost identical, indicating that a constant molal overflow is satisfactory for a mixture as abnormal as ethanol and water. It is obvious that both methods will give the same number of theoretical plates, since they give the same operating lines. Figure 52 indicates about 4.8 theoretical plates in addition to the still and total condenser.

Packed Towers.—Packed towers can be used in fractional distillation as well as bubble-plate columns. Instead of bubbling through a pool of liquid as in a bubble-plate tower, the interaction between vapor and liquid can be obtained by causing the reflux to flow over the surface of the packing material while the vapor flows up through the voids of the packing in the tower. The use of packed tower is generally limited to towers of small sizes or to special distillations such as the concentration of nitric acid. In small laboratory and pilot-plant size, the packed tower necessary for a given separation is, in general, less expensive than a corresponding bubble-plate tower; but in large diameter, the reverse may be true. Aside from the economic aspects, packed towers are easily constructed and can be made of noncorrosive

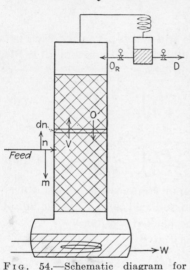

refractory earthenware, glass, and carbon as well as the usual metals used in bubble-plate tower construction. They have the disadvantage that it may be difficult to clean the tower without completely dismantling the unit, and often they channel badly; *i.e.*, the liquid flowing down the tower segregates on one side while the vapor passes up the other. In such cases, the efficiency of contact between liquid and vapor is very poor. The packed towers, in general, have very low pressure drops from top to bottom relative to an equivalent bubble-plate tower.

F I G. 54.—Schematic diagram for packed tower.

For tower packing, a wide variety of materials have been used, *e.g.*, coke, stone, glass, earthenware, carbon and metal rings, wood grids, jack chain, carborundum, and metal and glass helices, as well as a large number of other packings including many manufactured packings of special shapes.

Design of Packed Tower.—The interaction between vapor and liquid in packed towers is true countercurrent rather than the stepwise-countercurrent process of a bubble-plate tower with theoretical plates. Instead of finite steps, the true counter-current action should be treated differentially. Consider the schematic drawing of the packed tower in Fig. 54. Let O be the mols of overflow; V the mols of vapor; x and y the mol fraction in the liquid and vapor, respectively, n distance above and m distance below the feed. Focusing on the differential section dn, $V(dy/dn)$ must equal $O(dx/dn)$ for each component, and this transfer must be due to an exchange of components back and forth between the liquid and vapor. This transfer is due to the fact that the vapor and liquid at a given cross section are not in equilibrium with each other, and the rate of transfer will be proportional to the distance from equilibrium; thus,

$$V\frac{dy}{dn} = O\frac{dx}{dn} = kA(y^* - y) = k'A(x - x^*) \qquad (28)$$

where k and k' are proportionality constants, A is the area per unit height, y^* is the vapor in equilibrium with x, and x^* is the liquid in equilibrium with y. From which

$$n = \frac{V_n}{kA}\int_{y=y_{f'}}^{y=y_T}\frac{dy}{y^* - y} = \frac{O_n}{k'A}\int_{x=x_{f'}}^{x=x_T}\frac{dx}{x - x^*} \qquad (29)$$

Below the feed

$$m = \frac{V_m}{kA}\int_{y=y_n}^{y=y_{f'}}\frac{dy}{y^* - y} = \frac{O_m}{k'A}\int_{x=x_w'}^{x=x_{f'}}\frac{dx}{x - x^*} \qquad (30)$$

where x_f', y_f' are the liquid and vapor compositions in the tower at the level at which the feed is introduced, and x_w' is the liquid concentration at the bottom of the packed section.

A material balance above the feed gives

$$y = \left(\frac{O}{V}\right)x + \left(\frac{D}{V}\right)x_D \qquad (31)$$

By assuming values of y, values of x can be calculated by Eq. (31), and these used in Eq. (29) together with equilibrium data to evaluate the integrals. A similar material balance below the feed can be used with Eq. (30). The equilibrium curve and the material-balance equation can be plotted on the y-x diagram, and $x^* - x$ or $y - y^*$ read directly. In Fig. 55 is plotted the y-x equilibrium curve of benzene-toluene.

Consider the separation of an equimolal mixture of benzene and toluene into a product containing 95 mol per cent benzene and a residue containing 5 mol per cent benzene. An O/D of 3 will be used, and the feed will enter heated such that the mols of vapor above and below the feed are the same. The usual simplifying assumptions will be made.

The operating lines are identical with those for the stepwise diagram. The vertical distance between the equilibrium line and the operating line is $y^* - y$, and the horizontal distance between the operating line and the equilibrium line is $x - x^*$. In general, the integration must be performed graphically, although in cases where the equilibrium curve can be expressed as an algebraic relation between y and x the integration can be carried out algebraically, but the resulting equations are often complex and involved.

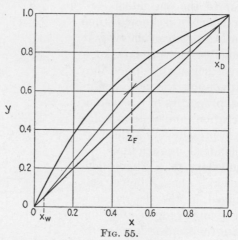

Fig. 55.

From Fig. 55, values of $y^* - y$ are read at various values of y. Such values are tabulated in the following table.

y	$y^* - y$	$\dfrac{1}{(y^* - y)}$
0.615	0.098	10.2
0.7	0.100	10.0
0.8	0.090	11.1
0.9	0.043	23.2
0.95	0.028	35.7

Values of $\dfrac{1}{(y^* - y)}$ are then calculated and plotted vs. y. The area under this curve from $y = 0.615$ to $y = 0.95$ is equal to kAn/V; so that if kA is known, n can be calculated. The values $\dfrac{1}{(y^* - y)}$ vs. y are plotted in Fig. 56. The value of $\dfrac{dy}{(y^* - y)}$ is the shaded area which is equal to 5.35. A similar procedure is used below the feed, and alternately the $x - x^*$ values may be used.

The only satisfactory method of evaluating kA and $k'A$ is the use of actual test data on a packed column similar to the one under consideration for which n is known, thus allowing kA or $k'A$ to be calculated. It should be possible to correlate such experimental coefficients by dimensionless groups involving the flow conditions, packing, properties of the system under consideration, and other similar variables, but at present very little progress has been made along such lines.

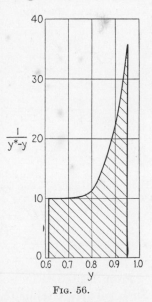

Fig. 56.

Height Equivalent to a Theoretical Plate.—In general, the graphical calculation involved in the design of a packed tower is more tedious and time consuming than the stepwise procedure used for plate towers. Actually, the equilibrium curve and operating lines on the y-x diagram are identical for the two cases, and one of the most common methods of designing packed towers has been to determine the number of theoretical plates required for the separation by the usual stepwise method and then to convert to the height of the corresponding packed tower, by multiplying the number of theoretical plates by the height of packing equivalent to one theoretical plate. This is abbreviated to H.E.T.P. (11) and is a height of packing such that the vapor leaving the top of the section will have the same composition as the vapor in equilibrium with the liquid leaving the bottom of the section. The use of the H.E.T.P. substitutes a stepwise countercurrent procedure for the true countercurrent operation and is therefore theoretically unsound; but when the concentration change between plates is small and the number of plates is large, the error introduced by its use will be small. Values of H.E.T.P. are determined experimentally by calculating the number of theoretical plates necessary to be equivalent to some actual packed tower; the height of the packed tower divided by the number of theoretical plates is then the H.E.T.P. Values of H.E.T.P. will be considered in the chapter on Column Performance (page 218).

Height of a Transfer Unit.—Chilton and Colburn (3) have proposed another design method for packed tower, based on the

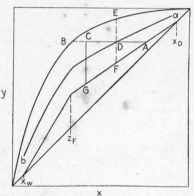

FIG. 57.—Diagram for H.T.U.

use of a unit called the height of a transfer unit H.T.U. The H.T.U. is the height of the tower divided by the number of transfer units, this latter number being defined above the feed as

$$\int_{y'_f}^{y_r} \frac{dy}{y^* - y} = \frac{kAn}{V};$$

and a similar expression can be obtained in terms of x. Over the height of one transfer unit, the value of $y^* - y$ does not ordinarily vary widely, and the arithmetic average may be used. Baker (1) has developed a relatively simple stepwise method for estimating the number of transfer units under these conditions. In the usual y-x diagram (Fig. 57), a line ab is drawn at the arithmetic mean of the equilibrium curve and the operating line. The H.T.U. corresponds to a step giving a change in y equal to the average value of $y^* - y$ over the step. Starting at A, one proceeds not to B but to C, such that $AD = DC$, and then steps from C to the operating line. If the curvature of the equilibrium curve is not too great, CG, the change in y, which is numerically equivalent to the EF, will be approximately equal to the average value of $y^* - y$ between A and G, and therefore the steps correspond to one transfer unit. This stepwise procedure is continued to the terminals of the tower, giving the number of transfer units in the tower. The step illustrated in

Fig. 57 is smaller than the corresponding H.E.T.P. which would extend from A to B; in general, if the equilibrium curve is flatter than the operating line, one theoretical plate will give a greater concentration change than one transfer unit; and if the equilibrium curve is steeper, the reverse will be true, and when the curves are parallel the two units are identical. The advantage of the H.T.U. relative to the H.E.T.P. is that it is defined on the basis of the true differential process rather than the incorrect stepwise countercurrent. Values of H.T.U. are used in the same manner as values of H.E.T.P.

References

1. BAKER, *Ind. Eng. Chem.*, **27**, 977 (1935).
2. BOSNJAKOVIC, "Technische Thermodynamik II," diagrams, Theodor Steinkopf, Dresden, 1937.
3. CHILTON and COLBURN, *Ind. Eng. Chem.*, **27**, 255, 904 (1935).
4. DODGE, *Chem. Met. Eng.*, **35**, 622 (1928).
5. FENSKE, *Ind. Eng. Chem.*, **24**, 482 (1932).
6. GUNNESS, Sc. D. thesis in chemical engineering, M.I.T., 1936.
7. KEESOM, *Bull. Internat. Inst. Refrig.*, **15** (1934).
8. LEWIS, *Ind. Eng. Chem.*, **14**, 492 (1922).
9. LEWIS and CAREY, *Ind. Eng. Chem.*, **24**, 882 (1932).
10. McCABE and THIELE, *Ind. Eng. Chem.*, **17**, 605 (1925).
11. PETERS, *Ind. Eng. Chem.*, **14**, 476 (1922).
12. PONCHON, *Tech. moderne*, **13**, 20 (1921).
13. SAVARIT, *Arts et metiers*, pp. 65, 142, 178, 241, 266, and 307 (1922).
14. SMOKER, *Trans. Amer. Inst. Chem. Eng.*, **34**, 165 (1938).
15. SOREL, "La rectification de l'alcool," Paris, 1893.

CHAPTER XIV

RECTIFICATION OF COMPLEX MIXTURES

As has been pointed out in previous chapters, the separation of binary and ternary mixtures into their substantially pure components or pure constant-boiling mixtures is a relatively simple matter and one that may be analyzed mathematically. The tremendous growth of the petroleum industry in recent years has introduced the problem of handling great quantities of extremely complex mixtures where the mathematical analysis becomes very much more involved and, in some cases, practically impossible.

It so happens, however, that it is possible to generalize from solutions of problems involving binary mixtures so that the solutions of problems in the separation of much more complicated mixtures become readily possible. The following generalizations have been drawn from a study of binary mixtures and are directly applicable to the study of mixtures of any complexity.

Generalization I.—In the rectification of a liquid mixture in the column of a continuous still, the liquid mixture being fed into the central portion of the column, the function of that portion of the column above the point at which the feed enters is solely to remove the remnants of the less volatile component from the more volatile components in the distillate.

Generalization II.—The function of that portion of the column below the point of introduction of the feed is solely to remove the remnants of the more volatile component from the less volatile components leaving the bottom of the column.

These two generalizations lead to the conclusion that in the fractional distillation of any volatile mixture, no matter how complex, so long as the object of the distillation is the separation of the mixture into two portions, one containing the more volatile components, and the other containing the less volatile components, the only way in which it is possible to effect the separation at all completely is to introduce the feed into the central portion of the column and not into the top or bottom. If this is not done, the liquid leaving the bottom of the column will not be completely stripped of the more volatile components if the feed enters the bottom of the column; whereas if the feed enters the top of the column, the distillate will contain some of the less volatile portion.

Generalization III.—Effective working of any part of a rectifying column is impossible without a supply of heat below and a removal of heat above the point in question.

The result of this is that a column will not function unless heat, usually in the form of latent heat in a rising current of vapor, is introduced into the bottom, and unless heat is removed from the top of the column usually by condensing part of the distillate and returning it to the top of the column. Any portion of the column below the lowest point of introduction of heat will be inoperative as a fractionating device, and any part of the column above the highest point at which heat is removed will also be inoperative.

Heat absorption may be due to the introduction of feed at a temperature below the temperature of the liquid on the feed plate. The introduction of low-boiling feed which vaporizes on entering the column, thereby abstracting heat from the contents, will also have the same effect. The downflowing feed, or reflux, which comes from a zone of lower temperature to one of higher temperature also removes heat in becoming heated up.

Heat may be introduced solely in the form of latent heat coming in the vapor from some other part of the equipment, or it may be furnished from heating coils at the bottom of the column. The result is the same so far as the supply of heat is concerned.

Generalization IV.—The use of a single total condenser at the top of the column for the complete condensation of the vapor leaving the top of the column and the return of part of that condensed vapor to the top of the column for reflux is, in general, more economical than the use of more complicated condenser design with the purpose of obtaining additional rectification by partial condensation, even though a somewhat higher column will be required. Of course, this does not apply to the cases where the feed to the column is partially preheated by using it as a cooling fluid in a partial condenser and then finishing the condensation in a final condenser.

Generalization V.—The permissible vapor velocities in a column are substantially independent of the composition of the mixture being distilled no matter how complex.   In other words, in a column of a given type, vapor velocities suitable for alcohol-water mixtures are equally suitable for complicated mixtures, such as petroleum products.   Of course, such a generalization implies that materials that foam or entrain badly must have special consideration.

Generalization VI.—Except under very special conditions, it is impossible to make more than one sharp cut per column; that is, it is impossible to take off of one column two or more products and one residue, each one of which is substantially free from the others.   This means that a continuous still must have as many columns less one as there are products into which the mixture is to be separated.

To give a specific example, to separate a crude petroleum into four products, gasolene, kerosene, gas oil, and fuel oil, and to effect sharp cuts cannot be done in a continuous still with less than three columns.

It should be understood in this connection, however, that sometimes several columns are combined into one shell so that externally it appears as one column.   The internal arrangements of such a combination column must include all of the requirements for separate columns in order for it to function successfully and give sharp separation.

Generalization VII.—If a known mixture is to be separated sharply into two fractions at some specific point, the temperature and the pressure at both the top and the bottom of the column are thereby automatically fixed.   If partial condensation is used, by the top of the column is meant the outlet of the partial condenser.

Generalization VIII.—Additional cooling at the top of the column will produce additional reflux; but if separation is good and the temperature in the condenser is not changed, the composition of the product will remain unchanged.   It will, however, lower the temperature at the inlet to the partial condenser and therefore the temperature on the top plate of the column.

Generalization IX.—When a partial condenser is used in the removal of a mixture of several components as the distillate, the outlet temperature of the condenser is always the condensing temperature of the distillate under the operating pressure and is always intermediate between the initial and final boiling temperatures of the distillate.

Such a system may be operated so that there is a sharp separation of the components of the feed into two fractions, the distillate and the residue, at the point required, although the boiling points of the components between which the separation is effected are far above the temperature at the outlet of the condenser. The low-boiling reflux washes out the high-boiling components from the vapor rising through the column, and the vapor entering the bottom of the column strips out the low-boiling components from the reflux running back into the bottom of the column. The result is that the low-boiling components up to a certain point are ejected from the top of the column, while the high-boiling components are rejected by the partial condenser and must go back to the bottom of the column.

Generalization X.—In testing complex mixtures of liquids of reasonably normal behavior from the standpoint of volatility by the determination of the ordinary boiling-point curve, such as the Engler or A.S.T.M. distillation curve, the initial boiling point of the mixture is always above the boiling point of the most volatile pure component, and the final boiling point of the mixture is always below the boiling point of the least volatile component, unless that component is present in very large amount in the original mixture. Furthermore, in distilling such a mixture, the initial boiling point of the distillate will be lower than the initial boiling point of the original mixture; and if the separation is good, the final boiling point of the distillate may be below the initial boiling point of the residue. This difference in temperature between the final boiling point of the distillate and the initial boiling point of the residue will be the greater the greater the difference in volatility between the most volatile and the least volatile components in the original mixture. With perfect separation, this difference will be a maximum for any particular case. In petroleum distillation, this "gap" is taken to be a sign of effective fractionation.

Generalization XI.—It is practicable to feed a column in a continuous still with either a liquid or a vapor or a mixture of the two. Feeding with liquid tends to overload the column with reflux below the feed plate, particularly if the liquid is cold. On the other hand, feeding with vapor overloads the upper part of the column unless the percentage of distillate in the feed is very large. The best point in the column at which to introduce the feed will be affected also by the proportion of liquid and vapor in it.

Generalization XII.—If the feed enters as a liquid and a small percentage of it is removed as distillate, the main task of the column is to strip all of the volatile constituents from the residue, which means the use of a large exhausting column. If most of the feed is taken off as distillate, the main function of the column is the removal of the traces of residue from the distillate which means that the rectifying section above the feed plate must be large.

Although it is true that these generalizations are qualitative in scope and are not readily made quantitative, nevertheless, a careful analysis of the problem in their light will make it possible to select the most suitable type of distilling equipment for the problem at hand and prevent the mistakes that are so likely to occur where there is no rational basis for comparison.

The following chapters will take up some features of the quantitative side of distillation calculations in the fractional distillation of complex petroleum mixtures. It is hoped that a study of the methods of calculation employed will be of assistance particularly to those on whom falls the duty of designing petroleum equipment.

CHAPTER XV

RECTIFICATION OF MULTICOMPONENT MIXTURES

Multicomponent mixtures are those containing more than two components in significant amounts. In commercial operations, they are encountered more generally than are binary mixtures. As with binary mixtures, they can be treated in batch or continuous operations, in bubble-plate or packed towers. Since the continuous operation is much more amenable to mathematical analysis, owing to the steady conditions of concentration and operation, it will be considered first.

Fundamentally, the estimation of the number of theoretical plates involved for the continuous separation of a multicomponent mixture involves exactly the same principles as those given for binary mixtures. Thus, the operating-line equations for each component in a multicomponent mixture are identical in form with those given for binary mixtures (see page 83). And the procedure is exactly the same; *i.e.*, starting with the composition of the liquid at any position in the tower, the vapor in equilibrium with this liquid is calculated; and then by applying the appropriate operating line for the section of the tower in question to each component, the liquid composition on the plate above is determined, and the operation repeated from plate to plate up the column. However, actually the estimation of the number of theoretical plates required for the separation of a complex mixture is more difficult than for a binary mixture. When considering binary mixtures, fixing the total pressure and one component in either the liquid or vapor immediately fixes the temperature and composition of the other phase; *i.e.*, at a given total pressure, a unique or definite relation between y and x allows the construction of the y-x curve. In the case of a multicomponent mixture of n components, in addition to the pressure, it is necessary to fix $(n - 1)$ concentrations before the system is completely defined. This means that for a given component in such a mixture the y-x curve is a function not only of the physical characteristics of the other components but also of their relative amounts. There-

137

fore, instead of a single y-x curve for a given component, there are an infinite number of such curves depending on the relative amounts of the other components present. This necessitates a large amount of equilibrium data for each component in the presence of varying proportions of the others, and, except in the special cases in which some generalized rule (such as Raoult's law) applies, these are not usually available, and it is very laborious to obtain them. One of the largest uses of multi-component rectification is in the petroleum industry; for a large number of the hydrocarbon mixtures encountered in these rectifications, generalized rules have been developed which give multicomponent vapor-liquid equilibriums with precision sufficient for design calculations. Such data are usually present in the form $y = Kx$, where K is a function of the pressure, temperature, and component. The use of equilibrium data in such a form usually requires a trial-and-error calculation to estimate the vapor in equilibrium with a given liquid at a known pressure. This results from the fact that the temperature is not known, so a temperature is assumed, and the various equilibrium constants at the known pressure and assumed temperature are used to estimate the vapor composition. If the sum of the mol fractions of all the components in the vapor, so calculated, add up to 1, the assumed temperature was correct. If the sum is not equal to 1, a new temperature must be assumed, and the calculation repeated until the sum is unity. Such a procedure is much more laborious than that involved in a binary mixture where the composition of the liquid and the pressure together with equilibrium data immediately gives the vapor composition without trial and error.

In the foregoing discussion of multicomponent systems, it was assumed that the complete composition of the liquid at some position in the column was known as a starting point for the calculation. The determination of this complete composition as a starting point is often the most difficult part of the whole multicomponent design. This difficulty arises since for a given feed composition, reflux ratio, and total pressure, it is possible to fix only two additional factors, such as two terminal compositions, before the system is completely defined.[1] In general, the

[1] The discussion assumes constancy of O/V in each section, definite feed location, definite thermal condition of the feed, and theoretical plates.

complete composition of neither the residue nor the distillate can be determined by using the two additional factors to fix two terminal conditions, in which case it is necessary to estimate the complete composition of either the product or the residue and then proceed with the calculations as before until the desired degree of separation is attained. If, then, the calculated product and residue compositions satisfy a material balance for each component, the estimated composition was correct. However, if a material balance is not satisfied by any one of the components, it is necessary to readjust the composition and repeat the calculation until the material balances are all satisfied simultaneously. This estimation is often simplified, owing to the fact that the degree of separation is so high that the heavier components will appear in the product in quantities so small as to be negligible, and the same will be true for the lightest component in the residue.

Several methods have been proposed for the design of multicomponent mixtures, but fundamentally they are based on Sorel's method. One of the best of these proposed methods is that due to Lewis and Matheson (2). This is exactly the application of Sorel's method together with the usual simplifying assumptions to multicomponent mixtures. The same operating lines as used on page 83 for binary mixtures are employed to determine the relation between the vapor composition and the composition of liquid on the plate above, this calculation together with vapor-liquid equilibrium data being sufficient for the determination of the number of theoretical plates for given conditions. The use of this method will be illustrated by the fractionation of a mixture of benzene, toluene, and xylene under conditions where the separation will be sufficiently good so that the determination of the terminal conditions will not be difficult.

Consider the rectification of a mixture containing 60 mol per cent of benzene, 30 mol per cent of toluene, and 10 mol per cent of xylene into a distillate or product containing not over 0.5 mol per cent of toluene and a bottoms or residue containing 0.5 mol per cent of benzene. A reflux ratio O/D equal to 2 will be used, and the feed will enter preheated so that the change in mols of overflow across the feed plate will be equal to the mols of feed. The usual simplifying assumptions will be made, and Raoult's law will be used. The distillation will be carried out at 1 atm. absolute pressure.

Since the concentration of toluene in the distillate D is low, the xylene will be practically zero and therefore will be essentially all in the residue W. Taking as a basis 100 mols of feed, a benzene material balance, input equals output, gives the following:

$$60 = Dx_{DB} + 0.005W = (100 - W)x_{DB} + 0.005W$$
$$= 100x_{DB} + (0.005 - x_{DB})W$$
$$x_{DB} = 0.995$$
$$60 = 99.5 - W(0.99)$$
$$W = \frac{39.5}{0.99} = 39.9$$
$$D = 60.1$$

where D = mols of product.

W = mols of residue.

x_{DB} = mol fraction of benzene in liquid distillate.

The terminal conditions are then

	Distillate		Residue	
	Mols	Mol per cent	Mols	Mol per cent
Benzene....................	59.8	99.5	0.20	0.5
Toluene....................	0.30	0.5	29.7	74.4
Xylene....................	0	.....	10.0	25.1
	60.1	100.0	39.9	100.0

Since $O/D = 2$, in the top part of the tower

$$O_n = 2 \times 60.1 = 120.2,$$

and $V_n = O_n + D = 180.3$, and $O_m = O_n + F = 220.2$, giving $V_m = 180.3$.

For the part of the column below the feed plate, the operating lines are

for benzene:

$$y_{mB} = \left(\frac{O}{V}\right)_m x_{(m+1)B} - \left(\frac{W}{V}\right)_m x_{WB} = \left(\frac{220.2}{180.3}\right)x_{(m+1)B} - \frac{39.9}{180.3}(0.005)$$
$$= 1.221x_{(m+1)B} - 0.0011$$

for toluene:

$$y_{mT} = 1.221x_{(m+1)T} - 0.164$$

for xylene:

$$y_{mX} = 1.221x_{(m+1)X} - 0.0555$$

Beginning with the composition of the liquid in the still, a temperature is assumed, and the partial pressure of each component is calculated using Raoult's law. If the sum of the partial pressure is 760 mm. Hg (the total pressure), the assumed temperature was correct. The vapor pressure of these components is given in Fig. 58. Assume $T = 115°C$.

	x_s	P	x_sP	$y_s = x_sP/\Sigma x_sP$
C_6	0.005	1990	10	0.0135
C_7	0.744	850	632	0.854
C_8	0.251	390	98	0.1325
			740	1.0000

Since the total is 740 instead of 760, the assumed temperature was too low, but a nearer correct temperature is easily found by determining the temperature from Fig. 58 at which the vapor pressure of toluene is $(760/740)(850) = 873$, giving $T = 116.0°C$. The calculation is then repeated for 116°C.

	x_o	P	x_sP	$y_s = x_sP/760$
C_6	0.005	2000	10	0.0131
C_7	0.744	873	650	0.855
C_8	0.251	400	100.4	0.132
			760.4	1.0000

With this assumed temperature, the sum of x_sP is seen to be very close to 760, and the temperature is satisfactory. Actually, such a recalculation is not necessary, since the values desired are y_s, and these values may be obtained from $y_s = x_sP/\Sigma x_sP$, where Σx_sP is the sum of the x_sP values. Thus, in the fourth column of the table for the first assumed temperature are given values of $y_s = x_sP/740$. These are seen to correspond closely to the values in the corrected table and agree well within the accuracy of such factors as the vapor pressures, the applicability of Raoult's law, etc. In general, such a simplified procedure is satisfactory when the sum of x_sP is within 10 per cent of the desired value; however, at times, such a simplification is not justified, and a preliminary check on the system in question should be made to determine the satisfactory limit of the sum of x_sP.

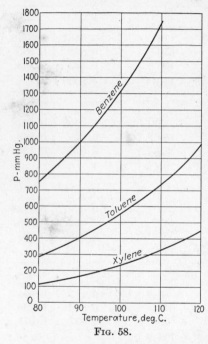

Fig. 58.

The calculation is now continued with the values of y_s just obtained, using the operating-line equations to determine x_1; and then y_1 is calculated from these values similarly to y_s.

The value of x_1 is obtained from y_s by the use of the appropriate operating-line equation applied to each component. y_1 is then calculated using Raoult's and Dalton's laws at an assumed temperature of 115°C., and x_2 is obtained from the values of y_1 by the use of the operating-line equation. The operation is repeated, making adjustments of the assumed temperatures such that ΣxP stays between 700 and 820. In making these adjustments of temperature, it is desirable to continue using one temperature until the value of ΣxP is about as much greater than 760 as it was less than 760 on the first plate on which the temperature was used. Thus, in the following table, the values of 110°C. were continued from $x_2P = 720$ to $x_4P = 804$, giving approximately an equal displacement on both sides of 760.

The table on page 143 carries these calculations up to the sixth plate.

However, as pointed out on page 138, the vapor-liquid data are more often given as $y = Kx$ rather than as Raoult's law. With

Component	T, °C. assumed	P_{mm}	x_s	x_sP	$y_s = x_sP/\Sigma x_sP$	x_1
C_6	115	1990	0.005	10	0.0135	
C_7	...	850	0.744	632	0.854	
C_8	...	390	0.251	98	0.1325	
				$\Sigma xP = 740$	$\Sigma y = 1.0000$	
						x_1
C_6	116	2000	0.005	10	0.0131	0.0116
C_7	...	873	0.744	650	0.855	0.835
C_8	...	400	0.251	100.4	0.132	0.153
				$\Sigma xP = 760.4$	$\Sigma y = 1.0000$	
			x_1	x_1P	y_1	x_2
C_6	115	1990	0.0116	23.1	0.0292	0.0248
C_7	...	850	0.835	709	0.895	0.868
C_8	...	390	0.153	59.7	0.0755	0.1065
				$\Sigma xP = 791.8$	$\Sigma y = 1$	
			x_2	x_2P	y_2	x_3
C_6	110	1740	0.0248	43	0.0597	0.0498
C_7	...	740	0.868	642	0.892	0.865
C_8	...	330	0.1065	35	0.0486	0.085
				$\Sigma xP = 720$		
			x_3	x_3P	y_3	x_4
C_6	110	1740	0.0498	86.7	0.115	0.095
C_7	...	740	0.865	640	0.848	0.830
C_8	...	330	0.085	28	0.037	0.075
				$\Sigma xP = 754.7$		
			x_4	x_4P	y_4	x_5
C_6	110	1740	0.095	165	0.205	0.169
C_7	...	740	0.830	614	0.763	0.759
C_8	...	330	0.075	25	0.031	0.071
				$\Sigma xP = 804$		
			x_5	x_5P	y_5	x_6
C_6	105	1520	0.169	257	0.336	0.276
C_7	...	645	0.759	489	0.638	0.657
C_8	...	280	0.071	20	0.026	0.067
				$\Sigma xP = 766$		

equilibrium data in such form, the method of calculation is similar. Given the values of x in the liquid on any plate, the temperature is assumed, and a value of K for each component is obtained from equilibrium data at the assumed temperature and the operating pressure. The value of y in equilibrium with this liquid is given by Kx. If the sum of the values of y is equal to 1, the assumed temperature was correct, and the x values on the plate above may be obtained from the y values just calculated by using the operating-line equation. If the sum of the values of Kx does not equal 1, the temperature should be readjusted; but as in the previous case, this adjustment is usually unnecessary if the sum of Kx is within 10 per cent of 1, in which case the values of y are calculated by $y_a = K_a x_a / \Sigma Kx$.

The benzene-toluene-xylene calculations will be continued, using the K method. For this particular mixture, where Raoult's and Dalton's laws are assumed to apply, the equilibrium constant is equal to the vapor pressure divided by the total pressure; e.g.,

$$y_a \pi = x_a P_a, \text{ or } y_a = \frac{P_a}{\pi} x_a, \text{ giving } K_a = P_a / \pi.$$

Component	T, °C. assumed	$K = P/760$	x_6	xK	$y_6 = xK/\Sigma xK$	x_7
C_6	100	1.745	0.276	0.482	0.49	0.402
C_7	...	0.735	0.657	0.482	0.49	0.535
C_8	...	0.316	0.067	0.021	0.021	0.063
				$\Sigma xK = 0.985$		
			x_7	$x_7 K$	y_7	x_8
C_6	95	1.52	0.402	0.612	0.635	0.521
C_7	...	0.628	0.535	0.336	0.348	0.420
C_8	...	0.263	0.063	0.016	0.017	0.059
				$\Sigma xK = 0.964$		
			x_8	$x_8 K$	y_8	x_9
C_6	95	1.52	0.521	0.793	0.738	0.605
C_7	...	0.628	0.420	0.264	0.246	0.336
C_8	...	0.263	0.059	0.016	0.015	0.058
				$\Sigma xK = 1.073$		

The ratio of x_{c_6} to x_{c_7} on plate 9 is approximately that in the feed, so this plate will be used as the feed plate. The proper feed-plate location for this column will be considered in a later section. Above the feed plate, the procedure is the same, except that the equation for the upper portion of the tower is utilized.

The operating-line equations above the feed are for C_6:

$$y_{nB} = \left(\frac{O}{V}\right)_n x_{(n+1)B} + \left(\frac{D}{V}\right)_n x_{DB} = 0.667x_{(n+1)B} + 0.332$$

for C_7:

$$y_{nT} = 0.667x_{(n+1)T} + 0.0017$$

for C_8:

$$y_{nx} = 0.667x_{(n+1)X}$$

Proceeding as before:

Component	T, °C. assumed	K	x_9	xK	$y_9 = xK/\Sigma xK$	x_{10}
C_6	90	1.33	0.605	0.805	0.807	0.712
C_7	..	0.533	0.336	0.179	0.180	0.267
C_8	..	0.221	0.058	0.013	0.013	0.020
				$\Sigma xK = 0.997$		
			x_{10}	$x_{10}K$	y_{10}	x_{11}
C_6	85	1.15	0.712	0.819	0.867	0.802
C_7	..	0.452	0.267	0.121	0.128	0.189
C_8	..	0.184	0.020	0.004	0.004	0.006
				$\Sigma xK = 0.944$		
			x_{11}	$x_{11}K$	y_{11}	x_{12}
C_6	85	1.15	0.802	0.923	0.914	0.873
C_7	..	0.452	0.189	0.085	0.084	0.123
C_8	..	0.184	0.006	0.0012	0.0012	0.0018
				$\Sigma xK = 1.009$		
			x_{12}	$x_{12}K$	y_{12}	x_{13}
C_6	85	1.15	0.873	1.005	0.947	0.922
C_7	..	0.452	0.123	0.055	0.053	0.0765
C_8	..	0.184	0.0018	0.0004	0.0004	0.0006
				$\Sigma xK = 1.061$		

Component	T, °C. assumed	K	x_9	xK	$x_9 = xK/\Sigma xK$	x_{10}
			x_{13}	$x_{13}K$	y_{13}	x_{14}
C_6	80	0.995	0.922	0.917	0.968	0.953
C_7	..	0.379	0.0765	0.029	0.032	0.045
C_8	..	0.153	0.0006	0.0001	0.0001	0.00015
				$\Sigma xK = 0.946$		
			x_{14}	$x_{14}K$	y_{14}	x_{15}
C_6	80	0.995	0.953	0.948	0.982	0.974
C_7	..	0.379	0.045	0.017	0.018	0.024
C_8	..	0.153	0.00015	0.00002	0.00002	0.00003
			x_{15}	$x_{15}K$	y_{15}	x_{16}
C_6	80	0.995	0.974	0.969	0.99	0.988
C_7	..	0.379	0.024	0.0091	0.0093	0.0114
C_8	..	0.153	0.00003	0.000005	0.000005	0.000007
			x_{16}	$x_{16}K$	y_{16}	
C_6	80	0.995	0.988	0.983	0.9956	
C_7	..	0.379	0.0114	0.0043	0.0044	
C_8	..	0.153	7×10^{-6}	10^{-6}	10^{-6}	

The vapor leaving the sixteenth plate, on being liquefied in the total condenser, will give a product containing slightly more than 99.5 per cent benzene.   Thus, approximately 16 theoretical plates together with a total condenser and still or reboiler are required to effect the desired separation under the operating conditions chosen.

In general, it is instructive to plot the compositions vs. the plates.   This type of figure is shown in Fig. 59 for the example just solved.   The benzene is seen to rise on a smooth curve, and the concentration of toluene in the liquid passes through a maximum two plates above the still and then falls off in a smooth curve with the exception of a slight break at the feed plate; the xylene drops rapidly above the still and then flattens out until the feed plate is reached and then drops rapidly to a negligible value.   The maximum in the toluene curve is a result of the fact that, in the still, toluene and xylene are the main components; and since toluene is the more volatile of the two, it tends to increase, and the xylene tends to decrease.   This increase in toluene concentration continues until the benzene concentration becomes appreciable; and since this latter component is very volatile, it increases rapidly and forces the toluene to decrease. This increase of benzene relative to the toluene continues up to the condenser. The xylene decreases up the column from the still because of its low volatility but cannot decrease below a certain value, since the 10 mols of xylene in the feed must flow down the column, and this sets a minimum limit on the concentration of

$$\frac{10}{O_m} = \frac{10}{220} = 0.0455;$$

actually the value will be slightly higher, since the small amount of xylene that passes upward in the vapor must again pass down the column. This is due to the fact that essentially no xylene leaves the top of the column. Above the feed plate, the amount of xylene passing in with the vapor to a plate must be equal to the xylene in the overflow from the plate, *i.e.*, $Vy_n = Ox_{n+1}$, since Dx_D is essentially zero. However, $y_n = Kx_n$, giving $x_{n+1} = \dfrac{VK}{O_n}x_n$; and for a heavy component such as xylene which does not leave the top of the column in appreciable amount, the composition of the liquid on one plate is related to that on the plate below by VK/O. In general, K is very small for such components and the concentration decreases rapidly as shown by the straight line in Fig. 59.

These concentration-gradient curves are typical of those generally obtained. The two main components between which the rectification is taking place tend to increase and decrease up the column, much as in a binary mixture. They are often called the key components. The concentrations of the components heavier than the heavier key component tend to decrease rapidly as one proceeds from the still up the column, but they tend to become constant because of the necessity of their flowing down the overflows in order that they may be removed at the still. These components then decrease rapidly above the feed plate, usually dropping to negligible values a few plates above this plate. The concentrations of components lighter than the light key component give the same type of curves from the condenser down the column as the heavier components do from the still upward. Thus, the concentrations of these light components decrease rapidly for a few plates down from the condenser but

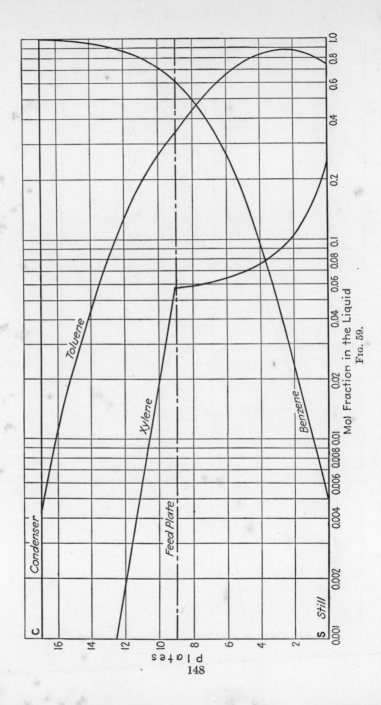

Fig. 59.

148

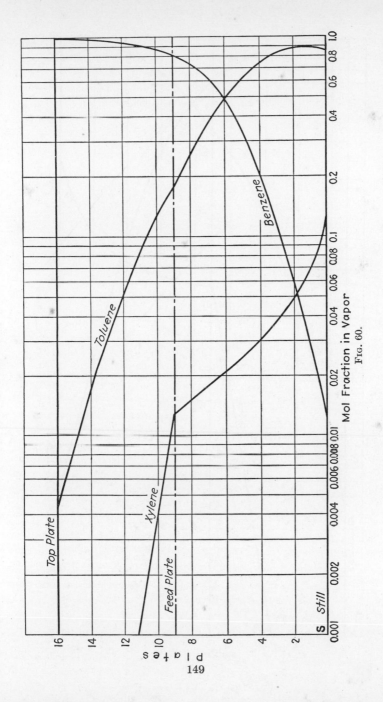

Fig. 60.

149

then flatten out, since by material balance essentially all of the mols of these components that are in the feed must flow up through the upper part of the column to be removed at the condenser, and this factor sets a lower limit on their concentration in this section. Below the feed plate, these light components

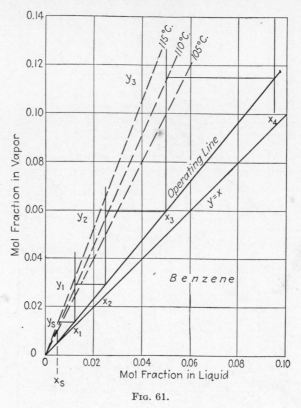

Fig. 61.

decrease rapidly and generally become negligible a few plates below the feed plate.

Lewis and Cope (3) applied the same method graphically, by constructing a separate y-x plot for each component. On these plots, the y-x line and the operating lines are drawn the same as for a binary mixture. The three plots for the previous examples are given in Figs. 61, 62, and 63. Only the lower portions of the benzene and xylene curves are given in order to increase the

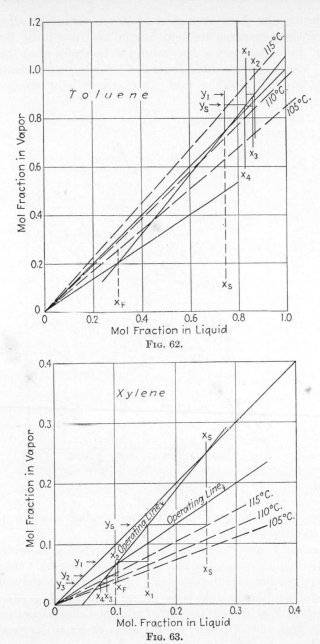

FIG. 62.

FIG. 63.

graphical accuracy.   It is interesting to note that for xylene and toluene the intersection of the operating line, which occurs at x_F, just as in the case of a binary mixture, falls below the y-x diagonal.   This is due to the fact that x_S is greater than x_D, and the components are both of lower volatility than the benzene.   If unique equilibrium curves could be drawn on the diagrams, the problem would become similar to the stepwise procedure for a binary mixture.   However, in general, such curves are not known. Lewis and Cope's method was to draw a series of equilibrium curves of the type $y = Kx$ which at constant temperature are in general straight lines through the origin of slope K.   Thus, in the present example, $K = P/760$, where P of any one component is a function of the temperature only.   Such equilibrium curves have been drawn in for the temperatures of 105, 110, and 115°C. Starting at x_S on each plot, vertical lines are drawn through this point cutting the equilibrium curves.   By trial and error, temperatures are tried until the sum of the y values at the intersection of the vertical line through x_S and the equilibrium curve for the assumed temperature adds up to unity.   Thus, if 115°C. is tried, the sum of the y values at the intersection of the 115°C. curve with the x_S lines is $0.013 + 0.837 + 0.13 = 0.98$, indicating that 115°C. is too low.   By interpolation at 116°C., the sum becomes $0.013 + 0.855 + 0.132 = 1.00$, indicating that this is the correct temperature, and the y values give the composition y_S of the vapor in equilibrium with x_S.   Horizontal lines are then drawn through the y_S values to the operating line, the abscissa of the intersection with the operating line being x_1.   Vertical lines are drawn through the x_1's; and by using the same procedure as for x_S, a temperature of 112.5°C. is found to give Σy equal to unity, and the step is then completed to the operating line.   In a like manner, steps are taken up the column.   The same operating line is used until the feed plate is reached, and then the change is made to the operating line for the upper portion of the column simultaneously for all three components.

A comparison of the values of these figures with those obtained in the previous algebraic calculation shows the close agreement. Actually, they have to give the same result, since they both are solutions of the same set of equations, one being algebraic and the other graphical.   Both methods have their advantages; in the algebraic method, as a rule, higher accuracy can be obtained than in the graphical method; this is especially true in the low-concentration region where the graphical diagram must be greatly expanded or replotted on logarithmic paper, such as was utilized in the binary mixtures. The advantage of the graphical method is that it gives a visual picture of the concentration gradients and operation of the tower. The amount of labor and time consumed is approximately the same for the two methods.

Numerous analytical methods (5) based on the foregoing methods have been proposed to simplify the trial and error required in the Lewis and Matheson method. However, all of these methods make assumptions that are not justified in all cases and, in general, leave the designer in doubt as to the exactness of his design. Generally, much is made of the difficulty of the trial-and-error calculations involved in the Lewis and Matheson method; but actually, by using $y = Kx/\Sigma Kx$ instead of making the Kx's add to exactly unity, the trial-and-error work is practically eliminated. In the example just solved, when ΣKx became larger than 1, the temperature was dropped, making ΣKx less than 1; and this temperature was used until ΣKx again became greater than unity, and then the temperature was again dropped. Thus, no actual trial and error was required, but merely successive drops of temperature of 5 to 10°. Such calculations require only a few hours more than the simplest of the approximate methods and only two or three such stepwise calculations at different reflux ratios together with the minimum number of plates at total reflux and the minimum reflux ratio are required to allow the construction of a curve of theoretical plates required vs. the reflux ratio. In general, the added confidence that may be placed in the stepwise calculations relative to the approximate methods more than justifies the extra work involved.

In using the stepwise method with the simplification that $y = Kx/\Sigma Kx$, the problem arises as to how much ΣKx can differ from unity and still not appreciably affect the values of y. The justification of this simplification is that for moderate changes in temperature the percentage change in the values of K for substances that do not differ too widely is approximately the same. A little consideration will show that if all the K values change the same percentage with temperature, then the values of y calculated by such a method will be independent of the temperature chosen. This relative variation in the K values is best expressed in the relative volatility. Thus, if $y_A = K_A x_A$ and $y_B = K_B x_B$, then $y_A/y_B = (K_A/K_B)(x_A/x_B)$, and (K_A/K_B) is the relative volatility of A to B, α_{AB} (see page 50). If the percentage change in both K_A and K_B is the same with temperature, α_{AB} will be a constant over this region, and a plot of α_{AB} vs. temperature will give immediately the region over which ΣKx can vary without appreciably altering the y value. Actually, the α's can be introduced into the equations, and the K's eliminated. Thus,

$$y_A + y_B + y_C + y_D + \cdots = 1$$

$$\frac{y_A}{y_B} + 1 + \frac{y_C}{y_B} + \frac{y_D}{y_B} + \cdots = \frac{1}{y_B}$$

using the relative volatility

$$\frac{\alpha_{AB} x_A}{x_B} + 1 + \frac{\alpha_{CB} x_C}{x_B} + \alpha_{DB}\frac{x_D}{x_B} + \cdots = \frac{1}{y_B}$$

which can be rearranged to give

$$y_B = \frac{x_B}{\alpha_{AB} x_A + x_B + \alpha_{CB} x_C + \alpha_{DB} x_D + \cdots} = \frac{x_B}{\Sigma \alpha x}$$

since

$$\frac{x_B}{y_B} = \alpha_{AB}\frac{x_A}{y_A}$$

$$y_A = \frac{\alpha_{AB} x_A}{\Sigma \alpha x}$$

Likewise,

$$y_C = \frac{\alpha_{CB} x_C}{\Sigma \alpha x}; \qquad y_D = \frac{\alpha_{DB} x_D}{\Sigma \alpha x} \tag{1}$$

A similar analysis starting with

$$x_A + x_B + x_C + \cdots = 1$$

leads to

$$x_A = \frac{y_A/\alpha_{AB}}{\Sigma y/\alpha}, \qquad x_B = \frac{y_B/\alpha_{BB}}{\Sigma y/\alpha}, \qquad x_C = \frac{y_C/\alpha_{CB}}{\Sigma y/\alpha} \tag{2}$$

where all the relative volatilities are with respect to the B component; and in the case of the y_B equation, a relative volatility does not appear with x_B, since α_{BB} is 1. Given the liquid composition on any plate, the values of x are multiplied by the α corresponding to the component in question, and the values of αx are totaled to give $\Sigma \alpha x$; then the value of y for any component is calculated by dividing αx for the component by $\Sigma \alpha x$. In general, it is desirable to take the volatilities relative to one of the key components; this will cause $\bar{\alpha}$ to be greater than 1 for the components that are lighter and less than 1 for the heavier components. This method will be most clearly brought out by its

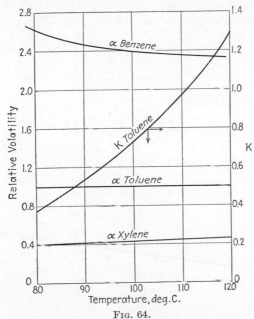

Fig. 64.

application to actual problems. First it will be applied to the benzene, toluene, and xylene problem previously solved. Figure 64 shows the volatilities relative to toluene plotted as a function of temperature and also shows the K for toluene as a function of the temperature. It will be noticed that the variation in the relative volatilities with temperature is very small and that for xylene in the lower part of the column a constant value of α equal to 0.43 is well within the design accuracy. The benzene volatility relative to toluene varies more, but even here the variation is small. In the previous example, starting at the still:

	x_S	α_{110}	αx_S	$y_S = \alpha x/0.869$	x_1	$\alpha_{110}x_1$	$y_1 = \alpha x/0.932$
C_6	0.005	2.36	0.0118	0.0136	0.012	0.0283	0.030
C_7	0.744	1.0	0.744	0.856	0.835	0.835	0.896
C_8	0.251	0.45	0.113	0.130	0.152	0.0684	0.074
			0.8688			0.9317	

$$K_T = 0.856/0.744 = 1.15 \qquad K_T = 0.896/0.835 = 1.07$$
$$T_S = 116°C. \qquad\qquad T_1 = 113.4°C.$$

	x_2	$\alpha_{110}x_2$	$y_2 = \alpha x/0.976$	x_3	$\alpha_{110}x_3$	$y_3 = \alpha x/1.02$
C_6	0.0254	0.06	0.061	0.0508	0.13	0.117
C_7	0.868	0.868	0.890	0.864	0.864	0.845
C_8	0.106	0.0477	0.049	0.086	0.039	0.038
		0.9757			1.023	

$$K_T = 1/0.9757 = 1.025 \qquad K_T = 0.978$$
$$T_2 = 111.8°C. \qquad\qquad T_3 = 110.2°C.$$

	x_4	$\alpha_{110}x_4$	$y_4 = \alpha x/1.086$	x_5	$\alpha_{110}x_5$	$y_5 = \alpha x/1.192$
C_6	0.096	0.226	0.208	0.171	0.403	0.338
C_7	0.826	0.826	0.760	0.757	0.757	0.636
C_8	0.076	0.034	0.031	0.071	0.032	0.027
		1.086			1.192	

$$K = 0.922 \qquad K = 0.84$$
$$T_4 = 108°C. \qquad T_5 = 104.8°C.$$

A comparison of the values calculated above with those previously obtained shows a very close agreement, as must be the case, since both calculations are fundamentally identical. In these calculations, the temperature has been determined on each plate by taking the K for toluene corresponding to the plate and determining the temperature from Fig. 64. Thus, K's were determined for the still and first plate by dividing the calculated y values by the value of x, $K_T = y_T/x_T$; thus for the still, x_T is 0.744, and y_T was calculated as 0.856, so that $K_T = 0.856/0.744 = 1.15$. From Fig. 64, the temperature is 116°C. at $K = 1.15$. A little consideration will show that K_T also is equal to $1/\Sigma\alpha x$, since $y = \alpha x/\Sigma\alpha x$; then $y/x = \alpha/\Sigma\alpha x$; but for the component to which the relative volatilities are taken, α is equal to 1, and $y/x = 1/\Sigma \alpha x$ for this component. This latter method was used for the second plate upward.

Continuing in this manner, the α's should probably be shifted when the temperature becomes about $100°C$. Taking the new values of α at $90°C$. should be satisfactory for finishing the column. Thus, no trial and error is needed, and only two sets of α values are employed. In order to speed computations, further modifications can be made. If, instead of calculating

	x_s	y_5	$4.52y_5$	$5.52x_6 = x_s + 4.52y_5$	$5.52\alpha_{110}x_6$	$4.52y_6 = (5.52\alpha x_6/7.411)(4.52)$
C_6	0.005	0.338	1.53	1.535	3.62	2.21
C_7	0.744	0.636	2.88	3.624	3.624	2.21
C_8	0.251	0.027	0.12	0.371	0.167	0.098
					7.411	

$$K = 5.52/7.411 = 0.746 \qquad T_6 = 100.7$$

	$5.52x_7$	α_{90}	$5.52\alpha x_7$	$4.52y_7 = (5.52\alpha x/8.56)4.52$	$5.52x_8$
C_6	2.215	2.47	5.46	2.89	2.895
C_7	2.954	1.0	2.954	1.56	2.304
C_8	0.349	0.42	0.147	0.078	0.329
			8.561		

$$K = 5.52/8.56 = 0.646 \qquad T_7 = 95.8$$

	$5.52\alpha x_8$	$4.52y_8$	$5.52x_9$
C_6	7.15	3.36	3.365
C_7	2.304	1.09	1.834
C_8	0.138	0.065	0.316
	9.592		

$$K = 0.577 \qquad T_8 = 92.2$$

	x_9
C_6	0.609
C_7	0.334
C_8	0.057

y_m, one calculates Vy_m, where V is the mols of vapor per mol of residue, then simply adding x_s to these values gives $O_m x_{m+1}$, where O_m is the mols of overflow per mol of residue. Then $O\alpha x_{m+1}$ is calculated, and $Vy_{m+1} = O\alpha x_{m+1}/\Sigma O\alpha x_{m+1}$, which materially shortens the time necessary per plate but has the disadvantage that the actual x and y values do not appear. Continuing by this method, V per mol of bottoms is $180.3/39.9 = 4.52$, and $O = 220.2/39.9 = 5.52$.

The values of x_9 are essentially those obtained previously, indicating that the trial-and-error calculation to determine plate temperature is, in general, not necessary and that the Lewis and Matheson method when carried out in such a manner does not possess any great obstacles. The use of the relative-volatility method also offers other advantages than the ease of determining the plate composition. Consider the fractionation in a vacuum column in which the overhead pressure is fixed and the pressure drop per plate is an appreciable percentage of the total pressure causing the absolute pressure to vary widely. In general, the K values are approximately inversely proportional to the pressure and therefore would vary with the change in pressure as well as with the changes in temperature. On the other hand, the relative volatility is often mainly a function of the temperature and only slightly affected by the moderate changes in pressure. In such cases, it is therefore possible to proceed by the α method, as in the constant-pressure calculations, without troubling with the pressure variation.

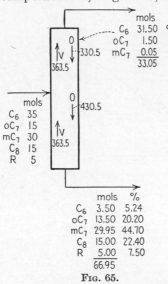

	mols	%
C_6	31.50	95.30
oC_7	1.50	4.55
mC_7	0.05	0.15
	33.05	

0
$\uparrow V \downarrow$ 330.5
363.5

0
430.5

mols		
C_6	35	
oC_7	15	
mC_7	30	
C_8	15	
R	5	

0
$\uparrow V$ 363.5

	mols	%
C_6	3.50	5.24
oC_7	13.50	20.20
mC_7	29.95	44.70
C_8	15.00	22.40
R	5.00	7.50
	66.95	

Fig. 65.

As another example of such calculations, consider the fractionation of a 35 mol per cent phenol, 15 mol per cent o-cresol, 30 mol per cent m-cresol, 15 mol per cent xylenols, and 5 mol per cent heavier. The overhead is to be 95 mol per cent phenol, and the phenol recovery is to be 90 per cent. The still pressure will be 250 mm. Hg absolute, and 4 mm. Hg pressure drop will be allowed per theoretical plate. A reflux ratio O/P equal to 10 will be employed.

The equilibrium data obtained by Rhodes, Wells, and Murray (4) for this type of system indicate that Raoult's law is followed, and thus the relative volatilities are independent of the pressure and a function of the temperature only. Thus, the relative-volatility method will be most suitable for estimating the number of theoretical plates.

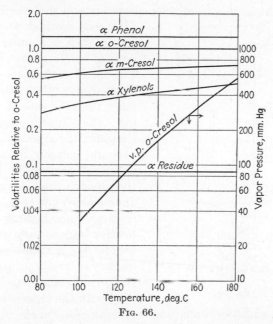

FIG. 66.

The result of over-all material balances is given in Fig. 65. The ratio of o-C_7 to m-C_7 in the distillate was assumed as 30 to 1.

Figure 66 gives the volatilities relative to o-cresol as well as the vapor pressure of o-cresol. In the calculations, the temperature is checked occasionally by determining the vapor pressure of o-cresol P_o on the plate. Since $y_o\pi = P_o x_o$, then

$$P_o = \frac{y\pi}{x} = \frac{\pi}{\Sigma\alpha x},$$

where π is corrected for pressure drop in the column. Below the feed, per mol of bottoms, the mols of vapor are 5.43, and the

mols of liquid are 6.43; above the feed, the corresponding figures
per mol of distillate are 11 and 10, respectively.

	x_s	α_{160}	αx_s	$5.43y_s = \alpha x_s(5.43)/0.685$	$6.43x_1$
C_6	0.0524	1.25	0.0656	0.521	0.573
$o\text{-}C_7$	0.202	1.0	0.202	1.60	1.80
$n\text{-}C_7$	0.447	0.7	0.312	2.48	2.93
C_8	0.224	0.44	0.099	0.79	1.01
R	0.075	0.087	0.006	0.048	0.123
			0.6846		

$$P_o = 250/0.685 = 365 \text{ mm.} \qquad T = 165°C.$$

	$6.43\alpha x_1$	$5.43y_1$	$6.43x_2$	$6.43\alpha x_2$	$5.43y_2$
C_6	0.716	0.775	0.828	1.035	1.045
$o\text{-}C_7$	1.80	1.95	2.152	2.152	2.18
$m\text{-}C_7$	2.05	2.22	2.667	1.865	1.89
C_8	0.444	0.48	0.704	0.310	0.31
R	0.011	0.012	0.087	0.008	0.008
	5.021			5.370	

	$6.43x_3$	$6.43\alpha x_3$	$5.43y_3$	$6.43x_4$	$6.43\alpha x_4$
C_6	1.097	1.37	1.32	1.372	1.72
$o\text{-}C_7$	2.38	2.38	2.30	2.50	2.50
$m\text{-}C_7$	2.34	1.635	1.575	2.02	1.41
C_8	0.53	0.233	0.225	0.45	0.198
R	0.083	0.007	0.007	0.082	0.007
		5.625			5.835

	$5.43y_4$	$6.43x_5$	$6.43\alpha x_5$	$5.43y_5$	$6.43x_6$
C_6	1.60	1.652	2.07	1.87	1.92
$o\text{-}C_7$	2.33	2.53	2.53	2.28	2.48
$m\text{-}C_7$	1.31	1.76	1.23	1.11	1.56
C_8	0.184	0.41	0.18	0.16	0.38
R	0.006	0.081	0.007	0.006	0.081
			6.017		

$$P_o = 230(6.43)/6.017 = 246 \qquad T_5 = 153°C.$$

	$6.43\alpha x_6$	$5.43y_6$	$6.43x_7$	$6.43\alpha x_7$	$5.43y_7$
C_6	2.40	2.12	2.17	2.72	2.36
$o\text{-}C_7$	2.48	2.20	2.40	2.40	2.08
$m\text{-}C_7$	1.09	0.96	1.41	0.99	0.86
C_8	0.17	0.15	0.37	0.163	0.14
R	0.007	0.006	0.081	0.007	0.006
	6.147			6.280	

	$6.43x_8$	α_{140}	$6.43\alpha x_8$	$5.43y_8$	$6.43x_9$	$6.43\alpha x_9$
C_6	2.41	1.26	3.04	2.61	2.66	3.35
$o\text{-}C_7$	2.28	1.0	2.28	1.95	2.15	2.15
$m\text{-}C_7$	1.31	0.675	0.88	0.76	1.21	0.82
C_8	0.36	0.392	0.14	0.12	0.34	0.13
R	0.081	0.087	0.007	0.006	0.081	0.007
			6.347			6.457

	$5.43y_9$	$6.43x_{10}$	$6.43\alpha_{10}$	$5.43y_{10}$	$6.43x_{11}$	$6.43\alpha x_{11}$
C_6	2.82	2.87	3.62	3.01	3.06	3.86
$o\text{-}C_7$	1.81	2.01	2.01	1.67	1.87	1.87
$m\text{-}C_7$	0.69	1.14	0.77	0.64	1.09	0.74
C_8	0.112	0.34	0.13	0.11	0.33	0.13
R	0.006	0.081	0.007	0.006	0.081	0.007
			6.537			6.607

	$5.43y_{11}$	$6.43x_{12}$	$6.43\alpha x_{12}$	$5.43y_{12}$
C_6	3.17	3.22	4.06	3.32
$o\text{-}C_7$	1.54	1.74	1.74	1.42
$m\text{-}C_7$	0.61	1.06	0.71	0.58
C_8	0.11	0.33	0.129	0.105
R	0.006	0.081	0.007	0.006
			6.646	

$$P_c = 202(6.43)/6.65 = 195; \qquad T_{12} = 146.5\,°C.$$

	$6.43x_{13}$	$6.43\alpha x_{13}$	y_{13}
C_6	3.37	4.25	0.634
o-C_7	1.62	1.62	0.242
m-C_7	1.03	0.70	0.104
C_8	0.33	0.129	0.019
R	0.081	0.007	0.001
		6.706	

The ratio of phenol to o-cresol in the liquid on the thirteenth plate is essentially that in the feed, and this plate was used as the feed plate. The calculations are then completed using a basis of one mol of distillate. On such a basis the operating line for each component $10x_n = 11y_{n-1} - x_D$ and the remainder of the table is set up in this manner.

	y_{13}	$11y_{13}$	$10x_{14}$	$10\alpha x_{14}$	$11y_{14}$
C_6	0.634	6.974	6.024	7.59	7.54
o-C_7	0.242	2.662	2.617	2.617	2.60
m-C_7	0.104	1.144	1.14	0.77	0.77
C_8	0.019	.209	.209	0.082	0.081
R	0.001	.011	.011	0.001	0.001
				11.060	

	$10x_{15}$	$10\alpha x_{15}$	$10y_{15}$	$10x_{16}$	$10\alpha x_{16}$	$11y_{16}$	$10x_{17}$	$10\alpha x_{17}$	$11y_{17}$
C_6	6.59	8.3	8.0	7.05	8.89	8.38	7.43	9.36	8.73
o-C_7	2.55	2.55	2.46	2.41	2.41	2.27	2.22	2.22	2.07
m-C_7	0.765	0.516	0.498	0.493	0.333	0.314	0.31	0.209	0.195
C_8	0.081	0.032	0.031	0.031	0.012	0.011	0.011	0.004	0.004
R	0.001	9×10^{-5}	8×10^{-5}	8×10^{-5}	7×10^{-6}	7×10^{-6}	7×10^{-6}	6×10^{-7}	6×10^{-7}
		11.398			11.645			11.793	

	$10x_{18}$	$10\alpha x_{18}$	$11y_{18}$	$10x_{19}$	$10\alpha x_{19}$	$11y_{19}$	$10x_{20}$	$10\alpha x_{20}$	$11y_{20}$
C₆	7.78	9.81	9.02	8.07	10.2	9.3	8.35	10.55	9.53
o-C₇	2.02	2.02	1.86	1.81	1.81	1.65	1.60	1.6	1.44
m-C₇	0.19	0.128	0.118	0.113	0.076	0.069	0.064	0.043	0.0399
C₈	0.004	0.002	2×10^{-3}	2×10^{-3}	8×10^{-4}	7×10^{-4}	7×10^{-4}	3×10^{-4}	3×10^{-4}
		11.960			12.086			12.193	

$$P_o = 178(10/11.96) = 149 \qquad T_{18} = 138°C.$$

	$10x_{21}$	$10\alpha x_{21}$	$11y_{21}$	$10x_{22}$	$10\alpha x_{22}$	$11y_{22}$	$10x_{23}$	$10\alpha x_{23}$	$11y_{23}$
C₆	8.58	10.8	9.74	8.79	11.08	9.91	8.96	11.30	10.1
o-C₇	1.39	1.39	1.25	1.20	1.20	1.07	1.02	1.02	0.91
m-C₇	0.035	0.024	0.022	0.018	0.012	0.011	0.007	4.7×10^{-3}	4.2×10^{-3}
		12.214			12.292			12.32	

	$10x_{24}$	$10\alpha x_{24}$	$11y_{25}$	$10x_{25}$	$10\alpha x_{25}$	$11y_{25}$	$10x_{26}$	$10\alpha x_{26}$	y_{26}
C₆	9.15	11.52	10.24	9.29	11.70	10.37	9.42	11.88	0.952
o-C₇	0.86	0.86	0.76	0.71	0.71	0.63	0.58	0.58	0.047
		12.38			12.41			12.46	

$$P_o = 154(10/12.38) - 124 \qquad T = 133°C.$$

The concentration of m-cresol in the distillate is less than the assumed value, but a recorrection of this value would not make enough difference to be significant, and a material balance on this component is in essence satisfied. The results of the calculations are plotted in Fig. 67.

It is interesting to consider what would happen if the feed had not been introduced on the thirteenth plate. This calculation has been carried out and the results plotted in Fig. 68. Up to the thirteenth plate, the results are obviously identical with those given in Fig. 67; but above this plate, the change of concentration per plate is much less in Fig. 68. By the twenty-sixth plate, all of the components have become almost asymptotic, and increasing the plates to an infinite number would make little difference in the concentrations from those for the twenty-sixth plate. Thus it is impossible to obtain the desired separation without having plates above the feed plate, since the asymptotic

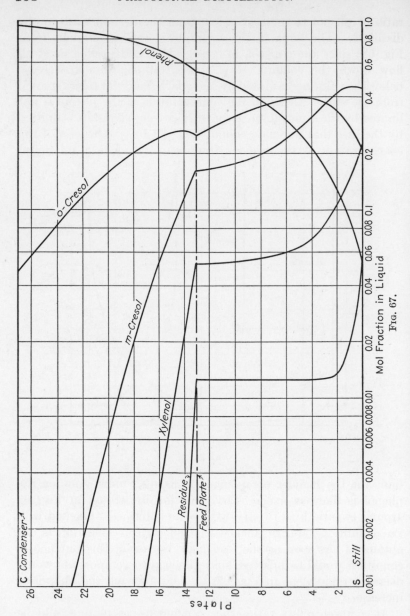

Mol Fraction in Liquid

Fig. 67.

ratio of phenol to o-cresol is less than the desired ratio in the distillate. The limit to this asymptotic ratio is obvious from Fig. 68; since the o-cresol, m-cresol, xylol, and residue must all flow down the column, their concentrations cannot decrease below the value necessitated by material balance for their removal from the still. Although the concentration of the phenol is not limited by the same factor as the heavier components, it is limited by the fact that its value cannot exceed 1 minus the sum of the concentration of the heavier fractions; and since a minimum

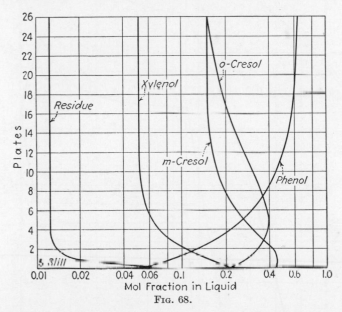

Fig. 68.

limit for the heavier components is fixed, a maximum for the phenol is likewise fixed. The condition illustrated in Fig. 68 around twentieth to twenty-sixth plate is termed "pinched in"; *i.e.*, conditions are so pinched that effective rectification is not obtained. As soon as the feed plate is passed, this pinched-in condition would be relieved, since the heavier components would decrease rapidly, as in Fig. 67, thereby allowing the phenol to increase.

At a lower reflux ratio, the enrichment per plate would be reduced, and more plates required for a given separation. Figure

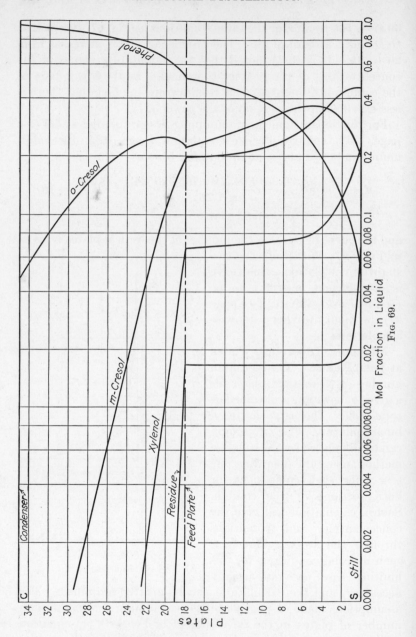

Mol Fraction in Liquid

Fig. 69.

69 gives the results for the same conditions as Fig. 67, except that O/D was 7 instead of 10. The number of plates increases from 26 to 35. It is to be noted that the asymptotic values of the concentrations of the heavier components in the lower part of the column also increase; this results from the fact that there is less overflow in this section of the tower.

For this separation, the minimum O/D is estimated at 5.6 (see page 174); and by Fenske's equation (page 167), the minimum number of plates at total reflux becomes

$$n + 1 = \frac{\log (0.95/0.0452)(0.202/0.0524)}{\log 1.26} = \frac{1.908}{0.1} = 19$$

$$n = 18 \text{ theoretical plates}$$

and the curve of O/D vs. the number of theoretical plates is given in Fig. 70. With only the two stepwise calculations, this curve is of sufficient accuracy to be used for cost estimates (see page 97) without further stepwise calculations.

Minimum Theoretical Plates at Total Reflux.—The minimum number of theoretical plates for a given separation is obtained at total reflux, the same as for a binary mixture. This minimum can be calculated by the stepwise method, using the operating line $y = x$ for each component for both sections of the column. Such a calculation will give the concentration and conditions through the tower. However, such internal conditions for this limiting case are not usually

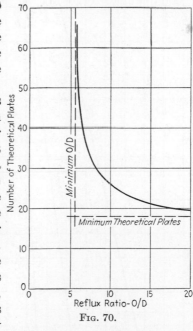

Fig. 70.

necessary, and the calculations can be greatly simplified. The assumptions made on page 94 for the calculation of the minimum number of plates in the development of Fenske's (1) equation apply to the components of a multicomponent mixture, and by its application this limiting condition is easily calculated. In general, when applying Fenske's equation to a multicomponent mixture, it is desirable to use the two components whose concentrations are most accurately known in the distillate and residue, and most often these two components are the key components.

Feed-plate Location.—The criterion for the optimum location of the feed plate is that the relative enrichment of the key components should be a maximum. As with binary mixtures, the feed plate corresponds to the step that passes from one operating line to the other. The change from one operating line to the other should be made just as soon as it will give a greater enrichment than continuing on the same operating line. In coming up from the still, the feed plate is the last step on the lower operating line; calling this the nth plate, and the key vapors entering, $y_{lk(n-1)}$ and $y_{hk(n-1)}$, for the light, or more volatile, and heavy, or less volatile, components, respectively, the foregoing criterion states that if the nth plate is the optimum position for the feed, then the x ratio on this plate should be greater when calculated by the lower operating line from the y_{n-1} values than by the upper operating line, or

$$\left(\frac{x_{lk}}{x_{hk}}\right)_n = \frac{y_{lk(n-1)} + \dfrac{W}{V_m}x_{wlk}}{y_{hk(n-1)} + \dfrac{W}{V_m}x_{whk}} \geqq \frac{y_{lk(n-1)} - \dfrac{D}{V_n}x_{Dlk}}{y_{lk(n-1)} - \dfrac{D}{V_n}x_{Dhk}}. \tag{3}$$

which by combining with $V_n = V_m + (p + 1)F$ and

$$Wx_w + Dx_D = Fz_F$$

becomes

$$\left(\frac{x_{lk}}{x_{hk}}\right)_n \leqq \frac{z_{Flk} + \dfrac{W(p + 1)}{V_m}x_{wlk}}{z_{Fhk} + \dfrac{W}{V_m}(p + 1)x_{whk}} \tag{4}$$

Also, by this criterion the x ratio on the $(n + 1)$th plate should be greater when calculated by the upper than by the lower operating line:

$$\left(\frac{x_{lk}}{x_{hk}}\right)_{n+1} = \frac{y_{nlk} - \dfrac{D}{V_n}x_{Dlk}}{y_{nhk} - \dfrac{D}{V_n}x_{Dhk}} \geqq \frac{y_{nlk} + \dfrac{W}{V_m}x_{wlk}}{y_{nlk} + \dfrac{W}{V_m}x_{whk}} \tag{5}$$

which gives

$$\left(\frac{x_{lk}}{x_{hk}}\right)_{n+1} \geqq \frac{z_{Flk} - \dfrac{D}{V_n}(p+1)x_{Dlk}}{z_{Fhk} - \dfrac{D}{V_n}(p+1)x_{Dhk}} \tag{6}$$

The right-hand sides of Eqs. (4) and (6) are equivalent and equal to $(x_{lk}/x_{hk})_i$ as given by the intersection of the operating line; thus, since n is now the optimum feed plate, the subscript may be changed, and the criterion for the feed-plate step becomes

$$\left(\frac{x_{lk}}{x_{hk}}\right)_{f+1} \geqq \frac{z_{Flk} + \dfrac{W}{V_m}(p+1)x_{wlk}}{z_{Fhk} + \dfrac{W}{V_m}(p+1)x_{whk}} = \left(\frac{x_{lk}}{x_{hk}}\right)_i \geqq \left(\frac{x_{lh}}{x_{hk}}\right)_f \tag{7}$$

where $(x_{lk}/x_{hk})_i$ is the ratio of the key components as given by the intersections of the operating lines. However, it should be emphasized that the feed plate does not necessarily step across the intersection of the operating lines, as it does for a binary, but simply that the ratio of the keys for the optimum feed-plate step passes over the ratio of the values given by the operating-line intersections. The absolute value of both key components may be several times the values given at the intersection, provided the ratio satisfies Eq. (7).

Minimum Reflux Ratio.—As in the case of binary mixtures, there is a reflux ratio below which it is not possible to obtain the desired separation of a multicomponent mixture even when an infinite number of plates is used. The calculation of this minimum for a multicomponent mixture is much more involved than for the corresponding binary mixture. This difficulty is due to the fact that, whereas in a binary mixture with a normal volatility curve, the "pinch," or "limit," so occurs that the concentration of the feed plate and the plate above are identical, in the multicomponent mixture this is not true, since large amounts of heavy, essentially nonvolatile components may be present on the feed plate, but the same components would appear in much smaller concentrations on the plate above, thereby causing a sharp concentration break between these plates even at minimum reflux.

However, the limit for a complex mixture of normal volatility does occur at the feed plate; thus, proceeding up from the still using the lower operating line at a given O/D, there is a maximum ratio in the vapor (or liquid) of the light key component to the heavy key component which can be attained even if an infinite number of plates are employed. This is very clearly illustrated in Fig. 68, where the ratio of the key components on the twenty-sixth has become practically asymptotic. Similarly, proceeding down from the condenser using the upper operating line at the same O/D, there is a minimum ratio of the key components in the vapor that can be attained even with an infinity of plates. For the column to be operable, at this given O/D, it is necessary that the maximum ratio of key components in the vapor from below the feed shall be equal to or exceed the minimum ratio obtained from above. If these limiting ratios are just equal, an infinite number of plates are required, and the O/D is the minimum reflux ratio for the separation. If the maximum exceeds the minimum, then a finite number of plates will accomplish the separation at the O/D employed. The calculation of the minimum O/D then involves the determination of the reflux ratio in such manner that the maximum ratio of key component exactly equals the minimum ratio.

In proceeding up from the still, at this pinch the ratio of the key component in the liquid is given by Eq. (7) as

$$\left(\frac{x_{lk}}{x_{hk}}\right)_f = \left(\frac{x_{lk}}{x_{hk}}\right)_i \tag{8}$$

The $<$ sign is omitted, since the size of the steps at this point is essentially zero. Likewise,

$$\left(\frac{x_{lk}}{x_{hk}}\right)_{f+1} = \left(\frac{x_{lk}}{x_{hk}}\right)_i = \left(\frac{x_{lk}}{x_{hk}}\right)_f \tag{9}$$

Equation (9) states that the ratios of the key components in the liquid on the feed plate and the plate above are equal at the minimum reflux ratio, a condition that is not true at reflux ratios greater than the minimum. However, this equation does not state that the concentrations on the two plates are equal: it is only the ratios that are equal. By making the following substitutions.

$$\left(\frac{x_{lk}}{x_{hk}}\right)_f = \frac{\alpha_{hk}}{\alpha_{lk}}\left(\frac{y_{lk}}{y_{hk}}\right)_f$$

and

$$\left(\frac{x_{lk}}{x_{hk}}\right)_{f+1} = \frac{V_n y_{lkf} - Dx_{Dlk}}{V_n y_{hkf} - Dx_{Dhk}}$$

Equation (9) becomes

$$\left(\frac{O}{D}\right)_{\text{min.}} = \frac{1}{(\alpha_{lk} - \alpha_{hk})}\left(\alpha_{lk}\frac{x_{Dlk}}{y_{lkf}} - \alpha_{hk}\frac{x_{Dhk}}{y_{hkf}}\right) - 1 \qquad (10)$$

Equation (10) gives the minimum O/D, but in general is difficult to use, because the absolute values of y_{lkf} and y_{hkf} are generally not known, only their ratios being defined. Equation (10) can be modified to

$$\left(\frac{O}{D}\right)_{\text{min.}} = \frac{\alpha_{hk}}{(\alpha_{lk} - \alpha_{hk})y_{hkf}}\left[\frac{x_{Dlk}}{(x_{lk}/x_{hk})_i} - x_{Dhk}\right] - 1 \qquad (11)$$

and y_{hkf} can be set equal to $K_{hfk}x_{hfk}$. x_{hkf} is calculated by

$$\left(\frac{y_{lk}}{y_{hk}}\right)_{f-1} = \frac{\alpha_{lk}}{\alpha_{hk}}\left(\frac{x_{lk}}{x_{hk}}\right)_{f-1} = \frac{(x_{lk})_f - (W/O)x_{lkw}}{(x_{hk})_f - (W/O)x_{hkw}}$$

and when the column is pinched in, $x_{lk(f-1)}$ is approximately equal to x_{lkf}, and the same holds for the heavy key, giving

$$x_{hkf} = \frac{\alpha_{lk}(W/O)x_{hkw}}{\alpha_{lk} - \alpha_{hk} + \alpha_{hk}(W/O)(x_{lkw})/x_{lkf}} \qquad (12)$$

In general, the last term of the denominator may be neglected, since α_h, W/O, and (x_{lkw}/x_{lkf}) all are small. Likewise, for all components heavier than the heavy key component,

$$x_{hf} = \frac{\alpha_{lk}(W/O)x_{hw}}{\alpha_{lk} - \alpha_h + \alpha_h(W/O)(x_{lkw}/x_{lkf})} \qquad (13)$$

A similar derivation for the components lighter than the light key component gives

$$x_{lf} = \frac{\alpha_{lk}(V/O)_m(D/V)_n x_{Dl}}{\alpha_1 - \alpha_{hk} + \alpha_{hk}(D/V)_n(x_{hkD}/y_{hkf})} \tag{14}$$

Equations (11) and (12) are combined to give

$$\left[\left(\frac{O_n}{D}\right)\left(\frac{W}{O_m}\right)\right]_{\min.} = \left[\left(\frac{O_n}{D}\right)\left(\frac{W}{O_n - pF}\right)\right]_{\min.}$$

$$= \frac{\alpha_{hk}}{K_{hkf}x_{hkw}}\left[\frac{x_{Dlk}}{(x_{lk}/x_{hk})_i} - x_{Dhk}\right] - 1 \tag{15}$$

Knowing the relative volatilities, p, and the terminal conditions, it is possible to solve the foregoing equation by trial and error. K and V_m are assumed, and $(x_{lk}/x_{hk})_i$ calculated from Eq. (7). If p equals -1, then only K need be assumed, since

$$(x_{lk}/x_{hk})_i = (z_{lk}/z_{hk})_F$$

for this condition. With these values of K and the intersection ratio, O_n is calculated from Eq. (15), and the assumed values of V_m can be checked. The assumed value of K is checked by calculating the feed-plate composition from Eqs. (13) and (14) together with the facts that $(x_{lk}/x_{hk})_f = (x_{lk}/x_{hk})_i$ and that the sum of the mol fractions must equal unity. In the use of Eqs. (13) and (14), the last terms of the denominators are, in general, neglected. Such a trial-and-error procedure is time consuming but in general a knowledge of the minimum O/D is of sufficient use to justify the expenditure of effort.

The trial-and-error procedure can be incorporated into Eq. (11). Using Eqs. (12), (13), and (14),

$$y_{hkf} = \frac{\alpha_{hk}\left(\dfrac{x_{whk}}{\alpha_{lk} - \alpha_{hk}}\right)}{\left\{\left[\alpha_{hk} + \alpha_{lk}\left(\dfrac{x_{lk}}{x_{hk}}\right)_i\right]\dfrac{x_{hkw}}{\alpha_{lk} - \alpha_{hk}} + \displaystyle\sum_{hk^+}\left(\dfrac{\alpha_h x_{hw}}{\alpha_{lk} - \alpha_h}\right) + \left(\dfrac{V_m}{W}\right)\left(\dfrac{D}{V_n}\right)\displaystyle\sum_{lk^+}\left(\dfrac{\alpha_l x_{Dl}}{\alpha_l - \alpha_{hk}}\right)\right\}}$$

which gives

$$
\begin{aligned}
\left(\frac{O}{D}\right)_{\text{min.}} + 1 = \\
\frac{\left\{\left[\alpha_{hk} + \alpha_{lk}\left(\dfrac{x_{lk}}{x_{hk}}\right)_i\right]\dfrac{x_{hkw}}{\alpha_{lk} - \alpha_{hk}} + \displaystyle\sum_{hk^+}\left(\dfrac{\alpha_h x_{hw}}{\alpha_{lk} - \alpha_h}\right) + \left(\dfrac{V_m}{W}\right)\left(\dfrac{D}{V_n}\right)\displaystyle\sum_{lk^+}\left(\dfrac{\alpha_l x_{Dl}}{\alpha_l - \alpha_{hk}}\right)\right\}\left[\dfrac{x_{Dlk}}{(x_{lk}/x_{hk})_i} - x_{Dhk}\right]}{x_{whk}}
\end{aligned}
\tag{16}
$$

where $\displaystyle\sum_{hk^+}$ signifies the sum of all such groups for the components heavier than the heavy key component, and $\displaystyle\sum_{lk^+}$ the sum of all such groups lighter than the light key component. Equation (16) involves no trial and error for the case of an all-liquid feed for which $V_m = V_n$. For feeds containing vapor, trial and error is involved, since $(x_{lk}/x_{hk})_i$ and V_m/V_n are not known until the reflux ratio is known.

In deriving Eq. (16), use was made of Eqs. (12), (13), and (14) together with the fact that the sum of the mol fractions was 1. In addition, there is also the condition that

$$(x_{lk}/x_{hk})_f = (x_{lk}/x_{hk})_i.$$

Only four of these five conditions are truly independent; but owing to approximations, the fifth does not quite reduce to an identity of the other four; and by using a different set of four out of the five, modifications of Eq. (16) may be obtained; but all give essentially the same result.

Equation (16) will be applied to some of the previous examples.

1. Benzene-toluene-xylene example (page 139). The key components are benzene and toluene, and the design conditions are given below.

$$p = -1 \qquad W = 39.9 \text{ mols} \qquad D = 60.1 \text{ mols}$$

	Residue	Distillate	Feed	Relative volatility
C_6	0.005	0.995	0.60	2.5
C_7	0.744	0.005	0.30	1.0
C_8	0.251	.....	0.10	0.45

Minimum O/D by Eq. (16):

$$\left(\frac{O}{D}\right)_{\text{min.}} + 1 =$$

$$\frac{\left\{\left[1 + 2.5\left(\frac{0.60}{0.30}\right)\right]\dfrac{0.744}{2.5 - 1} + \dfrac{(0.45)(0.251)}{2.5 - 0.45}\right\}\left[\dfrac{0.995}{(0.60/0.30)} - 0.005\right]}{0.744}$$

$$= 2.01$$

$$\left(\frac{O}{D}\right)_{\text{min.}} = 1.01$$

2. Phenol-cresol problem.

$$p = -1 \qquad W = 66.84 \text{ mols} \qquad D = 33.16 \text{ mols}$$

	Feed	Residue	Distillate	Relative volatility
C_6	0.35	0.0524	0.95	1.26
$o\text{-}C_7$	0.15	0.202	0.0452	1.0
$m\text{-}C_7$	0.30	0.447	0.0048	0.663
C_8	0.15	0.224	......	0.394
R	0.05	0.075	......	0.087

$$\left(\frac{O}{D}\right)_{\text{min.}} + 1 =$$

$$\frac{\left\{\left[1 + 1.26\left(\dfrac{0.35}{0.15}\right)\right]\dfrac{0.202}{1.26 - 1} + \dfrac{(0.663)(0.447)}{1.26 - 0.663} + \dfrac{(0.394)(0.224)}{1.26 - 0.394} + \dfrac{(0.087)(0.075)}{1.26 - 0.087}\right\}\left[\dfrac{0.95}{(0.35/0.15)} - 0.045\right]}{0.202} = 6.6$$

$$\left(\frac{O}{D}\right)_{\text{min.}} = 5.6$$

3. If, in the preceding example, p had been zero instead of -1, trial and error would have been required. The solution for the case of $p = 0$ is solved by assuming

$$\left(\frac{O}{D}\right)_{\text{min.}} = 7.0. \qquad V_m = D\left(\frac{O}{D} + 1\right) - F = 165$$

By Eq. (7)

$$\left(\frac{x_{lk}}{x_{hk}}\right)_i = \frac{0.35 + (66.84/165)(0.0524)}{0.15 + (66.84/165)(0.202)} = 1.603$$

$$\left(\frac{O}{D}\right)_{min.} + 1 =$$

$$\frac{\left\{[1 - 1.26(1.603)]\dfrac{0.202}{0.26} + \dfrac{(0.663)(0.447)}{0.597} + \dfrac{(0.394)(0.224)}{0.866} + \dfrac{(0.087)(0.075)}{1.173}\right\}\left[\dfrac{0.95}{1.603} - 0.045\right]}{0.202}$$

$$= 8.0$$

$$\left(\frac{O}{D}\right)_{min.} = 7.0$$

If the calculated value of O/D had not checked the assumed value, the calculation would have had to be repeated.

As a further illustration, the estimation of the number of theoretical plates for a gasoline stabilization will be considered. The feed composition is given in the table, on page 176 and the tower is to operate at 250 lb. per square inch gage. A reflux ratio of 2 will be used in the upper portion of the tower, and the feed will enter such that $(O/V)_m$ below the feed will be 1.5. It is desired to recover 96 per cent of the normal butane with the stabilized gasoline, but this bottom product is to contain not over 0.25 mol per cent propane.

In preparing this table, it was assumed that the concentrations of all components lighter than propane were negligible in the residue and that all components heavier than n-C_4 were negligible in the distillate. The isobutane is intermediate to the propane and n-butane and therefore will appear in appreciable quantities in both the distillate and residue. Since the i-C_4 is more volatile than n-C_4, the following table was prepared on the assumption that 20 per cent of the i-C_4 in the feed would appear in the overhead. The volatilities relative to n-C_4 are given in Fig. 71. These relative volatilities are based on the fugacity data of Lewis and coworkers.[1] The equilibrium constant K for n-C_4 is also

[1] *Ind. Eng. Chem.*, **25**, 725 (1933); *Oil Gas J.*, **32**, No. 45, pp. 40, 114 (1934).

Feed		Residue		Distillate	
	Mol per cent	Mols/100 feed	Mol per cent	Mols/100 feed	Mol per cent
CH$_4$	2.0	....	....	2.0	6.33
C$_2$H$_6$	10.0	....	....	10.0	31.60
C$_3$H$_6$	6.0	....	....	6.0	19.00
C$_3$H$_8$	12.5	0.0025W	0.25	12.5 − 0.0025W	39.00
i-C$_4$H$_{10}$	3.5	2.8	4.10	0.7	2.2
n-C$_4$H$_{10}$	15.0	14.4	21.10	0.6	1.9
C$_5$	15.2	15.2	22.20		
C$_6$	11.3	11.3	16.50		
C$_7$	9.0	9.0	13.20		
C$_8$	8.5	8.5	12.40		
360°F.	7.0	7.0	10.20		
		68.2 + 0.0025W		31.8 − 0.0025W	

$$68.2 + 0.0025W = W$$
$$W = 68.4; \qquad D = 31.6.$$

plotted in this figure. Since the overhead is very volatile, it will be removed as a vapor, only enough liquid being produced in the partial condenser to furnish reflux. It will be assumed that the reflux from the condenser leaves in equilibrium with the overhead vapor.

Starting at the composition of the overhead vapor, the calculations are carried down the column by the use of the equations given on page 154. These calculations are summarized in Table I. The first column of this table gives the components, the second column lists the vapor concentrations for the plate in question, and the third column gives the α values at the assumed temperature. The next column gives the values of the vapor concentrations divided by the relative volatility, and by using Eq. (2) on page 154, the liquid concentrations for this plate are obtained by dividing the values of the fourth column by the sum of all of the values in the fourth column. On the basis of 1 mol of overhead vapor or product, there are two mols of reflux, and for this reason the fifth column lists twice the concentrations obtained from column four and is therefore the actual mols of overflow for the basis chosen. There will be three mols of vapor to the plates and the mols of each component in the vapor to any

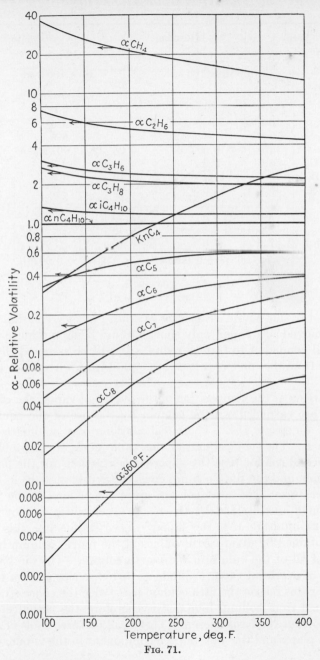

Fig. 71.

TABLE I
Basis: 1 mol overhead vapor; $O/D = 2$

	$y_{O.H.}$	α_{100}	$\dfrac{y_{O.H.}}{\alpha}$	$2X_R = \dfrac{2\dfrac{y_{O.H.}}{\alpha}}{\Sigma y/\alpha}$	$3y_T$
C_1	0.0633	36.5	0.00173	0.012	0.075
C_2	0.316	7.4	0.0427	0.296	0.612
C_3-	0.190	3.0	0.0633	0.440	0.630
C_3+	0.390	2.7	0.144	1.000	1.390
i-C_4	0.022	1.3	0.0169	0.117	0.139
n-C_4	0.019	1.0	0.019	0.132	0.151
			0.2876		

$$K_{\text{n-}C_4} = 0.2876 \qquad T = 98°\text{F.}$$

	$3y_T$	α_{100}	$3y_T/\alpha$	$2X_T$	$3y_{T-1}$
C_1	0.075	36.5	0.0021	0.004	0.067
C_2	0.612	7.4	0.0826	0.155	0.471
C_3-	0.630	3.0	0.210	0.394	0.584
C_3+	1.390	2.7	0.515	0.965	1.355
i-C_4	0.139	1.3	0.107	0.200	0.222
n-C_4	0.151	1.0	0.151	0.283	0.302
			1.067		

$$K_{\text{n-}C_4} = 1.067/3 = 0.356 \qquad T = 120°\text{F.}$$

	$3y_{T-1}$	α_{100}	$3y_{T-1}/\alpha$	$2X_{T-1}$	$3y_{T-2}$
C_1	0.067	36.5	0.0018	0.0029	0.066
C_2	0.471	7.4	0.0637	0.103	0.419
C_3-	0.584	3.0	0.195	0.316	0.506
C_3+	1.355	2.7	0.501	0.810	1.200
i-C_4	0.222	1.3	0.171	0.277	0.299
n-C_4	0.302	1.0	0.302	0.487	0.508
			1.2345		

$$K_{\text{n-}C_4} = 0.41 \qquad T = 130°\text{F.}$$

	$3y_{T-2}$	α_{150}	$3y_{T-2}/\alpha$	$2X_{T-2}$	$3y_{T-3}$
C_1	0.066	26	0.0025	0.003	0.066
C_2	0.419	6	0.070	0.091	0.407
C_3-	0.506	2.6	0.195	0.253	0.443
C_3+	1.200	2.3	0.522	0.678	1.068
i-C_4	0.299	1.23	0.243	0.315	0.337
n-C_4	0.508	1.0	0.508	0.660	0.679
			1.5405		

$$K_{\text{n-}C_4} = 0.51 \qquad T = 150°\text{F.}$$

plate above the fuel plate must equal the sum of the mols of that component in the product and in the overflow from that plate; *i.e.*, the sum of the values in column four plus the values in $y_{o.H.}$. These vapor values for the plate below are listed in the last column of the table. In Table II, for the calculation beginning at the still, a similar procedure was used employing Eq. (1) on page 154 and using a basis of 1 mol of residue.

A temperature of 100°F. was assumed for the partial condenser, and the calculated temperatures based on K_{n-C_4} are given for each plate. At the second plate below the top plate, the α values are shifted to 150°F. The liquid on the second plate below the top plate has a ratio of $C_3H_8/n-C_4$, a little higher than the feed ratio, and this plate will be made the last plate above the feed; *i.e.*, the feed plate will be the fourth from the top of the column. If an attempt is made to carry the calculations farther down the tower, a serious difficulty will be met in that no components heavier than n-C_4 have been considered, but they are much too large to be neglected below the feed plate. The most satisfactory solution to this difficulty is to drop to the still and calculate up to the feed plate. These calculations are presented in Table II. Such calculations are continued until the ratio of $C_3H_8/n-C_4$ in the vapor from some plate is approximately the same as the ratio in the vapor calculated from the feed plate in Table I. Thus, it is found that the vapor from plate 8 of Table II gives the ratio approximately equal to the ratio on the T-3 plate of Table I. Thus, approximately eleven theoretical plates in addition to the still and partial condenser are required. The vapors below the feed plate calculated from above and below do not appear to match very satisfactorily, because different components are present in the two calculations. This match can be made more satisfactory by allowing for the heavier components in the calculations a few plates above the feed plate and for the light components a few plates below the feed plate. The plates on which these components are first introduced into the calculations must be sufficiently far removed from the feed plate so that the material balances on these plates are not appreciably altered.

Thus, in Table III, the results of Table II are dropped back to the seventh plate, and the C_2 and C_3- added; and then on the

TABLE II

Basis: 1 mol residue; $(O/V)_m = 1.5$

	X_s	α_{300}	αX_s	$2y_s = 2\alpha X_s/\Sigma\alpha X$	$3X_1$
C_3+	0.0025	2.0	0.005	0.020	0.0225
i-C_4	0.041	1.18	0.048	0.191	0.232
n-C_4	0.211	1.0	0.211	0.840	1.051
C_5	0.222	0.58	0.129	0.513	0.735
C_6	0.165	0.38	0.0627	0.249	0.414
C_7	0.132	0.215	0.0284	0.115	0.247
C_8	0.125	0.12	0.0150	0.060	0.185
360°	0.102	0.038	0.0039	0.016	0.118
			0.503		

$$K_{\text{n-}C_4} = 1/0.503 = 1.99 \qquad T = 333°\text{F.}$$

	$3X_1$	α_{100}	$3\alpha X_1$	$2y_1$	$3X_2$
C_3+	0.0225	2.0	0.045	0.044	0.0465
i-C_4	0.232	1.18	0.273	0.269	0.310
n-C_4	1.051	1.0	1.051	1.035	1.246
C_5	0.735	0.58	0.426	0.420	0.642
C_6	0.414	0.38	0.157	0.155	0.320
C_7	0.247	0.215	0.053	0.052	0.184
C_8	0.185	0.12	0.022	0.022	0.147
360	0.118	0.038	0.005	0.005	0.107
			2.032		

$$K_{\text{n-}C_4} = 3/2.032 = 1.48 \qquad T = 285°\text{F.}$$

	$3X_2$	α_{300}	$3\alpha X_2$	$2y_2$	$3X_3$
C_3+	0.0465	2.0	0.093	0.082	0.0845
i-C_4	0.310	1.18	0.365	0.323	0.364
n-C_4	1.246	1.0	1.246	1.103	1.314
C_5	0.642	0.58	0.372	0.329	0.551
C_6	0.320	0.38	0.121	0.107	0.272
C_7	0.184	0.215	0.040	0.035	0.167
C_8	0.147	0.12	0.018	0.016	0.141
360	0.107	0.038	0.004	0.004	0.106
			2.259		

$$K_{\text{n-}C_4} = \frac{3}{2.259} = 1.33 \qquad T = 273°\text{F.}$$

Table II.—(*Continued*)

	$3X_3$	α_{250}	$3\alpha X_3$	$2y_3$	$3X_4$
C_3+	0.0845	2.03	0.172	0.147	0.1495
i-C_4	0.364	1.18	0.430	0.367	0.408
n-C_4	1.314	1.0	1.314	1.120	1.331
C_5	0.551	0.55	0.302	0.258	0.480
C_6	0.272	0.30	0.082	0.070	0.235
C_7	0.167	0.172	0.029	0.025	0.157
C_8	0.141	0.090	0.013	0.011	0.136
360	0.106	0.022	0.002	0.002	0.104
			2.344		

$$K_{\text{n-}C_4} = 1.28 \qquad T = 265°F.$$

	$3X_4$	α_{250}	$3\alpha X_4$	$2y_4$	$3X_5$
C_3+	0.1495	2.03	0.304	0.244	0.2465
i-C_4	0.408	1.18	0.481	0.386	0.427
n-C_4	1.331	1.0	1.331	1.070	1.281
C_5	0.480	0.55	0.264	0.212	0.434
C_6	0.235	0.30	0.071	0.057	0.222
C_7	0.157	0.172	0.027	0.022	0.154
C_8	0.136	0.090	0.012	0.010	0.135
360	0.104	0.022	0.002	0.002	0.104
			2.492		

$$K_{\text{n-}C_4} = 1.2 \qquad T = 256°F.$$

	$3X_5$	α_{250}	$3\alpha X_5$	$2y_5$	$3X_6$
C_3+	0.2465	2.03	0.500	0.380	0.382
i-C_4	0.427	1.18	0.504	0.383	0.424
n-C_4	1.281	1.0	1.281	0.975	1.186
C_5	0.434	0.55	0.238	0.181	0.403
C_6	0.222	0.30	0.067	0.051	0.216
C_7	0.154	0.172	0.027	0.021	0.153
C_8	0.135	0.090	0.012	0.009	0.134
360	0.104	0.022	0.002	0.002	0.104
			2.631		

$$K_{\text{n-}C_4} = 1.14 \qquad T = 250°F.$$

TABLE II.—*(Continued)*

	$3x_6$	α_{250}	$3\alpha x_6$	$2y_6$	$3x_7$
C_3+	0.382	2.03	0.776	0.556	0.558
i-C_4	0.424	1.18	0.501	0.359	0.400
n-C_4	1.186	1.0	1.186	0.850	1.061
C_5	0.403	0.55	0.222	0.159	0.381
C_6	0.216	0.30	0.065	0.047	0.212
C_7	0.153	0.172	0.026	0.019	0.151
C_8	0.134	0.090	0.012	0.009	0.134
360	0.104	0.022	0.002	0.001	0.103
			2.790		

$$K_{\text{n-}C_4} = 1.075 \qquad T = 241°F.$$

	$3x_7$	α_{250}	$3\alpha x_7$	$2y_7$	$3x_8$
C_3+	0.558	2.03	1.135	0.762	0.764
i-C_4	0.400	1.18	0.472	0.317	0.358
n-C_4	1.061	1.0	1.061	0.713	0.924
C_5	0.381	0.55	0.210	0.141	0.363
C_6	0.212	0.30	0.064	0.043	0.208
C_7	0.151	0.172	0.026	0.018	0.150
C_8	0.134	0.090	0.012	0.008	0.133
360	0.103	0.022	0.002	0.001	0.103
			2.982		

$$K_{\text{n-}C_4} = 1.01 \qquad T = 232°F.$$

	$3x_8$	α_{250}	$3\alpha x_8$	$2y_8$
C_3+	0.764	2.03	1.550	0.970
i-C_4	0.358	1.18	0.422	0.264
n-C_4	0.924	1.0	0.924	0.578
C_5	0.363	0.55	0.200	0.125
C_6	0.208	0.30	0.062	0.039
C_7	0.150	0.172	0.026	0.016
C_8	0.133	0.090	0.012	0.008
360	0.103	0.022	0.002	0.001
			3.198	

$$K_{\text{n-}C_4} = 0.94 \qquad T = 220°F.$$

TABLE III.—REMATCHING FEED PLATE FROM BELOW

	$3x_7$	α_{225}	$3\alpha x_7$	$2y_7$	$3x_8$
C_1	. . . . .	19.3	. . . . .	0.100	0.0045
C_2	0.036	5.1	0.181	0.240	0.100
C_3-	0.183	2.37	0.432	0.642	0.240
C_3+	0.559	2.07	1.155	0.262	0.644
i-C_4	0.400	1.18	0.472	0.590	0.303
n-C_4	1.061	1.0	1.061	0.112	0.801
C_5	0.381	0.53	0.202	0.032	0.334
C_6	0.212	0.27	0.057	0.013	0.197
C_7	0.151	0.15	0.023	0.006	0.145
C_8	0.134	0.072	0.010	0.001	0.131
360	0.103	0.016	0.002		0.103
			3.595		

$$K_{\text{n-}C_4} = 0.833 \qquad T = 205°F.$$

	$3x_8$	α_{200}	$3\alpha x_8$	y_8
C_1	0.0045	21	0.094	0.024
C_2	0.100	5.3	0.530	0.134
C_3-	0.240	2.4	0.576	0.146
C_3+	0.044	2.1	1.350	0.341
i-C_4	0.303	1.2	0.364	0.092
n-C_4	0.801	1.0	0.801	0.203
C_5	0.334	0.5	0.167	0.042
C_6	0.197	0.24	0.047	0.012
C_7	0.145	0.125	0.018	0.004
C_8	0.131	0.057	0.007	0.002
360	0.103	0.012	0.001	0.0003
			3.955	

$$K_{\text{n-}C_4} = 0.76 \qquad T = 188°F.$$

eighth plate the C_1 is introduced. It is obvious that the concentrations of these light components should be added such that the vapor from the eighth plate will give a match of these components with the T-3 vapor of Table I. This matching, in general, requires trial and error but can be simplified by the fact that for these light components $V_m y_m = O_{m+1} x_{m+1}$ giving $x_m = \Sigma \alpha x / \alpha (O/V)_m x_{m+1}$, which allows the change per plate to be easily estimated. Similarly above the feed Table I is dropped back to the T-1 plate in Table IV, and the C_5 and C_6 components added, and the C_7, C_8, and 360°F. components are introduced on the T-2 plate. After such adjustments, it is noted that the vapor y_8 of Table III and the vapor y_{T-3} of Table IV give a very

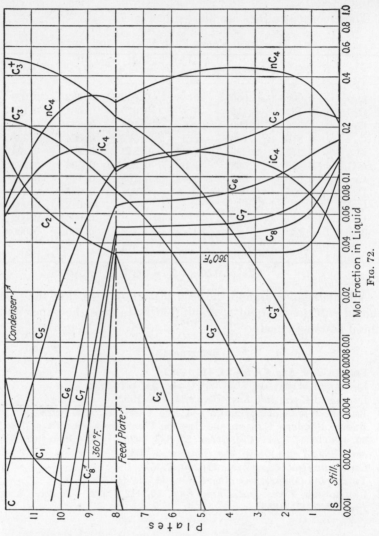

FIG. 72.

satisfactory match. The i-C_4 from Table IV is a little higher than in Table III, indicating that a little less than 20 per cent of the i-C_4 would go overhead, but the difference is so small that it does not justify readjusting. While this matching gives a more satisfactory-looking design, it, in general, does not alter the conclusion as to the number of theoretical plates as obtained from Tables I and II. These concentrations are plotted in Fig. 72.

TABLE IV.—REMATCHING FEED PLATE FROM ABOVE

	$2x_{T-1}$	$3y_{T-2}$	α_{150}	$3y_{T-2}/\alpha$	$2x_{T-2}$	y_{T-3}
C_1	0.0029	0.066	26	0.0025	0.003	0.022
C_2	0.103	0.419	6	0.070	0.084	0.133
C_3-	0.316	0.506	2.6	0.195	0.233	0.141
C_3+	0.810	1.200	2.3	0.522	0.624	0.338
i-C_4	0.277	0.299	1.23	0.243	0.290	0.104
n-C_4	0.489	0.508	1.0	0.508	0.606	0.208
C_5	0.045	0.045	0.43	0.105	0.125	0.042
C_6	0.005	0.005	0.18	0.028	0.033	0.011
C_7	......	.....	.....	......	0.012	0.004
C_8	......	.....	.....	......	0.006	0.002
360	......	.....	.....	......	0.0009	0.0003
				1.674		

$$K_{\text{n-}C_4} = 0.56 \qquad T = 163°F.$$

A heat balance around the feed plate indicates that the feed should enter as a liquid at about 130°F. to give the vapor and liquid flows assumed.

References

1. FENSKE, *Ind. Eng. Chem.*, **24**, 482 (1932).
2. LEWIS and MATHESON, *Ind. Eng. Chem.*, **24**, 494 (1932).
3. LEWIS and COPE, *Ind. Eng. Chem.*, **24**, 498 (1932).
4. RHODES, WELLS, and MURRAY, *Ind. Eng. Chem.*, **17**, 1200 (1925).
5. BROWN, SOUDERS, NYLAND, and HESLER, *Trans. Amer. Inst. Chem. Eng.*, **30**, 438 (1934). *Ind. Eng. Chem.*, **27**, 383, 1935. World Power Conference, 1936, *Trans. Chem. Eng. Congress*, **2**, 303.
6. GILLILAND, *Ind. Eng. Chem.*, **27**, 260 (1935).
7. THIELE and GEDDES, *Ind. Eng. Chem.*, **24**, 289 (1933).
8. UNDERWOOD, *Trans. Inst. Chem. Eng.*, **10**, 112 (1932). *J. Soc. Chem. Ind.*, **52**, 224T (1933).

CHAPTER XVI

RECTIFICATION OF COMPLEX HYDROCARBON MIXTURES

The analysis of distillation problems involving the usual mixtures met in petroleum refining is made particularly difficult on account of the fact that the composition of these mixtures with reference to their pure components is not definitely known.

The naphthas and oils of higher boiling point, however, are mixtures of members of many series of hydrocarbons, many of the substances present having boiling points so close together that it is practically impossible to separate them by fractional distillation. Therefore, there has been developed the use of the true-boiling-point curve of these complicated mixtures to give as good an indication as possible to their composition.

The technique of the determination of the true-boiling-point curve is simple. It consists merely of the distillation of the sample of oil in the laboratory in a flask that is fitted with a rectifying column and a reflux condenser. The column must be a relatively tall one, and the reflux ratio must be very great. It has been found that when distilling a liter sample, the distilling flask should be of about 2 liters capacity and the column should be of the filled type, about 2 in. in diameter and about 4 ft. high, well lagged with an excellent heat-insulating material. In a device of this sort, the ratio of reflux to distillate should be not less than 30 to 1.

The ordinary simple distillation of a complex mixture, such as is obtained approximately by the Engler or A.S.T.M. distillation, gives a boiling-point curve of the type shown in Fig. 73, curve *A*. The true-boiling-point curve for the same mixture would resemble curve *B* in the same figure if the constituents present were not too close together in boiling points. In most petroleum mixtures, however, the number of components is so great that the steps shown in curve *B* become very close together and disappear entirely. This type of curve is shown as curve *B* in Fig. 74.

It is customary to consider a short distance along such a true-boiling-point curve as representing a pure component; that is,

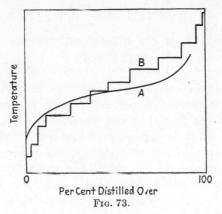

Fig. 73.

that fraction coming over as distillate between 39 and 40 per cent might be considered as a pure component, the boiling point of which, at the pressure at which the distillation was carried out,

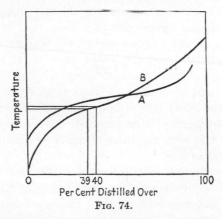

Fig. 74.

being the average of the two temperatures corresponding to 39 and 40 per cent.

If the distillate during such a true boiling-point distillation were to be divided into two fractions at some convenient point

A, corresponding to the temperature t_1, and simple distillation curves and true-boiling-point curves obtained for the two fractions, the results would resemble the curves shown in Fig. 75, where the curve B is the original true-boiling-point curve and B' the Engler distillation curve for the same mixture. The true and the Engler curve of the two fractions are shown as C and D curves for the more volatile and the less volatile fractions, respectively.

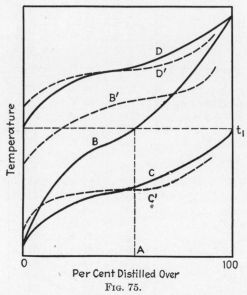

FIG. 75.

Such a separation into two fractions represents the maximum separation possible by fractional distillation. It is obvious that as many separate fractions as desired could have been made in such a true boiling-point distillation, each one of which would contain no substances that were present in any of the other fractions in so far as it would be possible to detect them by distillation means.

Commercial fractionation never gives such complete separation as is obtained in the laboratory apparatus just described, and it approaches it only in so far as it is desired to obtain as great a yield of a certain fraction as is commercially practicable. It will be of interest to indicate a method by which it is possible to estimate the requirements for commercial apparatus for specific separations.

The Method of Lewis and Wilde.[1]—This method makes use of the Sorel method for the determination of the number of plates in a rectifying column described in Chap. XIII, modified

SUMMARY OF DATA OBSERVED AT BATTERY AND IN LABORATORY

Item	Column temperature, degrees Fahrenheit	Gravity, degrees A.P.I.	Average boiling point, degrees Fahrenheit	Molecular weight	Rate, gallons per hour
Feed to battery...............	...	38.6	...	...	28,920
Total gasoline produced.......	...	58.4	......	...	10,200
Gasoline from still No. 4......	330	50.6	320	112	1,585
Feed to still No. 4.............	446	30.8	460	230	
Residuum from still No. 4.....	490	29.2	515	250	
Kerosene from still No. 5......	..	45.3	405	...	2,000
Liquid on plate 1.............	447	32.7	463		
Liquid on plate 2.............	442	32.6	457		
Liquid on plate 3.............	438	34.0	444	212	
Liquid on plate 4.............	391	44.8	402	141	
Liquid on plate 5.............	373	46.9	388	140	
Liquid on plate 6.............	370	47.5	380		
Liquid on plate 7.............	360	47.8	377		
Liquid on plate 8.............	358	48.1	372		
Liquid on plate 9.............	343	48.8	360		
Liquid on plate 10............	340	49.0	357		
Reflux to top plate...........	...	49.4	340		
Vapor from still to bottom of tower....................	485	43.2	419	150	

Gravity of cold oil through partial condenser........ 38.6° A.P.I.
Average rate of cold oil through partial condenser.... 10,600 gal. per hour
Average temperature of oil into partial condenser..... 77°F.
Average temperature of cold oil out of partial condenser 181°F.
Total steam in vapor from tower.................... 100 gal. per hour
Steam used in heating feed to tower................ 26 gal. per hour
Barometric pressure.............................. 758 mm. of Hg
Pressure at bottom of tower............. 16 mm. of Hg above barometer
Pressure at top of tower................ 23 mm. of Hg below barometer

[1] *Trans. Am. Inst. Chem. Eng.*, 1928.

to use a combination of Raoult's law and the true-boiling-point curves as described above.   These writers give the data obtained in a test on a fractionating column used in a petroleum refinery. They are reproduced as shown in the table on page 189.

The apparatus is shown diagrammatically in Fig. 76.

The plates in the column were 9 ft. in diameter and fitted with the usual type of boiling caps.

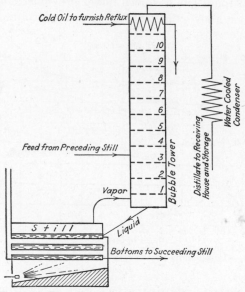

FIG. 76.—Flow sheet of still and tower used in test.

In the table of data, the column called "Average boiling point" is really the temperature at which the fraction as a whole boils and not the average that would be obtained during an Engler distillation.

The true-boiling-point curves for the feed, the distillate, and the residue are given in Fig. 77.

The curves for the liquids sampled from the plates are given in Fig. 78.

Lewis and Wilde's method consists of breaking the true-boiling-point curve of the feed up into fractions boiling within narrow temperature limits.   Thus the feed is divided into 10 or 20°F. fractions and expressed as a component boiling between definite temperature limits, such as 420 to 430°F. fraction which is present to the extent 1.5 weight per cent. Such cuts are then used as pure components by the methods used in Chap. XIV. The true-boiling-point curve on any plate in the tower is constructed from the calculations for that plate, by simply recombining the cuts in the proportion that the calculations indicate.

It has been found, as has been noted previously in this book, that the vapor above the plate of an actual column is not in

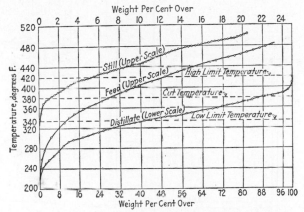

Fig. 77.—True-boiling-point curves of feed residuum distillate.

equilibrium with it, due to the fact that vapor from the plate below blows by the liquid in the plate and mixes with the vapor evolved from that liquid. The greater this blowby amounts to, the less efficient is the plate. In analyzing the behavior of a column, this plate efficiency must always be allowed for. Allowing a suitable plate efficiency, the writers of the article quoted estimated the proportion of the 420 to 430° component on the several plates above the bottom, and compared it with the actual amounts found in the test as a measure of the accuracy of their calculations. This is given in Fig. 79 where the curve represents the calculated concentration and the points the actual ones as found.

The details of this calculation may be found in the original article and in subsequent ones by the same writers.

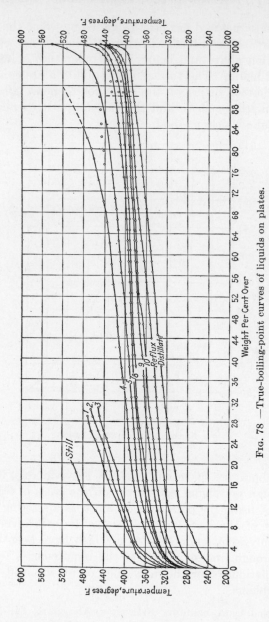

FIG. 78 —True-boiling-point curves of liquids on plates.

An alternate method[1] has been proposed by which the complex mixture is treated as a binary mixture of components, consisting of the fraction above and below the temperature at which the cut is being made. The vapor-liquid equilibria are constructed from the characteristics of the true boiling-point analysis or Engler distillation curves, and the calculation is carried out as in the McCabe-Thiele method.

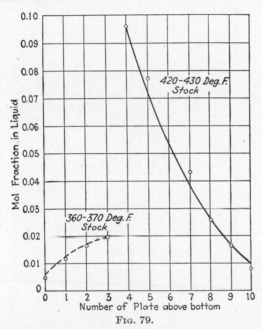

FIG. 79.

Where laboratory space and facilities are available, it is very wise to design petroleum equipment on the basis of laboratory experiments, using the data thus obtained as a starting point in calculations of the sort just indicated. It is believed that a rational analysis of laboratory data which have been collected with a thorough understanding of the requirements for subsequent calculations offers the safest method for the study of commercial problems.

[1] PETERS and OBRYADCHIKOV, Nestyanoe, *Klozyaistro,* **24,** 50 (1933). SINGER, WILSON, and BROWN, *Ind. Eng. Chem.,* **28,** 824 (1936). BROWN, *Chem. Eng. Congress,* World Power Conference, 1936, **2,** 324.

An illustration of such laboratory data, taken on a large scale by Smoley,[1] is given in the following pages.

A large-scale laboratory column with 10 plates was operated with total reflux, so that all of the distillate was returned to the top of the column. Under this condition, with infinite reflux and no distillate, the column was operating as an ideal continuous column with maximum separation per plate as described on pages 94 and 167.

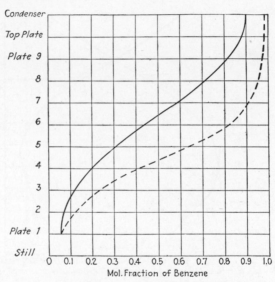

Fig. 80.—Operation of benzene-toluene column.

A mixture of benzene and toluene was distilled in this apparatus, and the composition of the liquid on the several plates determined, with the results shown by the solid line in Fig. 80. The curve of the mol fraction of benzene resembles the corresponding curve for alcohol in Fig. 28 (page 79) and is characteristic of the distribution of a binary mixture in a rectifying column, the most significant fact being the rapid change in the center and the slow change in composition at the top and bottom.

The effect of the efficiency of the actual plate as contrasted with the perfect plate is shown in the same figure. The dotted line was obtained from Fig. 15 (page 41) and shows the change in

[1] M. I. T. thesis, 1930.

composition when the vapor produced by the liquid has the same composition as the liquid on the next plate above, that is, when rectified in a perfect column with total or infinite reflux. The nearer the solid line comes to the dotted line the more nearly perfect is the plate. Thus to produce a 90 mol per cent distillate requires about 10 steps in the actual column, whereas the same effect is obtained in 6 steps in the perfect column, indicating a plate efficiency of around 60 per cent.

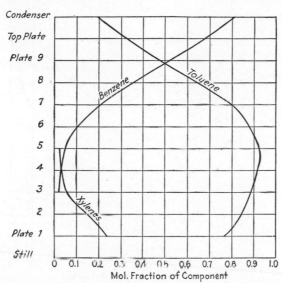

Fig. 81.—Operation of column on benzene-toluene-xylenes mixture.

The same column was then operated in the same way but using a mixture of benzene, toluene, and xylenes so as to produce as high a concentration of benzene as possible in the condenser and to segregate the xylenes in as concentrated a form as possible at the bottom. The results are shown in Fig. 81. The amount of xylenes was small so that a large proportion of toluene was present on the bottom plate. The highest concentration of toluene occurred on the fifth plate, this component thus tending to segregate in the column.   Under ordinary conditions, a column would be operated at a lower temperature level so that the benzene at the top would have contained less toluene, thus delivering the toluene and xylene together, from the bottom for subsequent separation in a second column. This experimental column had insufficient plates to do this.

The column was then operated with total reflux on a cracked petroleum distillate obtained from a Winkler-West Texas crude oil. The liquid samples from the several plates in the column

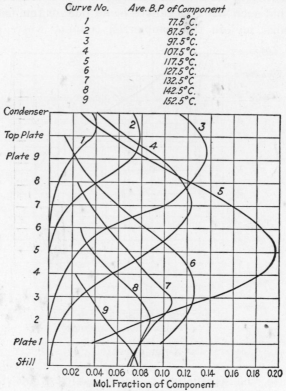

Curve No.	Ave. B.P of Component
1	77.5°C.
2	87.5°C.
3	97.5°C.
4	107.5°C.
5	117.5°C.
6	127.5°C.
7	132.5°C
8	142.5°C.
9	152.5°C.

Fig. 82.—Operation of column on petroleum distillate.

were then analyzed in a true-boiling-point still as described on page 187, being separated into components of 5°C. boiling-point range. Each of these components was indicated by its mid-temperature. Thus a component boiling on the true boiling-point apparatus between 75 and 80°C. was called the 77.5°C. component. The results of this experiment are given in Fig. 82, where each component is indicated by a concentration curve.

It will be noted that each component tends to segregate in the column, the segregation point depending on its boiling point. This segregation of a component in a continuous column is the basis for the type of still frequently found in petroleum refineries where streams or cuts are taken from the central portions of the column as well as from the top and bottom.   It is evident from Fig. 82 that such side cuts cannot be all pure or free from other components; and in the commercial column, where reflux is

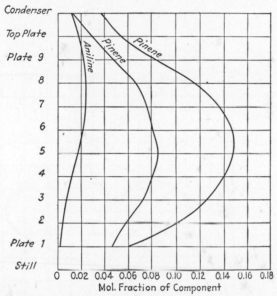

Fig. 83.—Operation of column on petroleum distillate containing aniline and pinene.

not infinite, the segregation is much less pronounced than is indicated in Fig. 82.

Figure 83 shows the behavior of aniline and pinene dissolved in a petroleum distillate.   Curve 2 represents the mol fraction of aniline, and curves 1 and 3 are for pinene in two different amounts.   Each of these was segregated in the column as in the previous cases, both aniline and pinene being soluble in the petroleum in all proportions but of different chemical structure so that the mixtures have no tendency to follow Raoult's law.

It should be emphasized that commercial columns will differ from this experimental column in that the commercial columns will not segregate so sharply on account of the relatively small, finite reflux ratio. Furthermore, the component that segregates in the column appears in greatest concentration on that plate where the temperature is the same as that of the pure component when boiling at the column pressure.

CHAPTER XVII

RECTIFICATION OF ABSORPTION NAPHTHA

Absorption naphtha as it is usually obtained consists of a mixture of the lower hydrocarbons, from methane, CH_4, to heptane,

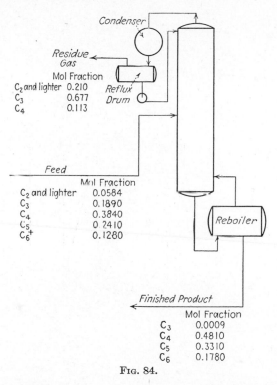

Condenser

Residue Gas

	Mol Fraction
C_2 and lighter	0.210
C_3	0.677
C_4	0.113

Reflux Drum

Feed

	Mol Fraction
C_2 and lighter	0.0584
C_3	0.1890
C_4	0.3840
C_5	0.2410
C_6^+	0.1280

Reboiler

Finished Product

	Mol Fraction
C_3	0.0009
C_4	0.4810
C_5	0.3310
C_6	0.1780

Fig. 84.

C_7H_{16}, and higher. It frequently contains such large amounts of the lower, more volatile members of this series that it is dangerous to handle and store, and it becomes necessary to subject it to a distillation to remove from it the bulk of the most volatile constituents, a process called stabilization.

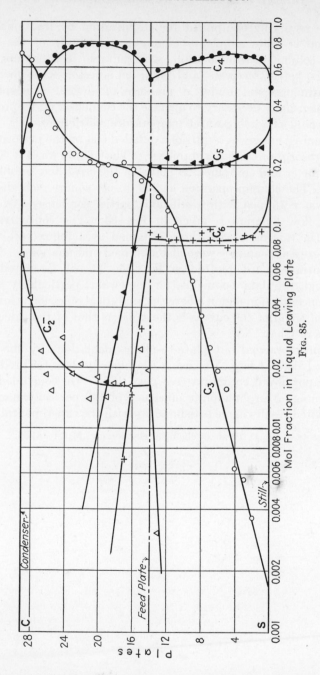

Fig. 85.

The rectifying equipment for stabilization by fractional distillation is quite simple in character, consisting of the usual single-column continuous still, with suitable feed heaters, condensers, kettle, receivers, and the usual accessories for operating a continuous still under a pressure of several atmospheres, it being usually necessary to operate the condenser under pressure on account of cooling-water temperature restrictions.

Gunness[1] has given results of a detailed test on the performance of an absorption-naphtha stabilizer. The column was 4 ft. $8\frac{1}{4}$ in. in diameter and contained 28 plates of the cross-flow bubble-cap type. The column operated at 265 lb. per square inch absolute and was equipped with a still and partial condenser. A schematic flow diagram is given in Fig. 84. The concentrations given in this figure are those obtained at a reflux ratio 2.57. Plate-to-plate samples were also obtained and analyzed. These concentrations are plotted in Fig. 85. It will be noted that although the data points scatter somewhat, particularly in the low-concentration region where the analytical precision is low, the general trend of the curves is the same as that of the calculated curves of Chap. XV.

Gunness carried out plate-to-plate calculations by the same methods as in Chap. XV, using the fugacity data for predicting the vapor-liquid equilibria (see page 175). He concluded that an average Murphree-plate efficiency of 100 per cent made the calculated results agree satisfactorily with the experimental data.

[1] GUNNESS, Sc. D. thesis in chemical engineering, M.I.T., 1936.

CHAPTER XVIII

TOPPING STILLS FOR CRUDE PETROLEUM

Crude petroleum as it comes from the oil wells usually contains sufficient material of the character of gasoline so that it is often subjected to a distillation to remove from it a gasoline cut. This operation is called "topping the crude." In recent years, it has become customary to remove several other fractions of higher boiling range at the same time. As an illustration of the

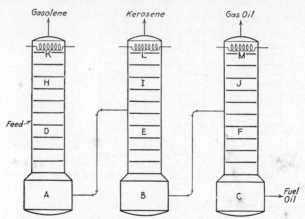

Fig. 86.—Topping still for four fractions.

principles previously given, some of the methods in common use for this purpose will be described diagrammatically.

Suppose that the crude oil to be distilled is to be topped to produce three overhead fractions or distillates and a residue, the distillates being gasoline, kerosene, and gas oil, the residue being taken off for fuel oil. Suppose, also, that this operation is to be efficiently conducted so that sharp cuts are obtained, each fraction containing very little of the components in the other cuts.

Considering the system, therefore, one of four components, there will be required three fractionating columns, each fitted

with a rectifying and an exhausting section and with reflux at
the top of the rectifying sections and supply of heat at the bottom
of the exhausting sections.

The simplest design for this purpose is given in Fig. 86, all
complications such as heat interchangers, etc., being omitted
from the drawing. It consists of a continuous battery of three
fire-heated stills *A*, *B*, and *C*, each surmounted by a distilling
column consisting of exhausting sections, *D*, *E*, and *F* and rectifying sections *H*, *I*, and *J*. In the top of each of the rectifying
sections are reflux condensers *K*, *L*, and *M*. The suitably

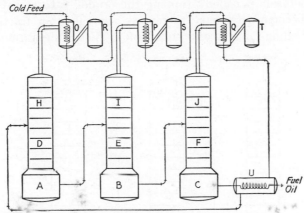

Fig. 87.—Continuous battery with heat recovery.

preheated feed enters the top of exhausting column *D* and flows
down through it into the still *A*, being stripped of its gasoline
which passes up through the column countercurrent to the
descending reflux. The latter removes from the vapor all of the
heavier components, so that the gasoline vapors issuing from
the top of the column are ready to pass to a condenser and be
collected as the gasoline cut.

The liquid reaching still *A*, freed from gasoline, is then pumped
into the top of the next exhausting column *E* as shown, and, in a
similar operation, the kerosene is taken off as the distillate. In
the same way, the gas oil is removed as distillate, freed from the
other fractions, from the top of the third column, while the residue
from the third still comprises the fuel oil.

Such a continuous battery, when properly designed with suitable heat-recovery equipment, is particularly satisfactory for work of this sort, as it has a maximum degree of flexibility, which is important where crude oils of different sources and compositions must be handled in the same equipment.

Figure 87 shows the same equipment with feed heaters and recuperator added. In this diagram, which is lettered the same as Fig. 86, there are three reflux condensers O, P, and Q through which the feed flows in series. It then passes to a recuperator U where it is further heated in countercurrent contact with the

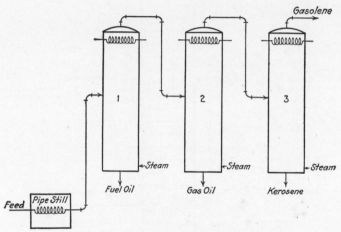

Fig. 88.—Single-flash topping unit.

hot fuel oil from still C, passing from that into the first column. The vapor from the three columns, after being partially condensed in the three feed heaters, passes to the water-cooled condensers R, S, and T, where the rest of it is condensed. The reflux to the top of each column may consist of part or all of the condensate from the feed heaters and, if necessary, part of that condensed in the final water-cooled condensers in addition, the return lines to the columns not being shown in the drawing.

The next device which may be applied for the purpose of obtaining four sharp cuts from a crude oil is shown in Fig. 88. This type of apparatus consists of three columns, as before, with exhausting and rectifying sections but without fire-heated stills.

The suitably preheated feed passes through a pipe still where it is heated to such a temperature that when its pressure is released on entering the first column, it nearly all flashes into vapor. This vapor passes up through the column where it meets the descending reflux which washes out of it the fuel oil so that the fuel oil passes out of the bottom of the column substantially free from

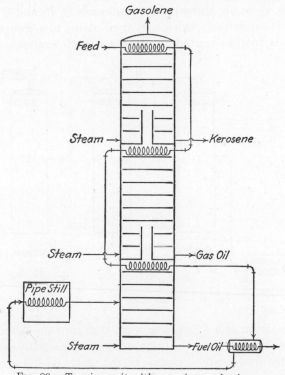

FIG. 89.—Topping unit with superimposed columns.

the more volatile fractions, superheated steam being injected into the bottom of the column to strip these fractions out of the descending fuel oil.

The vapors, containing the gas oil, kerosene, and gasoline, leave the reflux condenser at the top of the column and pass into the second column, where the process is repeated, the gas oil being removed from the bottom of this column.

The vapors from the second column then go to the third column where the separation of the gasoline and the kerosene takes place. The type of equipment is, of course, supplied with heat-recovery devices for the purpose of preheating the incoming feed.

An interesting modification of the preceding type of topping still, where the feed is superheated in a pipe still and the vapor

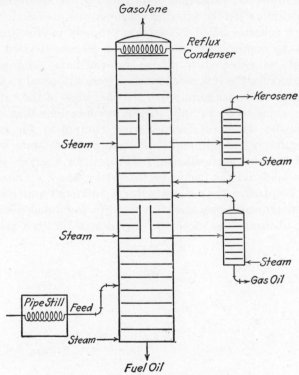

FIG. 90.—Five-column topping still.

passed successively through the columns, is given in Fig. 89. This device consists simply of the three columns described in Fig. 88, placed together to form one tall column, the internal arrangements being such that they function exactly as if separated. It will be noted that each column has its own reflux condenser, the drawing showing the incoming cold feed being used for the cooling medium, although any combination of feed or other cooling fluid may be used. Each column also has its own supply of heat in the form of superheated steam, exactly as in the previous case. The only advantage that this arrangement has over the preceding one is in construction.

It is especially interesting to note that combination columns somewhat like this type have been placed on the market for the purpose of separating crude petroleum into several fractions, differing, however, from that shown in Fig. 89, in that no provision for reflux for the internal columns was provided. Naturally such columns failed to function properly in effecting sharp cuts, so the combination shown in Fig. 90 was devised, where the fractions removed from the intermediate columns were taken to auxiliary columns where they were subjected to another fractionation in order to improve the sharpness of the cuts.

There seems to be no limit to the modifications that may be made in the design of fractionating equipment for complex mixtures like petroleum, and it is not possible to state which is the best for any particular purpose until an analysis of costs has been made for the particular problem at hand. The authors wish to emphasize the necessity for a thorough understanding of the fundamental principles involved in fractional distillation in order to insure the success of any design for such purposes.

CHAPTER XIX

COLUMN PERFORMANCE

Plate Efficiency.—The design calculations previously presented furnish a satisfactory method for determining the number of theoretical plates for a given separation, but the designer desires to know the number of actual rather than theoretical plates. The relation between the actual and the theoretical plates is given as plate efficiencies.

The mechanism of rectification involves the interaction of vapor with liquid. On a bubble plate, three types of interaction are involved: interaction of (1) vapor bubbles with the liquid, (2) vapor with free surface of the liquid, (3) vapor with liquid drops in the vapor space. The size of bubbles produced by a given bubble cap is mainly a function of the surface tension of the liquid and the size of the slots, and the effect of vapor velocity is mainly to increase the number of bubbles but not their size. Thus, for a given bubble cap and liquid on the plate the time of contact between the bubble and the liquid will be mainly a function of the liquid depth through which the bubble must rise. The efficiency of rectification would therefore be expected to increase with the liquid depth.

When a column is operating at low vapor velocities, the rectification must occur mainly by the first two methods of interaction, since little liquid is sprayed into the vapor space. As the vapor velocity is increased, the time of contact of the bubble rising through the liquid is substantially the same as before, but the effect of interaction with the free surface decreases, whereas the interaction of droplets in the vapor space increases. Likewise, the increased velocity causes entrainment of liquid drops from one plate to the next. This increase of vapor velocity may increase or decrease the efficiency of rectification, depending on whether the added interaction in the vapor space is able or not to compensate for the adverse effects of entrainment and

208

decreased interaction at the free surface. At very high velocities, the vapor may flow from the slots in an almost continuous stream and blow the liquid away from the cap and at the same time cause large quantities of liquid to be entrained from one plate to the next. When such action occurs, the plate efficiency decreases.

A number of different plate efficiencies have been proposed, but the two most commonly used are the over-all plate efficiency and the Murphree (20) plate efficiency. The over-all plate efficiency is simply the number of theoretical plates necessary for a given separation divided by the number of actual plates to perform the same separation expressed as a percentage; *i.e.*, it is the factor by which the number of theoretical plates is divided to give the actual number of plates.

The Murphree plate efficiency is defined as the ratio of the actual enrichment per plate divided by the enrichment that would be produced by a theoretical plate. Thus, if y_n is the concentration of some component entering the nth plate, y_{n+1} is the actual vapor leaving; and y^*_{n+1} is the vapor in equilibrium with the liquid x_{n+1} flowing from the $(n + 1)$ to the nth plate. The actual enrichment is $y_{n+1} - y_n$, whereas the theoretical enrichment is $y^*_{n+1} - y_n$, and the Murphree efficiency becomes

$$E_M = \frac{y_{n+1} - y_n}{y^*_{n+1} - y_n}(100) \tag{1}$$

Similarly, based on the liquid concentration,

$$E'_M = \frac{x_{n+1} - x_n}{x_{n+1} - x^*_n}(100) \tag{2}$$

where x^*_n is the liquid in equilibrium with y_n. Equation (1) should apply when the main resistance to mass transfer is in the vapor, whereas Eq. (2) should be more suitable when the transfer resistance is in the liquid phase. Murphree defined the concentration as the average values of x and y leaving a plate, and therefore these equations refer to the performance of an entire plate. Recently (15), the same equations have been used to define the point or local efficiency of a bubble rising through the liquid on a plate. This Murphree-point efficiency is based on corresponding x and y values defined by a vertical

Lewis Ind. Eng. Chem. 1936.

line through the plate. The Murphree-plate efficiency is the integrated effect of all the Murphree-point efficiencies on the plate.

The over-all plate efficiency is much simpler to use than the Murphree efficiencies, since only the terminal conditions are required; whereas in the calculation of the Murphree-plate efficiency, plate-to-plate compositions are required; and for the Murphree-point efficiency, complete liquid- and vapor-composition traverses are required on each plate. However, the Murphree efficiencies are based on a sounder theoretical basis than the over-all efficiencies.

By definition, a theoretical plate is one on which the average vapor leaving the plate is in equilibrium with the liquid leaving the plate. If the vapor and liquid upon a plate were completely mixed, it would be impossible to obtain better separation than that given by a theoretical plate. However, there is generally a concentration gradient of the liquid across the plate, whereas the vapors are probably fairly well mixed. In such a case, the average concentration of the liquid on the plate may be appreciably greater than the concentration of the liquid leaving the plate; and as a result of this greater concentration, the vapor actually leaving the plate may exceed the concentration of the vapor in equilibrium with the liquid leaving. It is thus possible for the concentration-gradient effect to give over-all and Murphree-plate efficiencies greater than 100 per cent; but since such gradients do not apply to the Murphree-point efficiency, this latter efficiency will never exceed 100 per cent. The theoretical effect of the concentration gradient has been studied by a number of investigators (12), (14), (15). Three cases were considered by W. K. Lewis, Jr.: Case I, vapor completely mixed, liquid unmixed; Case II, vapors do not mix, and the overflows are arranged such that the liquid flows in the same direction on all plates; Case III, the vapor rise from plate to plate without mixing, and the liquid flows in the opposite direction on successive plates. Using E and E_0 to represent the local and plate Murphree efficiencies, respectively, and setting the average slope of the equilibrium curve over the range of concentrations involved on the plate equal to K, Lewis gives the results tabulated in Table I, where the plate efficiency, E_0, for various assumed values of the point efficiency, E, is given as a function of the ratio of the slope of the equilibrium curve to the slope of the operating line, or $\dfrac{K}{O/V} = KV/O$.

TABLE I

E	E_0		
	$KV/O = 0$	$KV/O = 1.0$	$KV/O = 2.0$
	Case I		
20	20	22	25
40	40	49	61
60	60	82	116
80	80	123	198
100	100	172	319
	Case II		
20	20	22	25
40	40	50	63
60	60	86	125
80	80	133	226
100	100	200	392
	Case III		
20	20	22	25
40	40	49	60
60	60	81	110
80	80	116	173
100	100	150	247

It is noted that Murphree-plate efficiencies can be quite high. The usual bubble-plate towers probably fall somewhere between cases I and II.

The experimental data on plate efficiencies available at present are far too meager to allow any general correlations. Comparison between different investigators is complicated by differences of plate design, mixtures studied, and operating conditions employed. However, some of the more important of these investigations will be summarized.

Gadwa (10) has studied the plate efficiency in the fractionation of mixtures of (1) benzene-carbon tetrachloride, (2) methanol-isobutanol, (3) methanol-n-propanol, (4) isobutanol-water, (5) n-propanol-water, and (6) methanol-water. A small four-plate column containing one bubble cap per plate was employed. The bubble caps were $3\frac{1}{2}$ in. in diameter and 2 in. high containing 38 slots $\frac{1}{8}$ in. wide by $\frac{5}{8}$ in. high per cap. A vapor space of 5 by 5 in. was partitioned off from the overflow pipes, giving a ratio of slot area to superficial area of 0.12. The plates were spaced 11 in. apart, and overflow weirs were employed. Plate samples were taken so that the Murphree-plate efficiencies could be calculated. A portion of these results are given in Table II. The efficiencies in this table were calculated for the vapor [Eq. (1)].

TABLE II

System	Average Murphree-plate efficiency				
Average superficial vapor velocity, feet per second	1	2	3	4	5
Methanol-water....................	99	96	90	82	73
n-Propanol-water..................	83	85	88	88	80
Isobutanol-water..................	98	95	90	84	75
Methanol-n-propanol...............	90	88	87	87	87
Methanol-isobutanol...............	75	71	75	76	73
Benzene-carbon tetrachloride........	82	88	89	84	74

Gadwa concluded that for the mixtures he studied the Murphree-plate efficiency was substantially independent of the concentration and of the vapor velocity so long as foaming and entrainment did not occur but that when foaming and entrainment did occur, the efficiency decreased with increasing velocity.

Brown (4) and Gunness (11) both report Murphree-plate efficiencies of 100 per cent or greater for large commercial gasoline stabilizers. The tower studied by Gunness, operated at 250 lb. per square inch gage, was 4 ft. $8\frac{1}{4}$ in. in diameter and contained 28 plates each having 27 cast-iron bubble caps. The bubble caps were $6\frac{1}{4}$ in. in diameter and contained 32 1- by $\frac{1}{2}$-in. rectangular slots per cap. The plate spacing was 18 in. In these columns, there were a number of bubble caps per plate, and the liquid flowed in opposite directions on successive plates. Gunness analyzed his data by Lewis's cross-flow enrichment method (page 211) and concluded that the Murphree-point efficiency was between 70 and 80 per cent.

Lewis and Smoley (16) studied the plate efficiency in the rectification of mixtures of (1) benzene-toluene, (2) benzene-toluene-xylene, and (3) naphtha and mixtures of pinene and aniline in naphtha. An experimental column 8 in. in diameter with 10 plates spaced 16 in. apart was used. The bubble cap was rectangular, being 2 in. high and 2 in. wide and extended across the column. There were 24 slots $\frac{7}{8}$ by $\frac{3}{16}$ in. on each side of the cap, giving a ratio of slot area to superficial area of about 0.16. The investigators found average plate efficiencies of 60 per cent for the benzene-toluene mixture, 75 per cent for the ternary mixture, and 80 to 95 per cent for the naphtha mixtures.

In the same tower, Carey, Griswold, Lewis, and McAdams (5) found an average Murphree efficiency of 70 per cent when fractionating benzene-toluene. They found the efficiency substantially constant for superficial velocities from 0.2 to 4.5 ft. per second and independent of liquid composition. The same investigators report efficiencies of 50 to 99.75 per cent for the fractionation of an ethanol-water mixture in a 6 in.-diameter tower containing one plate. The logarithm of 100 minus the plate efficiency was found to be a linear function of the depth of submergence of the slots. A benzene-toluene mixture in the same one-plate tower gave an average Murphree efficiency of 58 per cent. A distillation of an aniline-water mixture in the 10-plate tower gave an average plate efficiency of 58 per cent at a vapor velocity of 2.77 ft. per second.

Lewis and Wilde (17) found an average plate efficiency of 65 per cent at a vapor velocity of 2.8 ft. per second for the rectification of naphtha in a 10-plate column 9 ft. in diameter. There were 115 bubble caps per plate containing slots $\frac{1}{4}$ by 1 in. The ratio of slot area to superficial area was 0.10, and the plate spacing was 2 ft.

Brown (3) reports efficiencies as high as 120 per cent for a commercial beer column using perforated plates. The same efficiency was reported for the rectification of an ethanol-water

mixture in a special laboratory column. The same investigator
3 reports efficiencies of about 20 per cent for naphtha-absorption towers.

Pressure Drop.—The pressure drop in bubble-plate towers is
made up of three main portions. First, the pressure drop
from the vapor space through the bubble cap riser to the slots.
This drop involves the entrance loss to the riser, the friction drop
in the riser, the reversal of flow at the top of the riser, and the
friction loss in the annular space between the riser and the inside
of the bubble cap. The second main pressure drop is that due
to the flow through the slots. The third is the pressure that
must be maintained to support the head of liquid above the top
of the slots.

For caps with the area of the riser, the clearance area at the
top of the riser, and the area of the annular space between the
riser and cap all equal, Dauphiné and Schneider (8) found the
following equation for flow of air:

$$\Delta p_u = 0.0118 \frac{Q^2}{D^4} \tag{3}$$

where Δp_u = pressure drop, inches of water.
Q = cubic feet of air per minute per cap.
D = diameter of riser, inches.
The diameter of the riser was varied from 2 to 4 in. Since the
loss is largely entrance, exit, and reversal losses, the pressure
drop for other gases should fit this equation if the constant is
increased in the ratio of the density of the gas to that of air.
Obviously, this loss should not be affected to any great degree
by the liquid on the plate.

These same investigators found that for air-water, the pressure drop through the slots could be expressed as

$$\Delta p_s = K \left(\frac{Q}{L} \right)^{0.4} \tag{4}$$

where Δp_s = pressure drop through slots, inches of water.
Q = cubic feet of air per minute per cap.
L = total slot width per cap, inches.
K = constant depending on cap design.

A number of different caps were studied, and values of K for some of these are listed below.

Cap	K
6-in.-diameter galvanized-iron cap:	
Slots, ⅛ by (0.5, 1.0, 1.5, and 2.0) in. ⎫	
Slots, ³⁄₁₆ in by (0.5, 1.0, and 1.5) in. ⎬	0.31
6-in.-diameter cast-iron cap:	
Slots, ¼ by (0.5 and 1.0) in......................	0.37
4-in.-diameter copper cap	
Slots, ⁵⁄₃₂ by ½ in..............................	0.25
4-in.-diameter cast-iron cap	
Slots, ³⁄₁₆ by (0.5 and 1.0) in....................	0.28

The pressure drop for other vapors can probably be estimated by the equation with the constant increased in the ratio of the vapor densities. Mayer (19) found that when using liquids such as water, glycerin, acetylene tetrachloride, and salt solutions, the pressure drop in the slots was proportional to the 0.6 power of the density of the liquid.

The third pressure drop, due to the liquid above the slots, will be proportional to the density of the liquid and its depth, its depth being the equivalent static depth when the liquid is stirred up.

Entrainment.—Entrainment is the carrying of the liquid from one plate to the plate above by the flow of the vapor. It is usually defined as the weight of liquid entrained per weight of vapor. Entrainment is undesirable, since it reduces plate efficiency by tending to destroy the countercurrent action of the tower, and it also may affect the distillate adversely from the standpoint of color.

The entrainment of the liquid is due to two main causes: (1) the carrying of liquid droplets due to the mass velocity of the gas and (2) the splashing of the liquid on the plate. The latter of these depends on the slot-vapor velocity and a function of the plate spacing.

Several investigators have published quantitative data on the amount of entrainment in bubble-plate columns. Most of these investigations have been on systems involving air and water. In Fig. 91, some of these experimental results are presented.

Curve A is based on the data of Ashraf, Cubbage, and Huntington (1) for the entrainment in a 7- by 30-ft. commercial absorber. The tower contained 10 trays 22 in. apart. The tower was operating on a gas oil-natural gas system at 45 lb. per square inch absolute. The investigators obtained a maximum entrainment of 0.0017 at a mass velocity of 23.4 lb. per minute per square foot. The same investigators also studied entrainment in a laboratory column 12½ in. in diameter containing two 3⅜-inch bubble caps per plate. The caps contained

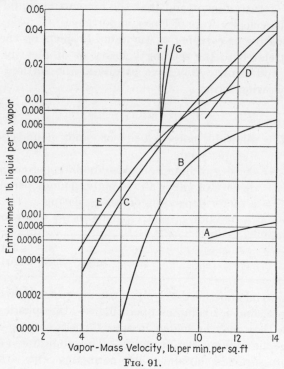

Fig. 91.

32 slots ³⁄₁₆ by 1 in., giving a ratio of slot area to superficial area of 0.0975. Curve C is based on their data for this tower when operating on kerosene-natural gas absorption at atmospheric pressure.

Curve B is based on the air-water results of Sherwood and Jenny (23). The tower contained two plates and was 18 in. in diameter. Four-inch caps were employed having 33 notched-type slots. The slots were ¾ in. high and tapered from ³⁄₁₆ in. at the bottom to ⅛ in. at the top.

Curves *D*, *F*, and *E* are also for water and air, the first curve being taken from Chillas and Weir (6), and the last two from Strang (26).

Holbrook and Baker (13) studied entrainment in an 8-in. bubble-plate column using steam and water. Curve *E* is based on a portion of their data. They conclude that the plate spacing and vapor velocity were the main factors in determining the amount of entrainment and that the amount of liquid flow and slot-vapor velocity were of lesser importance.

The floating or carrying of the liquid droplets by the vapor is directly related to the settling velocity of droplets in a vapor. Souders and Brown (25) have expressed the settling equation in the following form:

$$W = C[d_2(d_1 - d_2)]^{1/2} \qquad (5)$$

where W = allowable mass velocity of vapor, pounds per square foot per hour.

d_1 = density of liquid on plate, pounds per cubic foot.

d_2 = density of vapor above plate, pounds per cubic foot.

C = a factor depending on plate spacing.

C is given as a function of plate spacing in the following table.

Plate spacing, inches	10	15	20	30	40
C	150	420	560	700	740

Commercial superficial velocities usually range between 0.5 to 3 ft. per second for columns operating at atmospheric pressure, although they may be higher in special cases without adversely affecting the column performance. The allowable velocity at other pressures is obtained by correcting the atmospheric allowable velocity by the method of Souders and Brown.

Overflow Weirs and Down Pipes.—In small columns, the overflow from plate to plate is usually carried in pipes, the upper end of the pipe projecting above the plate surface to form an overflow weir and maintain a liquid seal on the plate. The lower end extends into a well on the plate below, thereby sealing the pipe so that vapor may not pass upward through it. In larger columns, straight overflow weirs placed on a chord across the tower are often used.

Locke (18) from a study of circular down pipes concluded that at least three types of liquid flow were possible in circular down pipes with liquid seals at the bottom. At low rates of liquid flow, the top of the pipe acted as a weir, and the liquid flowed down in a film. As the liquid head was increased, the pipe became full and sucked vapor bubbles down with it; whereas at still higher liquid rates, the pipe ran full but did not entrap vapor. The first type of flow occurred for liquid head less than one-sixth to one-fifth of the pipe diameter, and this type of flow could be represented by the familiar Francis weir formula

$$q = KLH^{1.5} \tag{6}$$

where q = cubic feet of liquid per second.

L = perimeter of inside surface of pipe, feet.

H = head of liquid above pipe, feet.

K = constant, decreasing from 5.4 to 4.7 as pipe size was increased from 0.87 to 2.07 in.

Rowley (21) recommends the following equation for the last two types of flow:

$$h = \left[\frac{1.5}{2g} + \frac{2fl}{gD} \right] V^2 \tag{7}$$

where h = total head of liquid above the liquid level in the seal box, feet.

g = acceleration due to gravity, feet per second squared.

D = inside diameter of pipe, feet.

l = length of overflow pipe, feet.

V = linear velocity of liquid in pipe, feet per second.

f = a proportionality constant of Fanning friction equation (see Walker, Lewis, McAdams, and Gilliland, "Principles of Chemical Engineering," 3d ed., p. 78).

For large rectangular weirs, when the downspouts are not running full, the Francis weir equation may be used. For such overflows running full, it is recommended that Eq. (7) be used, employing for D four times the hydraulic radius, which is equal to the cross-sectional area of the downspout divided by the perimeter.

Efficiency of Packed Towers.—The efficiency of packed towers is generally expressed as the height equivalent to a theoretical plate. Most of the reported values of H.E.T.P's. are for small laboratory columns, since this is one of the largest uses of packed columns. H.E.T.P. is a function of the packing dimension and construction, tower size, vapor velocity, and system being rectified. The efficiency of packed towers may be seriously impaired by the liquid's tending to pass down one side while the vapor flows up the other. This channeling of vapor and liquid prevents effective interaction between the vapor and liquid.

Baker, Chilton, and Vernon (2) report the results of tests on the distribution of water over various packing materials with air flowing up through the packing. The water rate was 500 lb. per hour per square foot in all tests. They found that a ratio of tower diameter to packing size greater than 8 to 1 gave a fairly uniform liquid distribution. At values of the ratio less than 8, the liquid tended to run down the tower walls and leave the center of the column nearly dry. A multiple-point liquid distributor at the top improved the liquid distribution at the top portion of the tower. The results of these investigators indicate the desirability of having the tower diameter over eight times the size of the packing material and of using multiple-point liquid distributors; this latter is most important in short towers.

Fenske, Tongberg, and Quiggle (9a) give the results of a large number of tests on packed laboratory towers. A comparison of some of their results for the distillation of a carbon tetrachloride-benzene mixture is given in the following table:

Packing	Tower dimensions, inches	H.E.T.P., inches
Straight $\frac{7}{32}$-in carding teeth	0 76 by 27	1.5
Straight $\frac{5}{32}$-in. carding teeth	0.76 by 27	1.7
Bent $\frac{1}{4}$-in. carding teeth	0.76 by 27	1.7
Miscellaneous carding teeth	0.76 by 27	2.2
Double-cross wire form	0.76 by 27	2.1
Hollow-square wire form	0.80 by 55	5.4
No. 20 single-link iron jack chain	2.0 by 53	5.2
No. 2 cut tacks	0.8 by 55	2.4
6-turn No. 24 Lucero wire helix	0.8 by 66	8.0
No. 18 single-link iron jack chain	2.0 by 53	6.5
Glass tubes	0.78 by 27	5.5
No. 16 single-link iron jack chain	0.76 by 27	4.2

The investigators conclude that (1) the best packings are one-turn and two-turn wire or glass helices, carding teeth, and No. 19 jack chain; (2) the efficiency of the packing decreases when the tower diameter is increased or when the height of the packed section is increased; and (3) different hydrocarbon mixtures give approximately the same value for H.E.T.P.

Weimann (27) has published results on the fractionation of ethanol-water mixtures in packed towers. Using a superficial velocity of 1 ft. per second at $O/D = 1.0$ with 8- by 8-mm. porcelain Raschig rings in a 0.11-m. (4⅓-in.) diameter tower, H.E.T.P. values of 6 to 8.5 in. were obtained for packing heights of 3.5 to 13 ft. A larger tower, approximately 1 ft. in diameter, using a 7-ft. depth of the same packing gave an H.E.T.P. of 8.5 in. at a superficial vapor velocity of 1¼ ft. per second.

Jantzen (13a) has presented the results of fractionating an ethanol-water mixture in a 13.5-cm. (1.37-in.) tower packed to a depth of 1 m. with either 1- or 0.46-cm. Raschig rings. The values of H.E.T.P. calculated from his data range from about 3 to 6 in., for superficial vapor velocities ranging from 0.15 to 2 ft. per second. The H.E.T.P. values increased as the 0.2 power of the vapor velocity and were about 50 per cent larger for the large than for the small rings. These values were found to be independent of the liquid concentration and of the reflux ratio (experimental values of O/D ranged from 4 to 10).

Fenske and coworkers (9) have also made an extensive study of the efficiency of packings when used for the separation of a n-heptane-methyl cyclohexane mixture in a 2-in.-diameter glass tower at total reflux. The tower was 114 in. high and was operated at atmospheric pressure. A few of their results are summarized in the following table.

These data indicate that H.E.T.P. values as low as 1.5 in. have been obtained, making it possible to obtain the equivalent of a large number of theoretical plates in a relatively short height. Because of their efficiency and simplicity, packed towers are widely used for laboratory columns. However, when larger sized packed towers are used, the efficiency in general decreases, and H.E.T.P. values of a few feet are more common for columns of commercial size.

Packing	Vapor velocity, feet per second	H.E.T.P., inches
Open tower.............................	0.25 to 1.7	25.5 to 29.2
½- by ½-in. carbon Raschig rings.........	0.25 to 1.45	6.0 to 11.3
½- by ½-in. stoneware Raschig rings.......	0.8 to 1.55	5.0 to 8.5
⅜- by ⅜-in. stoneware Raschig rings......	0.3 to 1.1	3.8 to 7.3
¼- by ¼-in. carbon Raschig rings.........	0.15 to 0.5	4.7 to 6.0
¼- by ¼-in. glass Raschig rings...........	0.4 to 0.9	4.3 to 6.8
No. 19 aluminum jack chain...............	0.1 to 1.65	4.2 to 8.9
½-in. clay Berl saddles...................	0.05 to 1.6	5.8 to 7.0
½-in. aluminum Berl saddles..............	0.3 to 1.75	4.1 to 7.0
6-mesh carborundum.....................	0.1 to 0.35	1.6 to 5.1
¼-in. aluminum single-turn helices.........	0.7 to 2.1	5.0 to 10.7
³⁄₁₆-in. aluminum single-turn helices........	0.1 to 1.8	3.7 to 6.2
⁵⁄₃₂-in. single-turn stainless-steel helices.....	0.3 to 1.25	4.0 to 5.4
⁵⁄₃₂-in. single-turn nickel helices............	0.55 to 1.65	2.9 to 5.5
⅛-in. single-turn nickel helices.............	0.1 to 1.0	2.9 to 5.5
³⁄₃₂-in. single-turn stainless-steel helices.....	0.15 to 0.95	1.5 to 2.3
⅛- by ⁷⁄₃₂-in. carding teeth...............	0.4 to 1.35	2.0 to 4.2

Pressure Drop.—Although the pressure drop through packed towers is usually small and is generally a negligible factor at atmospheric pressure, it may become a limiting factor in vacuum distillations.

Chilton and Colburn (7) have published a method for predicting such pressure drop for solid packings, based on the Fanning equation for friction in pipes. They modify the friction equation to

$$\Delta p = \frac{2fA_w A_L \rho u^2 h}{gd} \tag{8}$$

where Δp = pressure drop in height h.

A_w = a correction factor for wall effect.

A_L = a correction factor for wetting of the packing, by the liquid.

ρ = density of the vapor.

g = acceleration of gravity.

u = superficial gas velocity, *i.e.*, linear gas velocity based on the total cross section of the tower.

d = size of packing, nominal.

μ = viscosity of vapor.

f = function of $\left(\dfrac{du\rho}{\mu}\right)$ as given in Eqs. (9) and (10).

Chilton and Colburn gave a plot of f as a function of the Reynolds number $(du\rho/\mu)$. The data of this plot may be approximated by the following equations:

For $(du\rho/\mu)$ less than 40, use

$$f = \frac{850}{(du\rho/\mu)} \qquad (9)$$

For $(du\rho/\mu)$ greater than 40,

$$f = \frac{38}{(du\rho/\mu)^{0.15}} \qquad (10)$$

All of these equations are dimensionally sound, and any consistent set of units may be used. The following table contains values of the factor A_w.

Packing diameter	A_w	
Tower diameter	$\left(\dfrac{du\rho}{\mu}\right) < 40$	$\left(\dfrac{du\rho}{\mu}\right) > 40$
0	1.0	1.0
0.1	0.83	0.72
0.2	0.74	0.65
0.3	0.71	0.57

The correction for the wetting of the packing A_L is 1 for dry packing and increases with increased rates of liquid flow. Sherwood (22) presents plots of this factor indicating that the value of A_L has increased to 1.5 to 2.0 for water flowing over the packing at the rate of 1,000 lb. per hour per square foot.

The pressure drop with hollow packings is less than given by the equation for solid packings. The data on this effect are not very conclusive as to absolute magnitude but do indicate that, for hollow packing, the smaller the packing size the larger the pressure drop. For a detailed discussion of this factor, the reader is referred to Sherwood's summary (22).

Allowable Gas and Liquor Velocities.—The capacity of packed towers is limited by the tower's becoming flooded with liquid. The flooding can be caused by increasing either the liquid or the gas flow. This flooding is a result of the pressure drop through the tower exceeding the gravity head of the liquid flowing down.

These pressure drops per foot of height are given by the modified Fanning equation:

$$\Delta p_G = \frac{f_G V_G^2 \rho_G}{2gm} \qquad \Delta p_L = \frac{f_L V_L^2 \rho_L}{2gm}$$

where f = proportionality factor, a function of $mu\rho/\mu$.

V_G = actual linear gas velocity = u_G/FA_G.

V_L = actual linear liquid = u_L/FA_L.

ρ = density.

g = acceleration of gravity.

μ = viscosity.

F = fraction of tower that consists of voids.

S = surface of packing, square foot per cubic foot of packing.

m = hydraulic radius = free volume/contact area = F/S.

A_G, A_L = fraction of free cross section occupied by gas and liquid, respectively.

u = superficial velocity.

The flooding occurs when $\Delta p_L = \rho_L - \Delta p_G$ is a small fraction of Δp_G, since under such conditions a slight increase in the rate of flow of either stream or an uneven surge in the tower will increase A_L and decrease A_G, because of increased liquid holdup. This decrease in A_G will increase V_G and thereby Δp_G. If Δp_L is large relative to Δp_G, this increase in Δp_G will affect the liquid flow only slightly; however, if Δp_L is small compared to Δp_G, a small increase in Δp_G will make a large percentage decrease in Δp_L, causing the holdup to increase and the tower to flood.

Combining the pressure-drop equations,

$$\frac{A_G}{A_L} = \frac{A_G}{1 - A_G} = \sqrt{\frac{f_G u_G^2 \rho_G}{f_L u_L^2 \rho_L}} \sqrt{\frac{\rho_L - \Delta p_G}{\Delta p_G}}$$

NOTE.—For data on the values of S and F for various packings, the reader is referred to references (9a) and (22) at the end of the chapter.

Setting the ratio $(\rho_L - \Delta p_G)/\Delta p_G$ equal to b and noting that at flooding Δp_G becomes approximately equal to ρ_L modifies the previous equation to give

$$\frac{u_G^2 \rho_G}{2gm\rho_L F^2} = \frac{b\left(\dfrac{u_G}{u_L}\right)^2 \dfrac{\rho_G}{\rho_L f_L}}{[1 + b^{1/2}(u_G/u_L)(\rho_G f_G/\rho_L f_L)^{1/2}]^2} \tag{11}$$

At low values of $(u_G/u_L)^2 \rho_G/p_L$, the denominator of the right-hand side becomes 1, and the limiting gas velocity is a function of $(u_G/u_L)(\rho_G/\rho_L)$, the tower dimensions, and f_L, the latter term being chiefly a function of μ_L. It is interesting to note that in this region the gas viscosity is not a factor; but when the last term of the denominator is not negligible, the viscosity of the gas becomes a factor in the limiting gas velocity.

At very high values of this group, the right hand reduces to f_G. This would be the case when a very low liquid rate was employed and the gas occupied essentially the whole free cross section of the tower. For convenience in plotting, the right-hand side will be taken as a function of $(u_G/u_L)(\rho_G/\rho_L)^{1/2}/\mu_L^N$. The data of a

Packing	System	Reference
No. 19 aluminum jack chain....	Heptane-methyl cyclohexane	9
1-in. Raschig rings............	Air-water	19a
1-in. Berl saddles.............	Air-water	19a
8-mm. Raschig rings..........	Air-water	19a
½-in. Raschig rings...........	H_2-water	24
½-in. Raschig rings...........	Air-water	24
½-in. Raschig rings...........	CO_2-water	24
½-in. Berl saddles............	Air-water	24
½-in. Raschig rings...........	Air-methanol	24
½-in. Rachig rings............	Air-(50% H_2O + 50% CH$_3$OH)	24
½-in. Raschig rings...........	Air-glycerin	24
½-in. Raschig rings...........	Water + butyric acid-air	24
$\frac{7}{32}$-in. carding teeth..........	Benzene-carbon tetrachloride	9a
¼-in. bent carding teeth.......	Benzene-carbon tetrachloride	9a
0.23- by 0.27-in. glass rings.....	Benzene-carbon tetrachloride	9a
0.18-in. glass rings............	Ethanol-water	13a
0.47-in. glass rings............	Quinoline (distillation at 10 mm. Hg absolute)	13a

number of investigators are correlated in this way in Fig. 92, using a value of $n = 0.21$.

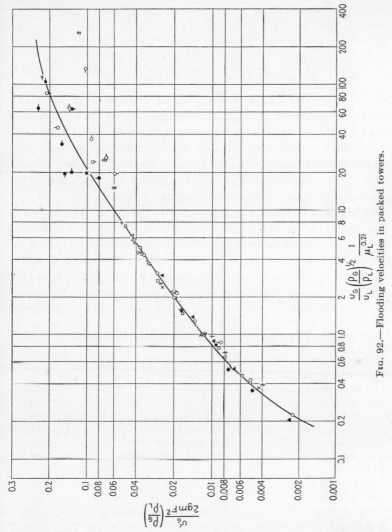

FIG. 92.—Flooding velocities in packed towers.

The data are seen to correlate well except at high values of the abscissa. This deviation may be due to the fact that the f_G factor in the denominator is neglected in the method of plotting of this figure.

References

1. ASHRAF, CUBBAGE, and HUNTINGTON, *Ind. Eng. Chem.*, **26**, 1068 (1934).
2. BAKER, CHILTON, and VERNON, *Trans. Amer. Inst. Chem. Eng.*, **31**, 296 (1935).
3. BROWN, World Power Conference, 1936, *Trans. Chem. Eng. Congress*, **2**, 330.
4. BROWN, SOUDERS, NYLAND, and HESLER, *Ind. Eng. Chem.*, **27**, 383 (1935).
5. CAREY, GRISWOLD, LEWIS, and McADAMS, *Trans. Amer. Inst. Chem. Eng.*, **30**, 504 (1934).
6. CHILLAS and WEIR, *Trans. Amer. Inst. Chem. Eng.*, **22**, 79 (1929).
7. CHILTON and COLBURN, *Trans. Amer. Inst. Chem. Eng.*, **26**, 178 (1931).
8. DAUPHINÉ and SCHNEIDER, see Schneider, Sc. M. thesis in chemical engineering, M.I.T. (1938).
9. FENSKE, LAWROSKI, and TONGBERG, *Ind. Eng. Chem.*, **30**, 297 (1938).
9a. FENSKE, TONGBERG, and QUIGGLE, *Ind. Eng. Chem.*, **26**, 1169 (1934).
10. GADWA, Sc.D. thesis in chemical engineering, M.I.T. (1936).
11. GUNNESS, Sc.D. thesis in chemical engineering, M.I.T. (1936).
12. HAUSEN, *Forschung*, **7**, 177 (1936).
13. HOLBROOK and BAKER, *Ind. Eng. Chem.*, **26**, 1063 (1934).
13a. JANTZEN, *Dechema Mon.*, **5**, No. 48 (1932).
14. KIRSCHBAUM, *Forschung*, **8**, 63 (1937).
15. LEWIS, *Ind. Eng. Chem.*, **28**, 399 (1936).
16. LEWIS and SMOLEY, *Bull. Amer. Pet. Inst.*, **11**, sec. 3, No. 1, p. 73 (1930).
17. LEWIS and WILDE, *Trans. Amer. Inst. Chem. Eng.*, **21**, 99 (1928).
18. LOCKE, S. M. thesis in chemical engineering, M.I.T., 1937.
19. MAYER, S. M. thesis in chemical engineering, M.I.T., 1938.
19a. MACH, *Forschungsheft*, **375**, p. 9 (1935).
20. MURPHREE, *Ind. Eng. Chem.*, **17**, 747 (1925).
21. ROWLEY, S. B. thesis in chemical engineering, M.I.T., 1938.
22. SHERWOOD, "Absorption and Extraction," p. 141, McGraw-Hill Book Company, Inc., New York, 1937.
23. SHERWOOD and JENNY, *Ind. Eng. Chem.*, **27**, 263 (1935).
24. SHIPLEY, S. M. thesis in chemical engineering, M.I.T., 1937.
25. SOUDERS and BROWN, *Ind. Eng. Chem.*, **26**, 98 (1934).
26. STRANG, *Trans. Inst. Chem. Eng.*, **12**, 169 (1934).
27. WEIMANN, *Die chemische Fabrik*, **6**, 411 (1933); see also *Beiheft z. ver. deut. Chem.*, No. 6 (1933).

CHAPTER XX

THE CONDENSER

The condenser receives all of the vapors leaving the top of the fractionating column. Some of the factors influencing the design of the condenser have been discussed previously. The decision as to the number of condensers to be used often depends on circumstances.

The capacity of the condenser system is often the controlling factor in determining the capacity of the whole distilling system. In many cases, the condensation of the product of the still and the condensation of the vapor for reflux are carried out separately in different condensers; whereas in other cases, both of these operations are performed by a single condenser which may act as a cooler as well. Condensers in distilling equipment are always of the surface type. It is felt that under ordinary circumstances a single condenser, large enough to take care of all of the reflux and condensation required, is the most economical design for a batch fractionating still. Continuous stills usually have multiple condensers.

It is customary to cool the condensed distillate below its boiling temperature, since a hot distillate is readily volatilized and is therefore likely to suffer loss by evaporation on standing; and, furthermore, in case the vapor is inflammable, a hot distillate is a considerable source of fire risk. In small distilling apparatus, it is customary to make the condenser large enough to furnish the necessary cooling. It is sometimes simpler, however, to furnish a supplementary cooler to receive the distillate from the condenser.

The vapors received by the condenser may consist almost entirely of the vapors of a single component, or they may be a mixture of several. In addition, there are always present in these vapors air or other not easily condensable gases. In the case of a nearly pure vapor, condensation takes place at nearly constant

227

temperature; whereas the condensation of mixed vapors may occur over a wide temperature range. It should be remembered that constant-boiling mixtures condense like pure vapor. The presence of the noncondensable gases makes the condensation more difficult both by lowering the condensing temperature and by interfering with the heat removal through the condensing surface.

Factors Influencing Condenser Design.—The design of a suitable condenser necessitates knowledge of the probable conditions under which it will operate. These include the composition of the vapors to be condensed; the required rate of condensation; the temperatures and pressures involved; and the quality, temperature, and amount of cooling water available or of other cooling medium, as the case may be. The type and location of the condenser must also be known. The specific data needed for the design are listed as follows:

1. The amount of vapor entering the condenser from the fractionating column.

2. The amount of heat that must be removed by the condenser in condensing the vapor.

3. The amount of heat that must be removed by the condenser in cooling the condensed vapor.

4. The amount of inert gas or other noncondensable vapors present in the vapors entering the condenser.

5. The temperature of the vapor entering the condenser.

6. The temperature of the noncondensable gases leaving the condenser.

7. The temperature of the condensed vapor leaving the condenser.

8. The amount of cooling liquid available.

9. The temperature of the cooling liquid available.

10. The temperature at which the cooling liquid should leave the condenser.

11. The velocity of the vapors by the cooling surface.

12. The velocity of the cooling liquid by the cooling surface.

13. The removal of the noncondensable gases from the condenser.

14. The physical characteristics of the condensed vapor.

15. The physical characteristics of the cooling fluid.

16. The arrangement of the condensing and cooling surfaces.
With all of this information, it is then possible with the present
knowledge of heat transmission to design a condenser that will
function properly for the specified conditions. Designers, however, are faced with the prospects of varying conditions about
which they know little or nothing, and, in order to allow for these
unknown variables, there are usually introduced factors of safety
the magnitude of which depend on the experience of the designer.

The principal problem to be solved is that of the removal of the
latent heat of condensation from the condensing vapors. In a
continuously operating condenser, where conditions are reasonably steady, the rate at which the heat will be removed is
expressed by the formula

$$\frac{Q}{\theta} = UA\Delta$$

where Q represents the heat removed in the time θ, U is the heat-
transfer coefficient, A is the area of the cooling surface, and Δ
is the difference in temperature between the condensing vapor
and the cooling medium. When the temperatures vary from
point to point in the condenser, it is necessary to use an average
value of Δ and of U. Very complete directions for the calculation
of these average values are available in books devoted to the
subject of heat transmission, and only a short outline will be
included in this work.

The value of the heat-transfer coefficient U depends on the
composition of the condensing vapors and the rate of removal of
condensate from the condensing surface; the material and thick-
ness as well as the arrangement of the condenser walls; and the
composition, temperature, and velocity of travel past the condenser walls of the cooling fluid. The amount of noncondensable
gas and the degree of fouling of the condenser walls are also very
important.

The following table gives the values of U for condensing steam
at atmospheric pressure outside a 1-in. thin copper tube through
which water at 100°F. is flowing at various velocities. These
values are expressed as B.t.u. (British thermal units) per degree
Fahrenheit temperature difference per square foot of condenser
surface per hour. They are based on steam entirely free from

noncondensable gases and condenser walls quite free from scale or other incrustation.

Water velocity, ft./sec	0.1	0.5	1.0	2.0	3.0	5.0	10.0
B.t.u./(sq. ft.) (°F.) (hr.)	50	170	275	440	560	730	1,000

The effect of the size of tubing on condensers is shown in the following table which gives values of U for condensing steam outside thin copper tubes of various diameters through which water at 100°F. is flowing at a velocity of 3 ft. per second, scale and noncondensable gases again being absent.

Pipe diameter, in	$\frac{1}{4}$	$\frac{1}{2}$	1	2	5	10
B.t.u./(sq. ft.) (°F.) (hr.)	720	610	560	500	440	390

The composition of the condensing vapor affects the value of U to a marked degree, the values in the following table being for a 1-in. thin copper tube placed horizontally with water at 100°F. flowing through it at a velocity of 3 ft. per second and with the pure vapor condensing on the outside at atmospheric pressure.

Condensing Vapor	U B.t.u./(sq. ft.) (°F.) (hr.)
Water vapor (nondropwise)	560
Carbon bisulfide	435
Methyl alcohol	340
Ethyl alcohol	270
Carbon tetrachloride	190
Benzene, C_6H_6	180

For liquids in the lower portion of this table, the effect of liquid velocity and tube diameter is less important than for those in the upper portion of the table.

The values of U for condensing vapors outside vertical pipes are somewhat smaller than for horizontal pipes, being smaller for long pipes than for short ones.

Scale and other solid deposits on condenser walls are often serious. If $\frac{1}{8}$ in. of hard sulphate scale is present on the 1-in. thin copper tube mentioned above, the value of U for condensing steam to 100°F. cooling water flowing at 3 ft. per second may be cut from 560 down to 20. The effect of noncondensable gases in considerable amount in the condensing vapor is equally serious.

The problem of condensing the vapors from petroleum distillation is sometimes complicated by the use of petroleum liquids as cooling fluids instead of water. Many of these liquids are of relatively high viscosity, low thermal conductivity, and low heat capacity, and the resulting coefficients of heat transfer are correspondingly low as compared with those obtained with water as the cooling fluid. The computation of the area of heating surface needed for such conditions is difficult, but a considerable amount of information on this point is to be found in the heat-transfer literature, to which the reader is referred.

The value of the temperature difference Δ between the condensing vapor and the cooling water or other medium may be determined if the temperature of the condensing vapors on the one side of the condenser walls and that of the cooling water on the other side are known. When a practically pure vapor is condensing at constant pressure without subsequent cooling, its temperature remains constant. The temperature of the cooling water usually rises considerably as it passes through the tubes. The value of Δ is therefore a variable, and it is customary to calculate an average value for it and use this as a constant. In the case of the condensation of a vapor at constant temperature where an average value of U may be taken, the proper average value of Δ is the logarithmic mean

$$\Delta_{\text{log mean}} = \frac{\Delta_1 - \Delta_2}{\log_e \dfrac{\Delta_1}{\Delta_2}}$$

where Δ_1 and Δ_2 are the values of Δ at the inlet and outlet of the condenser.

Where condensation is followed by cooling of the condensate, the logarithmic mean is only an approximation, and it is better to consider the condensation and cooling as two separate consecutive operations. Where condensation and cooling are taking place at the same time, as is the case when the condensed vapor is a mixture of components of varying boiling points, there is no simple method for determining the proper value of Δ average.

As an example of the method of calculating the area of condenser surface needed for a specific case, take the problem of condensing the alcohol vapors from a continuous still which is producing 250 lb. of high-strength alcohol per hour, using a 3 to 1 reflux ratio. The condenser is to be made up of 1-in. thin copper tubes in parallel, the cooling water passing through them at an average velocity of 3 ft. per second, entering at 75°F. and leaving at 125°F., so that the average cooling-water temperature is 100°F. The alcohol vapor is condensing outside the tubes at 173°F. and falling off them before it is cooled to any appreciable extent.

Referring to the table given above, it is seen that the average value of U for this case is 270 B.t.u. per square foot per degree Fahrenheit per hour. The logarithmic mean of Δ is

$$\frac{(173 - 75) - (173 - 125)}{\log_e \dfrac{173 - 75}{173 - 125}} = 70.2°$$

The latent heat of condensation of ethyl alcohol at 173°F. is 370 B.t.u. per pound. Since the reflux ratio is 3 to 1, there must be condensed $4 \times 250 = 1,000$ lb. of alcohol per hour.

Substituting these values in the heat-transmission formula gives

$$1,000 \times 370 = 270 \times 70.2 \times A$$

whence $A = 19.5$ sq. ft. of surface needed. This area must be divided up among sufficient tubes to satisfy the condition that the water velocity is 3 ft. per second and its rise in temperature, 50°F.

The area of cross section of a 1-in. tube is 0.785 sq. in., or 0.00545 sq. ft. The weight of water flowing through one tube per hour will therefore be $0.00545 \times 3 \times 3,600 \times 62\frac{1}{2} = 3,680$ lb.; and using a value of 1. for its specific heat, this water will absorb $3,680 \times 50 = 184,000$ B.t.u. Since 370,000 B.t.u. must be absorbed per hour, the number of tubes in parallel required in this condenser will be $370,000/184,000 = 2$ approximately. The surface of a 1-in. tube per foot of length is $\pi/12 = 0.262$ sq. ft. The length of each tube will therefore be $19.5/(2 \times 0.262) = 37$ ft., approximately. A suitable design of such a condenser would be a four-pass condenser with two tubes each 9 ft. long per pass, or eight 9-ft. tubes in all.

Removal of Noncondensable Gases.—As the thirteenth factor, the removal of noncondensable gases must be positive. There must be no pockets or dead spaces in the vapor space of the condenser, to permit these gases to accumulate. There must be a steady flow of vapor through all portions of the condenser, forcing all gases to the vent, which should be arranged in such a way that there is no possibility of its being sealed shut by distillate collecting in the vent pipe.

It is preferable, if possible, to operate the condenser under a pressure slightly greater than that of the atmosphere, so that there will be a positive flow of gases from the condenser into the atmosphere. This has the added advantage that the air under these circumstances cannot work its way back into the condenser and partially insulate the cooling surfaces. If the pressure difference between the inside of the condenser and the atmosphere is great, a certain amount of the condensed vapor will escape through the vent, and provision must be made by means of a supplementary cooler, scrubber, or condenser to retain this.

Characteristics of Vapor.—The fourteenth factor, the physical characteristics of the condensed vapor, is of importance in two respects:

First, the specific heat of this condensed vapor must be known in order to calculate the cooling, as was done above.

Furthermore, if the condensed vapor has excessive viscosity, which will tend to make it flow slowly over cooling surfaces, this must be allowed for in proportion to these surfaces.

Characteristics of Cooling Water.—The fifteenth factor, the physical characteristics of the cooling liquid, is especially important when the cooling liquid is water and that water comes from a relatively impure source. Many chemical plants are so located that they must use, for cooling water, water containing all sorts of sediment, scale-forming materials, etc.; and invariably under these conditions, the cooling surface becomes coated with layers of material that usually act as excellent heat insulators. It is, therefore, necessary under these circumstances to design the condenser so that the cooling surfaces on the water side can be readily cleaned. This is usually done by making the water flow through the tubes; and in the case of a vertical tubular condenser, it is possible, by removing the top of the condenser, to run a swab down through the tubes and clean them out. In the case of certain types of stills where the material that is to be distilled is run through a vapor heater which is part of the condensing system, the material may deposit scale or dirt on heating in the same way, and similar precautions must be taken.

The simplest design of condenser for a still of moderate size is the single-pass, vertical-tube type illustrated in the following sketch.

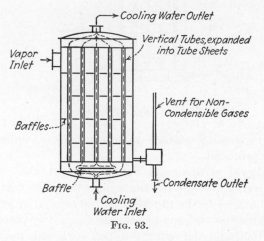

Fig. 93.

This type is characterized by low water velocities and corresponding low values of U. Its advantages are simple, inexpensive construction and ease of cleaning the inside surfaces of the tubes.

In order to increase the capacity of surface condensers, the usual change is to increase the velocity of the water flowing through the tubes. This is done by making the condenser multipass on the water side, as shown in the sketch (Fig. 94).

The insertion of the four baffles in the headers makes the condenser as drawn a five-pass type on the water side, and the water velocity is therefore five times greater than a single-pass condenser of the same size, with the corresponding increase in capacity as indicated in the table on page 230.

Condensers are frequently made multipass on the vapor side as well, and any type may be either vertical or horizontal, whichever is more convenient.

In distilling apparatus requiring unusually high coefficients of heat transfer, the double-pipe type of condenser frequently seen used for heat interchangers is sometimes used. It is likely

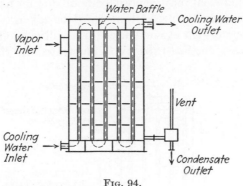

Fɪɢ. 94.

to flood the cooling surface with condensate, unless positive removal is provided.

In equipment of moderate size and height, the condenser is usually placed above the fractionating column so that the reflux can drain back on to the top plate of the column by gravity. In larger installations, the condensers are frequently placed at some lower position, and the reflux pumped back into the top of the column by a suitable pump.

CHAPTER XXI

ACCESSORIES

A fractionating still must have numerous accessories and attachments in order to permit of its accurate control. It is essential, in the first place, that a constant supply of steam be assured. This can be accomplished only by having a constant steam pressure available at the steam coil. Since in most chemical plants the load on the boiler plant fluctuates, and since the firing of such boiler plants is likely to be irregular, the boiler pressure almost always is variable, and this variability will be transmitted to the heating coils of the distilling apparatus unless special precautions are taken. These precautions are usually in the form of constant-pressure reducing valves between the boiler and the still, whereby a constant pressure on the steam coils may be assured no matter what variations may occur in the boiler pressure itself.

The condensed steam in the coils of the kettle must be removed as rapidly as it collects; otherwise, the water will collect in the tubes and blanket the surface, causing the rate of evaporation in the still to drop off immediately. This means that there should be efficient steam traps attached to the coils, and these traps must always be kept in perfect working condition.

Indicating Valves.—The throttle valve which controls the steam pressure on the coils should preferably be constructed in such a way that the amount of opening of the valve can be registered by means of an indicator on a dial or some device of that type. This enables the still operator to reproduce his valve opening and therefore his still pressure from charge to charge without necessitating the inspection of steam gages, etc. In the same way, the valves that control the flow of cooling water to the condenser should be fitted with indicating devices for the same purpose.

Testers or Weir Boxes.—The rate of flow of the distillate from the condenser to the receiving tank must be measured. This is usually done by means of so-called testers, weir, or look boxes, where the rate of flow is measured by the depth of liquid flowing through a suitable slot or opening.   It is also necessary to take samples of distillate from time to time, and the piping should be arranged with suitable connections so that this may be done conveniently, since in the fractional distillation of many liquids, it is not possible to rely entirely on temperature readings in order to determine the quality of the distillate obtained, and it is necessary to withdraw samples from time to time and test them in the chemical laboratory in order to determine exactly the degree of purity of the distillate.

Location of Controls.—Finally, for the convenience of the operator and for general efficiency of the distilling apparatus, all control valves should be located at one spot.   The operator must not be required to climb three or four stories of the building in order to operate the steam-control valves and water-control valves and inspect the rate of flow of distillate, but all of these valves, testers, etc., should be so arranged that the operator, standing in one place, can have the still under complete control.

Special Designs.—It should be remembered that the design of all chemical engineering machinery depends to a very great extent indeed upon local and special conditions, and, therefore, it is not possible for a designer to produce a machine suitable for everybody at every place.   This accounts for the fact that most manufacturers rarely carry so-called standard equipment in stock and must, in nearly every case, design special equipment suited for the particular requirements of the problem involved.

CHAPTER XXII

CONTINUOUS DISTILLATION

Continuous distillation differs from intermittent distillation in that the material to be distilled is fed continuously into the machine, the products of the distillation are withdrawn continuously, and the state of the components in the mixture being distilled remains a constant at any point in the system. That is, the temperature, pressure, and composition of the liquid and vapor at any point in the apparatus remain unchanged so long as external influences are constant.

Requirements for Continuous Distillation.—The requirements for the suitable utilization of continuous distillation are three in number:

1. The feed of material to be distilled must be constant in quality, temperature, and rate.

2. The source of heat or other form of energy used in operating the still must be constant.

3. There must be available cooling fluid for condensers, etc., constant in both amount and temperature.

Constant Rate of Feed. *Requirement 1.*—The constant feed assumes that the rate of flow of feed liquor to the still must be arranged so that it does not change from one time interval to another, and it also assumes that the quality or composition of this liquor remains unchanged. It is therefore obvious that, in general, continuous distillation is suitable especially for the handling of relatively large amounts of a fairly uniform material. Since, also, continuous distillation involves careful regulation of the apparatus at the beginning, and since such regulation is sometimes difficult, it is advisable to use continuous distillation only where large amounts of fairly uniform material are expected over extended periods of time.

The most satisfactory arrangement to insure a constant flow of feed to the still is the use of the constant-level feed tank.

238

This consists of an overhead tank, feeding by gravity to the still and arranged with a float valve on its supply line such that the level in this tank remains constant. Another method is to pump an excess of feed to this tank and have the excess overflow back to storage through a constant-level overflow pipe.

Constant-rate pumps are necessary for stills working under high pressure.

Constant Steam Supply. *Requirement 2.*—Constant source of heat supply for operating the still is essential so long as the still is to be semiautomatic in operation; that is to say, if steam is to be used for heating, there must be some suitable device in connection with the steam lines such that the steam pressure may be automatically kept constant. Usually, the source of steam available for distillation is the steam boiler; and since the boiler pressure is a variable quantity, depending upon firing conditions and demands on the boiler from other units, it is essential to use steam pressure sufficiently below that of the boiler pressure available so that suitable reducing valves placed on the line will function properly, giving a reasonably constant steam pressure at the still. Furthermore, most continuous stills are very sensitive to slight changes in the steam pressure applied, and it is therefore necessary to use, in addition to the constant-pressure reducing valve mentioned above, some sort of sensitive steam regulator which will automatically maintain a constant pressure in the still. It is no exaggeration to state that a sensitive steam regulator is perhaps the most important accessory for a continuous still.

Constant Water Supply. *Requirement 3.*—Constant supply of cooling fluid, usually water, implies constancy with regard to both amount and temperature, since the quality and amount of distillate obtained are functions of the amount of reflux which depends largely on the dephlegmation obtained in the reflux condenser.

Results of Continuous Distillation.—In general, the results obtained in continuous distillation are:

1. Constant products of distillation.
2. Constant conditions at any point in the system.

So far as the first result is concerned, constancy of production infers, of course, that the amount of distillate and waste obtained from the unit remains constant and that the quality of these products is unchanged, assuming, of course, that the requirements noted above are fulfilled.

The second result, constant conditions at any point in the system, is perhaps the chief reason why continuous distillation has been so successful, as it is possible so to design the distilling equipment as to take care of the conditions to be expected at any point in the system, since these conditions remain unchanged; i.e., in the fractionating column of a continuous still, the composition of the liquid on any plate and of the vapor above any plate will remain unchanged so long as the requirements for continuous distillation are fulfilled.

Essential Parts of a Continuous Still.—The essential parts of a unit for continuous distillation are, in general:

1. A fractionating column.
2. Source of heat.
3. Source of cooling liquid, which usually cools the condenser.

In addition, most continuous stills are supplied with a feed heater and a recuperator, or waste-heat interchanger.

Feed Heater.—The function of the feed heater is to raise the temperature of the continuously incoming feed liquor to as near the boiling point, under the conditions obtained in the still, as is possible. This feed heater may be in several parts, depending upon circumstances. For instance, the condenser receiving the vapor from the fractionating column may be divided into several units, one or more of these units being utilized for preheating the feed liquor by allowing the feed liquor to pass through it instead of cooling water. Usually, however, the temperature obtained in such a vapor heater, as it is called, is not sufficiently high, and it is therefore usual to allow the partially preheated liquor to pass then to a recuperator where it receives heat from the hot waste liquor discharged from the bottom of the still, this recuperator usually raising the temperature of the feed nearly to its boiling point. In some special cases, usually when either the vapor heater or the recuperator is dispensed with for manufacturing or operating reasons, it is customary to heat the incoming feed by means of a steam-heated preheater. This last method, however, is uneconomical and used only under special circumstances. It is, of course, possible to run the cold feed liquor directly into the still without preheating at all. Since the feed liquor is always run into the fractionating column on to a proper plate, the heating of the liquor to boiling will take place in the column, and the corresponding cooling obtained in the column will have the effect of additional dephlegmation, or reflux, and will therefore improve the degree of fractionation obtained from the point of entrance of feed down to the bottom of the column. Since, however, the most efficient distilling column is that one where the maximum reflux traverses the entire length of the column, the heat, thus taken out of the lower portion of such a column, will be of no assistance in improving the fractionation in the upper portion of the column; it is, therefore, better practice to take care of any excess reflux required by means of the reflux condenser and preheat the incoming feed by means of the waste heat of the vapor or the discharge from the bottom of the still.

The condensing units used in continuous stills are similar to those used on intermittent stills and are designed in similar fashion.

Fractionating Column.—The fractionating column of continuous stills are, in general, similar to those used in intermittent stills, the design depending, of course, upon special conditions in the particular unit. Quite often in the more complicated continuous stills, the fractionating column is divided into several units which are operated semi-independently of each other, and some of these will be discussed later under special applications of continuous distillation.

The utilization of the source of heat, however, is usually different from that of the intermittent still. In general, there are two methods of heating where steam is to be the source of heat. Where other sources of heat are used, *e.g.*, direct fire, in general the rules laid down for steam will apply with suitable modifications. Closed steam, or steam within steam coils or pipes, is usually used for nonaqueous solutions, where it is not desired to bring water into direct contact with the liquor that is being distilled; or closed steam is used for the distillation of aqueous solutions where the water is taken off as distillate and does not remain in the residue, the introduction of water vapor into the residue, of course, defeating the purpose of the distillation.

Open Steam.—The second method of heating with steam is to use open steam, *i.e.*, blowing water vapor into direct contact with the liquid in the still. This is usually used for aqueous solutions having water or other aqueous residue, as the less volatile portion of the liquid being distilled or where the introduction of water into the less volatile product from the still will do no harm. Superheated steam is used where the temperature at the point of introduction is well above the temperature of boiling water at that pressure.

In the continuous still, the fractionating column is usually divided into two portions which are called, respectively, the exhausting portion and the rectifying portion, the feed entering the column always being taken in at the dividing point between these two sections.

The function of the exhausting column is to remove from the less volatile material discharged from the bottom of the still the more volatile material present in the feed, while the function of the rectifying column is to separate the more volatile component as nearly as possible from the less volatile component, discharging the more volatile component from the top of the rectifying column and returning the less volatile component to the exhausting column.

The rectifying column is usually placed above the exhausting column so that the reflux passing down through the rectifying column can flow by gravity into the top of the exhausting column.

The design of the exhausting column depends, of course, upon the same things that were noted in the previous discussion of the rectifying column, the number of plates to be used being a function of the relative ease or difficulty of the separation of the more volatile component from the less volatile component, a function of the temperature and composition of the feed entering the top of the exhausting column, and the composition of the waste liquor discharged from the bottom. The volume of the column is a function of the time of contact desired between the liquor and the vapor, the exhausting column usually being made sufficiently great in diameter and having a sufficient depth of liquor on the plates to insure that the liquor descending through the column is in contact with the vapor a sufficiently long time so that practically all of the volatile component will be removed from it. The character of the plates to be used in the exhausting column is a function of the character of the liquor passing down through them;

for instance, if the liquor being distilled contains solids, as is frequently the case, the plates must be so designed that the solids will not deposit out on the plates and stop up the vapor openings.

In working out the design of the rectifying column, it must be remembered that the number of plates required is not a function of the ease or difficulty of separating one pure component from another pure component, but the rectifying column has to separate the more volatile component from a mixture of the composition of the feed entering the top of the exhausting column, and therefore, as a rule, fewer plates would be required in a rectifying column of a continuous still than would be the case in the rectifying column of an intermittent still. Since, however, the exhausting column of the continuous still usually is designed to insure that the discharge from its bottom contains practically none of the more volatile component, the total number of plates in the continuous still will often be greater than in the intermittent still designed for the same work.

Diagram of Continuous Still.—The accompanying diagram (Fig. 95) will give an idea of the essential features of a continuous still for the separation into its parts of a two-component system, where *A* represents a constant-level feed tank for supplying feed at uniform rate to the apparatus; *B* represents a vapor heater where the cold feed is heated part way to its boiling point by the hot vapor coming from the top of the fractionating column; *C* represents the recuperator where the partially preheated feed is raised nearly to its boiling point by means of the hot discharge from the bottom of the fractionating column; *D* represents the exhausting column where the feed enters on the top plate and the less volatile liquid gradually runs down from plate to plate and is discharged from the bottom passing through the recuperator; *E* is the rectifying column where the vapor from the top of the exhausting column is subjected to a fractional distillation, the more volatile component being discharged through the vapor pipe *F* to the feed heater *B*, and the less volatile component running back into the exhausting column; *G* is the condenser that receives the vapor not condensed in the feed heater *B* and condenses it completely, the liquid thus obtained being either run back into the top of the rectifying column together with the condensed vapor from the feed heater or carried off to a suitable receiving tank *H*, as indicated. Cooling water would be required for the condenser *G* only. In case it was necessary to cool the less volatile component discharged from the bottom of the exhausting column to a temperature below that at which it leaves the recuperator, it would be necessary to put an additional cooler on the waste line; and in case the condenser *G* failed to cool the distillate to a sufficiently low temperature, it would be necessary

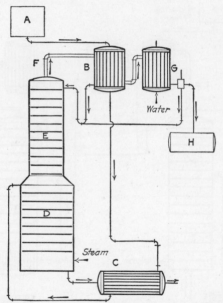

Fig. 95.—Diagram of a simple continuous still.

to introduce a suitable cooler into the line, taking the distillate from the condenser to the receiving tank. The steam used for heating the still would be introduced into the bottom section of the column *D*, either closed or open steam being used, depending upon circumstances as noted above.

Stills for Three-component Mixtures.—Continuous stills are of particular value in handling systems containing more than two components, *e.g.*, three-component systems. It will therefore be interesting to discuss such a system, taking for example the actual case of the system ethyl-ether, ethyl-alcohol, water, it being possible to separate the ether completely from the alcohol and water by fractional distillation, and it being possible to obtain about a 96 per cent alcohol from the water in the same way. If we consider the 96 per cent alcohol which is the constant-boiling mixture of alcohol and water to be for our purposes a pure component, spoken of as alcohol, since it behaves exactly as a pure component would, it will be possible to discuss a suitable

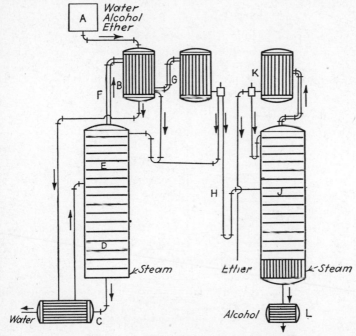

Fig. 96.—Type A—continuous still for three components.

continuous unit for separating almost completely these three components from each other.

In any continuous still for the separation from each other of three components, one component is always separated first from the other two, and these are also separated from each other by a subsequent operation. In the system noted above, ether, alcohol, and water, it is possible to obtain the separation of the three components in several ways. For instance, in Fig. 96, *A* represents a constant-level feed tank containing the mixture of alcohol, ether, and water. The liquid is allowed to pass through a feed heater, which, in this case, will consist of first a vapor heater B and then a waste recuperator C, the heated feed then passing into the central portion of a continuous fractionating column, the exhausting section being represented by the portion D, and the rectifying section by the portion E. The vapor from the top of the rectifying section passes through the vapor line F to the feed heater B and from there to the total and reflux condenser G. In this column, the ether and alcohol are separated from the water, the water being the less volatile component, and the ether and alcohol the more volatile components. The composition of the liquor approaching the bottom of the exhausting column increases in water, until, at the bottom, only water is obtained, and hot water is discharged from the exhausting column through the recuperator to the sewer, live steam being blown into the bottom of the column to supply the vapor and heat necessary for the vaporization of the alcohol and ether.

The rectifying column E has the problem of separating entirely the water from the ascending vapor, so that the liquid condensed in the condensers B and G consists of a mixture of alcohol and ether only. This condensed distillate then passes through the line H into the central portion of another continuous fractionating column J. This fractionating column J differs from the preceding column in that the source of heat at the base is not open steam but closed steam in the form of some sort of tubular or coil steam heater. In this column, there are to be separated only two components, the alcohol and the ether. The ether, being more volatile, passes up while the alcohol being less volatile, passes down, the alcohol at the bottom being substantially ether-free, and the ether at the top substantially alcohol-free; the ether vapor being condensed by means of the condenser K, and the alcohol withdrawn hot from the bottom of the column and passed through a suitable cooler L to a receiver.

Another method of accomplishing the same result is indicated in Fig. 97, where a mixture of ether, alcohol, and water is held in a constant-level feed tank A and flows from there through a preheater B to a recuperator C and into the central portion of the column DE as before, the difference being that the recuperator operates on the second column instead of the first. The column

DE in this case separates the most volatile component, ether, from the alcohol and water, the ether passing up through the column, and the alcohol and water passing down. The heat and vapor necessary for operating this column are supplied by open steam introduced at the base, as before. The ether passing out of the top of the rectifying column as vapor is condensed in the condensers and is collected in a suitable ether-receiving tank; and

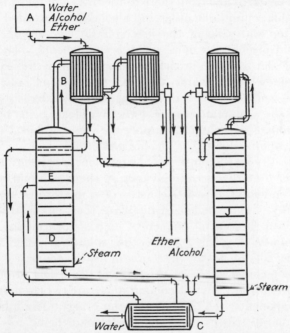

Fig. 97.—Type B—continuous still for three components.

the hot liquor being discharged from the bottom of the exhausting column, which consists of a mixture of alcohol, water, and condensed steam, flows by gravity into the central portion of the second column *J* where the alcohol and water are separated continuously, the alcohol going to the top and the water to the bottom as indicated.

The third method of separating the three components is indicated in diagram Fig. 98, which is similar to the diagram of Fig. 96, except that the mixture of ether and alcohol passing from the top of the first column to the central portion of the second consists of alcohol-ether vapor instead of condensed alcohol and ether, and therefore it is unnecessary to revaporize these liquids in the second column. It is necessary, however, to furnish a certain amount of heat and vapor in order to obtain the fractionation required in the second column, and therefore a closed heater at the base of the column is used, as in the first case.

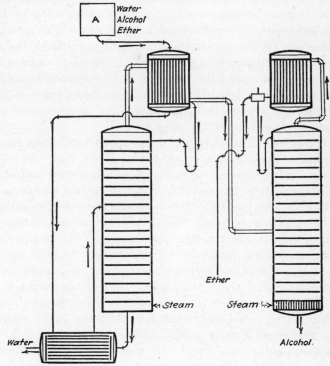

Fig. 98.—Type C—continuous still for three components.

Nonaqueous Solutions.—These preceding diagrams indicate the possible designs when water is one of the three components. Where the nonaqueous solutions are to be distilled, the method to be followed is similar in all respects except that live steam is not introduced into the system at any point, closed heaters being used. There are, however, exceptions to this rule where the material being distilled is insoluble in water, and the introduction of steam into this material will not cause any harmful dilution, since any water vapor that condenses in the material discharged from the column can be separated afterward continuously by suitable decanting apparatus.

Multicomponent Systems.—In the case of systems of more than three components, it is usually necessary to add an additional section for each component, and the systems, of course, become more and more complicated. It should be realized also that as systems become more and more complicated it is necessary to furnish so-called flywheels with them which will permit the equalization of the operation of different portions of the apparatus. Such flywheels usually consist of large intermediate receiving tanks where the liquid may be collected temporarily while subsequent units of the machine are being regulated, as it is manifestly impossible to regulate all of the sections of the complicated machine at the same time.

Accessories.—The successful operation of continuous fractionating stills depends to a considerable extent upon the suitable selection of accessories. Among these accessories perhaps the most important is the so-called steam regulator which has the function of maintaining constant steam pressure automatically on the distilling column. Since the rate of distillation in a distilling column is a function of the pressure of the vapor in the column, and since the quality of the product depends upon the rate at which the distillation is carried out, it is essential that the steam regulator be of the highest degree of sensitiveness, and the variation in pressure in the column to a fraction of an inch of water must be noted and counteracted by the steam regulator. These regulators usually operate on the principle of the U tube, or balanced columns of liquid, the pressure on the one side of the U being maintained by the column, while the pressure on the other side is usually atmospheric. The change in the relative pressures, therefore, will affect the level of the liquid in the two sides of the tube, and by means of suitable floats this change in level can be made to operate control valves on the steam supply, etc. In the same way, the method of controlling the feed supply and cooling-water supply is of great importance.

Feed Control.—In complicated continuous distilling apparatus, a slight change in the feed often has no appreciable effect on the product of the distillation until after a considerable period of time—sometimes as much as an hour being required to detect any change in the quality of the product.   It is therefore essential that the feed control be very sensitive so that the regulation may be made very exact and that very small changes in the rate of feed may be made.   In handling large quantities of liquids, it is essential to use large piping and large apparatus where it is very difficult to obtain careful regulation, and it is therefore customary to use the by-pass system of feed control where most of the liquid fed into the still passes through the main line through a large valve which can be opened to some point approximately correct, whereas the finer regulation is obtained by means of a by-pass and a needle valve which can be controlled very exactly.   These valves are usually fitted with indicating devices by which it is possible to tell by inspection the degree of opening of the valves.

Testers.—The products obtained from the apparatus also must be under constant observation.   This is usually accomplished by means of overflow devices which are called testers.   These testers usually consist of glass bell jars or other designs of a similar nature where the distillate flows continuously through an opening, the rate of discharge often being measured by the level of liquid passing through a weir under the bell jar.   It is also possible to observe the quality of the distillate continuously in such testers where the specific gravity of the liquor is a measure of its quality by having suitable hydrometer arrangements within the testers so that the specific-gravity reading may be observed at any time.

Slop Testers.—The waste liquor discharge from the bottom of the still is usually tested by a device known as the slop tester which takes the vapor from a section near the bottom of the exhausting column and condenses it by means of a small condenser in such a way that the condensed vapor flows through a small hydrometer tester where its specific gravity can be observed continuously.   These testers, feed valves, steam regulators, etc., are usually located at one point so that the operator in charge of the machine is able to operate all the controls and observe the operation of the machine without moving from one position.

Advantages and Disadvantages of Continuous Distillation.—
Continuous distillation has numerous advantages and also certain disadvantages. In general, the advantages may be classed under three headings:

1. Uniform quality and high grade of product.
2. Heat economy.
3. Labor saving.

The uniformity of the quality of the product and the high grade that can be obtained are due to the fact that the continuous still operates with uniform conditions at all points in the system, and it is therefore possible to design the system in such a way that impurities may be taken care of much more satisfactorily than can be done in the case of the intermittent distilling apparatus, where the quality and quantity of a product vary continuously during the distillation of each successive batch.

The heat economy obtained in the continuous still comes from two sources. In the first place, the heat required to raise the liquor to the boiling temperature may be recovered in the continuous still by suitable heat interchangers; whereas in the intermittent still, all this heat is lost; and, in the second place, the production of large amounts of intermediate fractions which must be redistilled in order to recover from them valuable constituents means that a large amount of heat must be supplied for this purpose. In the same way, the labor saving on the continuous system is effected in that there are no intermediate fractions to be redistilled. There is no labor in connection with filling and emptying and cleaning out kettles, and the operation involves very little attention after the machines have been suitably regulated, one operator usually being able to care for a number of continuous stills without undue exertion.

The disadvantages of the continuous system, however, are sometimes serious. They are, in general:

1. Excessive first cost.
2. Sensitiveness to external conditions.
3. Complicated construction and operation.

The excessive first cost of the continuous system lies chiefly in the fact that the accessories necessary to permit automatic operation are frequently complicated and expensive; and although the fractionating columns usually are similar to those used in intermittent stills, and there usually is no distilling kettle, the steam regulators, slop testers, and other accessories frequently increase the cost of the equipment considerably. Also, the continuous still is very sensitive to external conditions. As has been noted above, the continuous still operates successfully only where the quality and quantity of liquor fed to it are uniform and when steam and water supply remain constant; and, if in the operation of the process producing the material to be distilled, there are changes from time to time, where the material to be handled is variable, then the continuous still usually must undergo certain modifications in its design in order to handle the change in material. Whereas in the case of the intermittent still, it is usually possible to handle in a more or less satisfactory manner almost any material of nature similar to that for which the still was designed.

Finally, the continuous system is complicated in construction, and the operation requires a man trained for the work; since frequently the operation of distilling equipments must be entrusted to relatively unskilled labor, therefore continuous stills are frequently avoided on this account. In general, however, it may be said that, other things being equal, the continuous still is much to be preferred.

APPENDIXES

APPENDIX I

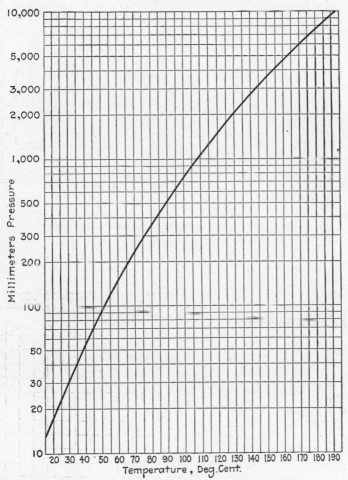

App. I.   Fig. 1.—Vapor-pressure curve of water.

x

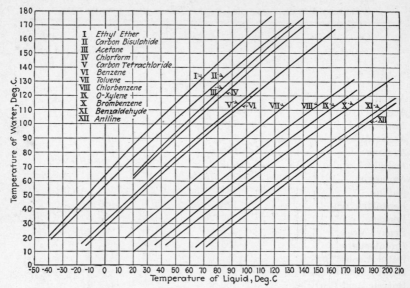

App. I. Fig. 2.—Temperature relations between certain liquids and water at the same pressure. (Explanation: ethyl ether (curve I) at 50°C. has the same vapor pressure as water at 114°C., which by reference to App. I, Fig. 1, is seen to amount to 1,300 mm.)

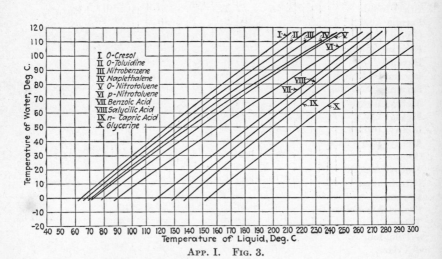

App. I. Fig. 3.

APPENDIX II

Substance	Boiling point, degrees, Centigrade	Molecular weight	Latent heat in calories per gram at boiling point
Acetal	104.0	118.1	66.2
Acetaldehyde	20.8	44.0	134.6
Acetic Acid	118.7	60.0	89.8
Acetic Anhydride	136.4	102.1	66.1
Acetone	56.6	58.1	125.3
Acetyl Chloride	55.6	78.5	78.9
Ammonia	− 34.7	17.0	341.0
Aniline	183.9	93.1	109.6
Benzaldehyde	178.3	106.1	86.6
Benzene	80.2	78.1	93.5
Benzyl Alcohol	205.0	108.1	98.5
Brombenzene	155.5	157.0	57.9
Butyl Alcohol (n)	117.6	74.1	143.3
Butyl Alcohol (iso)	107.9	74.1	138.9
Butyric Acid (iso)	162.2	88.1	114.0
Carbon Tetrachloride	76.8	153.8	46.4
Chlorbenzene	131.8	112.5	75.9
Chloroform	61.2	119.4	58.9
Cresol (m)	200.5	108.1	100.5
Ethyl Bromide	38.2	109.0	60.4
Ethyl Iodide	72.3	155.9	47.6
Formic Acid	100.8	46.0	120.4
Glycol	197.1	62.1	190.9
Heptane	98.4	100.2	74.0
Hexane	69.0	86.1	79.2
Iso amyl Alcohol	130.1	88.1	125.1
Iso propyl Alcohol	82.9	60.1	161.1
Methyl Alcohol	64.7	32.0	261.7
Methyl Chloride	− 24.1	50.5	96.9 (at 0°C.)
Methyl Iodide	42.4	141.9	46.0
Methyl Ethyl Ketone	81.0	72.1	103.5
Octane	125.8	114.2	71.1
Methyl Aniline	193.8	107.1	95.5
Nitrobenzene	208.3	123.1	79.2 (at 151.5°C.)
Pentane	36.3	72.1	85.8
Propyl Alcohol (n)	97.4	60.1	162.6
Toluene	110.4	92.1	86.8
o-Toluidene	203.3	107.1	95.1
o-Xylene	144.0	106.1	82.5
Water	100.0	18.0	536.6

APPENDIX III

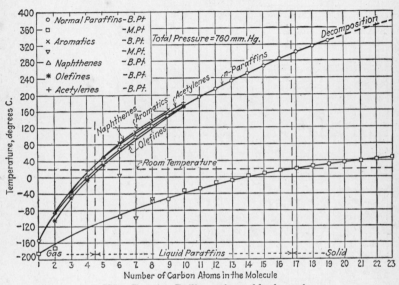

APP. III.   FIG. 1.—Boiling points of hydrocarbons.

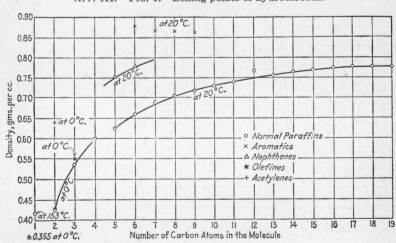

APP. III.   FIG. 2.—Density of hydrocarbons.

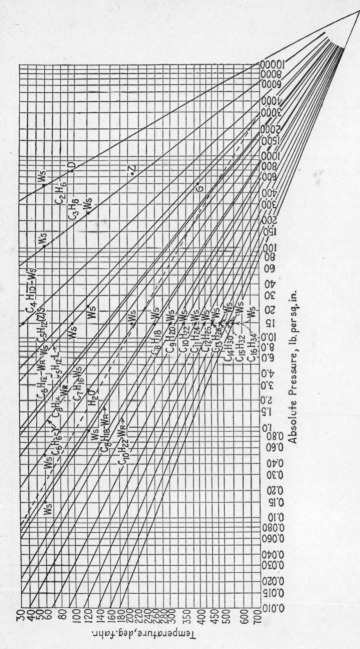

App. III. Fig. 3.—Ccx chart for vapor pressure of hydrocarbons.

INDEX

A

Absolute zero, 26

Absorption naphtha (*see* Rectification).

Accessories, 236

Acetic acid-water, vapor compositions relations, 48

Acetone-methyl alcohol, constant-boiling mixture, 67

Acetone still, 68

Air, composition of, 29
  in condensers, 233
  distillation of liquid, 110

Alcohol-ether-water, phase-rule system, 21

Allowable gas and liquor velocities, 217, 233

A.S.T.M. distillation, 135, 186

Ammonia, 53–58
  continuous still, diagram of, 54
  impurities in, sources of, 53
  partial pressure over water, 36
  removal of hydrogen sulphide and carbon dioxide, 55
  removal of oils, 57
  removal of water, 58
  scrubbers, 57
  treatment with lime, 56

B

Barbet, 160

Beer still, 72

Benzene, application of Clapeyron equation, 31

Benzene-toluene mixtures, 38–42
  boiling-point curve for, 41
  distillation of, 40
  partial-pressure curves for, 40

Benzene-toluene mixtures, rectification of, 87–89
  vapor-composition curves for, 42
  vapor-pressure curves for, 38

Benzene-toluene-xylene mixtures, distillation of, 140–158

Benzolized wash oil, 59–65
  boiling-point curve for, 60
  light-oil recovery, 59
  temperature-composition diagram, 61
  vacuum wash-oil still, 62
  wash-oil still, diagram of, 64

Binary mixtures, classes of, 18
  diagram of, 18
  of maximum boiling point, 18
  of minimum boiling point, 19

Boiling point, calculation from Raoult's law, 41
  curve for acetone and chloroform, 18
  curve for benzene-toluene, 41
  curve for benzene wash-oil, 60
  mixtures of maximum, 18
  mixtures of minimum, 19

Boyle's law, 25

Butane-hexane, effect of pressure on system, 43

C

Chemical combinations, 36

Clapeyron equation, 31

Column performance, 208
  allowable gas and liquid velocities, 223–225
    diagram for, 225
  effect of mixing of vapor and liquid on plate efficiency, 210–211

261